12/02

D1248976

Mystery in Children's Literature

Mystery in Children's Literature

From the Rational to the Supernatural

Edited by

Adrienne E. Gavin
Principal Lecturer
Canterbury Christ Church University College
Canterbury
Kent

and

Christopher Routledge

First published 2001 by
PALGRAVE
Houndmills, Basingstoke, Hampshire RG21 6XS and
175 Fifth Avenue, New York, N.Y. 10010
Companies and representatives throughout the world

PALGRAVE is the new global academic imprint of
St. Martin's Press LLC Scholarly and Reference Division and
Palgrave Publishers Ltd (formerly Macmillan Press Ltd).

ISBN 0–333–91881–9

This book is printed on paper suitable for recycling and
made from fully managed and sustained forest sources.

A catalogue record for this book is available
from the British Library.

Library of Congress Cataloging-in-Publication Data
Mystery in children's literature : from the rational to the supernatural /
edited by Adrienne E. Gavin and Christopher Routledge.
    p. cm.
Includes bibliographical references and index.
ISBN 0–333–91881–9
    1. Children's stories, English—History and criticism. 2. English fiction–
–20th century—History and criticism. 3. American fiction—20th
century—History and criticism. 4. Children's stories, American–
–History and criticism. 5. Detective and mystery stories—History and
criticism. 6. Horror tales—History and criticism. 7. Supernatural in
literature. 8. Rationalism in literature. 9. Mystery in literature. I. Gavin,
Adrienne E., 1962– II. Routledge, Christopher, 1968–
    PR888.C513 M9 2000
    823'.0872099282—dc21

                                                    00–062697

10   9   8   7   6   5   4   3   2
10   09 08 07 06 05 04 03 02

Printed in Great Britain by Antony Rowe Ltd, Chippenham, Wiltshire

To the mysteries with whom we share our lives, Dewayne and Siobhan.

Contents

Notes on Contributors

Troy Boone received his PhD from the University of Rochester and is an Assistant Professor of English at the University of Pittsburgh, USA, where he teaches on the Children's Literature Program. He has published articles on Bram Stoker, Daniel Defoe, the Marquis de Sade, and George Bernard Shaw in *Studies in the Novel, The Eighteenth Century: Theory and Interpretation, Nineteenth-Century Contexts,* and the anthology *Historicizing Christian Encounters with the Other* (Macmillan). He is completing a book titled *Youth of Darkest England: the Working Class in the Heart of Empire*, which examines the way in which popular culture, especially youth culture, negotiated unstable constructions of nation, class and urbanism in a variety of Victorian and Edwardian texts and contexts.

Clare Bradford is an Associate Professor in the School of Literary and Communication Studies at Deakin University in Melbourne, Australia. She completed her BA and MA degrees in New Zealand before moving to Sydney, where her PhD was in the field of fourteenth-century prose. She teaches and researches in literary studies and children's literature and has particular interests in the semiotics and ideologies of picture books and in colonial and postcolonial literatures for children. She has published four books: two children's books, a book for teachers, *Genre in Perspective* and an edited collection of essays on Australian children's texts, *Writing the Australian Child* (University of Western Australia Press, 1996). Her articles on children's literature have appeared in *Children's Literature in Education, Children's Literature Association Quarterly, Ariel, The Lion and the Unicorn, Papers,* and *New Literatures Review*, among other journals. She is the editor of Australia's only scholarly journal in children's literature, *Papers: Explorations into Children's Literature* and is currently President of the Australasian Children's Literature Association for Research.

Karen Coats is an Assistant Professor of English at Illinois State University, USA, where she teaches children's literature. She holds a Master's Degree in English from Virginia Tech and a PhD in Human Sciences from The George Washington University. Her research is primarily focused on contemporary theory and children's literature. She has published articles in *Para*doxa* and *Children's Literature* on psychoanalysis and children's books and is currently working on a book on the role of children's literature in the development of subjectivity.

Adrienne E. Gavin is Principal Lecturer in English at Canterbury Christ Church University College, UK, where she is course director for Victorian Literature and Children's Literature. She was educated and has taught in New Zealand, Canada, and Britain and has a background in law and criminology as well as in English literature. She has published articles on Elizabeth Gaskell, D. H. Lawrence, Anna Sewell, and Charles Dickens, and has written entries on a number of children's writers for *The Cambridge Guide to Women's Writing in English* (1999). She is engaged in research arising out of her PhD dissertation on the body in Dickens's novels and is also working on Anna Sewell and *Black Beauty*. She has wide-ranging research interests in the fields of children's literature, Victorian literature, the short story, and women's writing, and is interested in links between literature, law, and crime.

Valerie Krips, who did her PhD in Australia, now teaches in the Department of English at the University of Pittsburgh, USA, where she is Director of the Children's Literature Program. The author of work on fantasy and narrative, her most recent writing on children's books has appeared in *Children's Literature, The Lion and Unicorn,* and *Signal*; most recently she contributed to a special edition of *Critical Quarterly* which was concerned with the end of childhood. That paper drew on her current research interests in memory and heritage. Her book *The Presence of the Past: Memory, Heritage, Childhood* is forthcoming from Garland.

Robyn McCallum is a Lecturer in English at Macquarie University, Sydney, Australia. She has published several articles about children's literature, picture books, and film. She is author of *Ideologies of Identity in Adolescent Fiction* (1999) and co-author of *Retelling Stories, Framing Culture: Traditional Stories and Metanarrative in Children's Literature* (1998). Her primary research interests are in adolescent fiction, children's film and television and picture books.

Mary Jeanette Moran is working on her doctoral dissertation at the University of Iowa, USA, where she works on women's literature and portrayals of women in eighteenth- and nineteenth-century novels. Her projects have included a narratological analysis of female characters in *Dombey and Son* and *Little Dorrit*, a feminist critique of images of veiling in eighteenth-century texts and a discussion of human–animal interactions in children's fantasy literature. She has presented papers at the 1997 MMLA and the 1997 Conference on Modern Critical Approaches to Children's Literature and has a review essay pending in the *Southern Humanities Review* on Louisa May Alcott's *The Inheritance*. In addition to children's literature, her research interests include feminist approaches to ethics, narrative, psychoanalysis, and pedagogy.

Robin Amelia Morris is a poet as well as a scholar and won First Prize in the Academy of American Poets Contest for 1990 at the University of California at Davis. Her poetry has appeared in *Lilith* as well as in numerous literary journals including *American Literary Review, The Lowell Review* and online in the Summer/Fall 1998 issue of *Salt River Review* at www.mc.maricopa.edu/users/cervantes/SRR. The forthcoming *Cambridge Guide to Children's Books* includes her entries on poets who also wrote children's books: John Ciardi, Rosemary Carr Benét and Stephen Vincent Benét. Her article, 'Looking Back at the One Who Looks: Jorie Graham's Orpheus Sequence' appears in the Spring 1997 edition of *Religiologiques*. Robin Amelia Morris, who thought she would grow up to be a spy, is instead completing a doctoral dissertation on 'Poetic Strategies for Placing the Self' at the University of Massachusetts at Amherst, under the direction of Dr Paul Mariani. She has research interests in nineteenth- and twentieth-century poetry in English, as well as children's literature.

Pat Pinsent is a Senior Research Fellow in the English Department at Roehampton Institute London, UK, where she was for many years a Principal Lecturer. She has worked on the MA in Children's Literature since its inception in January 1993 and is currently convening the Distance Learning mode of delivery of the MA, tutoring the pilot group of students and devising much of the course material. Her five books include two concerned with children's literature: *The Power of the Page: Children's Books and their Readers* (1993) and *Children's Literature and the Politics of Equality* (1997). She has also published a number of articles in this area, on topics including school stories, teenage magazines, information books for children, Enid Blyton's Bible stories, and the depiction of Jewish themes in children's books. Her other research interests include children's reading development, seventeenth-century poetry, particularly the work of George Herbert and feminist theology. She has recently edited the papers from the 1998 Conference of the International

Board on Books for Young People (IBBY), which took as its topic 'Pop Fictions'.

Christopher Routledge is a full-time writer based in Lancashire, UK. He received his PhD from Newcastle University, has published academic articles on Raymond Chandler, G. K. Chesterton, and Paul Auster and is collaborating on a project which examines genre through the relationship between pragmatic theory and literature. He is a reviewer of secondary works on twentieth-century American detective fiction for the CD-ROM *Annotated Bibliography of English Studies* (Swets & Zeitlinger, 1995–) and has contributed entries on a range of American popular culture topics to the *St James Encyclopedia of Popular Culture* (1999). He has taught English and American literature at several British universities and has written on education issues for *The Daily Telegraph* and *The Guardian* newspapers.

David Rudd is a Senior Lecturer at Bolton Institute, UK, where he teaches courses in children's literature for the Humanities Division and is employed in the Communication Skills Unit. In 1997 at Sheffield Hallam University he completed the first doctorate on Enid Blyton's work. His books include *A Communication Studies Approach to Children's Literature* (Sheffield Hallam University, Pavic Press, 1992), concentrating on Roald Dahl and *The Famous Five: A Guide to the Characters* (Norman Wright, 1997). His *Enid Blyton and the Mystery of Children's Literature* will be published by Macmillan in early 2000. He has published numerous articles on aspects of children's literature, most recently on the 'Harry Potter' phenomenon and has given papers at conferences in the UK and America. He has also published on study and communication skills and is a founder of the Bolton Discourse Network, which published its first volume, *Critical Textwork: An Introduction to Varieties of Discourse and Analysis* (Open University Press) in 1999.

John Stephens is an Associate Professor in English at Macquarie University, Sydney, Australia, where his main teaching commitment is children's literature, but he also teaches and supervises postgraduate research in medieval studies, postcolonial literature, and discourse analysis. He is the author of *Language and Ideology in Children's Fiction* (1992), two books about discourse analysis and around sixty articles about children's (and other) literature. More recently, he has co-authored, with Robyn McCallum, *Retelling Stories, Framing Culture: Traditional Story and Metanarratives in Children's*

Literature (1998). His primary research focus is on the relationships between texts produced for children and young adults (especially literature and film) and cultural formations and practices. He is particularly interested in ideologies pertaining to gendering and multiculturalism and their impact on the representations of subjectivity. He was President of the International Research Society for Children's Literature 1997–99.

1
Mystery in Children's Literature from the Rational to the Supernatural: an Introduction

Adrienne E. Gavin and Christopher Routledge

> *The most beautiful experience we can have is the mysterious. It is the fundamental emotion which stands at the cradle of true art and true science. Whoever does not know it and can no longer wonder, no longer marvel, is as good as dead and his eyes are dimmed.*
>
> (Albert Einstein 11)

> *And when I asked them if they preferred books to be funny or exciting, they all with one accord said that what they liked best was a mystery.*
>
> (Joan Aiken 30)

> *I have grown to love secrecy. It seems to be the one thing that can make modern life mysterious or marvellous to us. The commonest thing is delightful if one only hides it.*
>
> (Oscar Wilde 4)

Mystery lies in both the knowable but as yet unknown and in the unknowable. Mystery provokes questions: who? how? why? Mystery demands answers: solution, in the form of those questions being answered, or resolution, in the form of acceptance of mystery as an insoluble but integral element of life. As Albert Einstein suggests, the mysterious is a 'fundamental emotion', central to human experience. It lies at the heart of all human endeavour, scientific as well as artistic and, as Basil Hallward in Oscar Wilde's *The Picture of Dorian Gray* suggests, it makes life 'delightful'. It is also fundamental to the texts which first stimulate our imaginings of our world, and writers of children's literature have great freedom to enhance and foreground the mysterious in their work. Perhaps because adulthood is a mystery to children and childhood has become a mystery to adults and neither can ever 'solve' the other state, mystery has a particularly strong presence in children's texts. Despite this presence, however, mystery has had surprisingly little critical attention paid to it in connection with children's litera-ture; this book seeks to redress that lack by examining the ways in which mystery is used in children's literature. Delving into the secrets of literary mystery and assessing critically the functions of mystery in writing for children, the essays in this collection suggest critical 'solu-tions' to the questions that mysteries raise.

In creating this book we elicited the responses of literary critics to mystery in children's literature (here used broadly to include young adult literature). We sought essays that would reveal the variety of mystery in writing for children and which would demonstrate the range of critical and theoretical responses mystery can provoke. The essays included here analyse mystery in detective, spy, and horror fictions, as well as in stories of religious mystery, the uncanny, and the supernatural. They approach their subject matter from a wide range of critical and theoretical perspectives, offering innovative and challeng-ing readings of both canonical children's fictions and popular contem-porary texts.

In their essays our contributors use their own definitions of mystery, but as a whole the collection's understanding of mystery is broad, including all secret or unexplained experiences, things, or occurrences and anything which, as the *Collins English Dictionary* states, 'arouses suspense and curiosity because of facts concealed'. We see mystery writing as falling into two categories: the 'rational' in which mysteries are solved to the satisfaction of a character's and/or reader's intellect, causing the mystery to disappear, and the 'supernatural' in which mysteries are generally resolved to the satis-faction of a character's or reader's instincts and in which the mystery remains. Rational mysteries involve explanation of the mystery; supernatural mysteries involve acceptance of mystery as an inexplicable element of human life.

The collection is structured so as to suggest a roughly chronological shift in the use of mystery in children's literature that can be described as a shift from certainty to hesitation. Maria Nikolajeva states that 'clear boundaries and rational explanations in early fantasy for chil-dren were conscious or unconscious compromises with prevailing edu-cational views. To leave a child reader in uncertainty was pedagogically wrong' (71). Like early fantasies, children's 'rational' mysteries also conclude in certainty and a reassuring solution, at least as far as revelation of the mystery goes. Again reflecting our observations of mystery, Nikolajeva suggests of fantasy that

> in the 1950s ... the fantasy code begins to change. In books by the British authors Lucy M. Boston and Philippa Pearce, for example, the mechanism of the marvelous events is not revealed and both readers and characters are confronted with mystery and hesitation as to the reality of the magic. (71)

In the same way, more recent children's mysteries provide room for more than one truth. In these 'supernatural' works, mysteries are resolved by being accepted or acknowledged as an inherent and insoluble part of life.

A key difference between fantasy and mystery is that mystery has a question mark in it. There is, however, a confluence between fantasy and mystery, particularly in mysteries from the latter half of the twentieth century. Like fantasy, too, mystery is an element in writing rather than a discrete genre. Although mystery appears most obviously in genres such as detective, horror, or supernatural fiction, it also finds a presence, in some form or another, in almost all children's literature.

John Daniel Stahl points out that for characters within children's texts '[s]ecrecy is a means ... to create a meaningful sense of self, frequently in productive, not necessarily hostile, opposition to grown-ups or rivals' (44). 'The presence of something unexplained', he writes, 'the effort to find clues about the explanation and finally the discovery of the desired answer: this sequence in a story is appealing because it is in fact the pattern of such a large part of growing up' (42). Mystery is, as Joan Aiken reports, what children look most for in a book. She suggests that 'children ... have a feeling for mystery' (30), yet there is little mystery to be found in the instructional children's literature written before the mid-nineteenth century, which taught moral certainties based on a fixed social order. Since then, children's literature increasingly has shied away from overt moral judgement, preferring instead to make truths of all kinds into things to be discovered on an individual basis. It does not seem a coincidence, then, that most of the primary texts addressed in this collection come from the twentieth century. The loss of moral and religious certainties that characterized the twentieth century exposed the universe as inherently mysterious and inexplicable.

The current proliferation of series mystery novels such as R. L. Stine's Goosebumps and the Point Horror series, together with the complex work of writers such as Gary Crew and Margaret Mahy, testify to a contemporary burgeoning of children's mystery literature. Adopting the postmodernist tropes of uncertainty, intertextuality, and narrative instability, these works reveal mysteries without solving them and their mysteries tend to be supernatural in nature. They are part of the 're-enchant[ment of] the universe' that Brian Inglis suggests characterizes children's literature from 1968 onwards (234). They are also influenced by and react against, earlier mysteries for children in which neater, more certain solutions are reached. These earlier texts such as the Nancy Drew series or Enid Blyton's Famous Five series and works by writers such as Frances Hodgson Burnett and Erich Kästner establish mysteries which are solvable (and are solved) through rational methods and fall broadly within the category of detective fiction. The change from what we are calling rational mysteries to what we term supernatural mysteries comes in the post-Second World War period in the work of writers like Philippa Pearce, whose *Tom's Midnight Garden* (1958), often regarded as the most significant children's novel of the twentieth century, becomes a catalyst for later children's fictions in which mystery becomes unsolvable.

Rational and supernatural mysteries are not opposites, nor does one completely eradicate the other; they lie along a continuum which has its roots in an even earlier manifestation of mystery. Mystery's earliest meanings are connected with the inexplicability of God and with the mysteries of religion. The entry of mystery into children's literature occurs through accounts of religious mystery such as those discussed in the first essay in this collection. However, as David I. Grossvogel claims in his book *Mystery and Its Fictions*, '[m]ystery extends beyond god: god represents only man's most strenuous effort to overcome mystery' (4). Grossvogel suggests a movement in mystery writing from texts that describe the mysterious, through those that reflect upon mystery and its effects upon individual consciousness and the limits of the self, to metaphysical mystery fiction which conveys mystery rather than analyses it and which is open-ended in nature. His pattern roughly parallels the movement described by this collection: a move from religious mysteries which attempt to describe mystery or provoke religious awe, through rational solvable mysteries which try to contain and explain mystery, to supernatural irresolvable mysteries which reveal the instability and shifting nature of knowledge, the self and truth.

Mystery, then, might be identified as a feature of a particular type of fiction. Yet E. M. Forster goes further, suggesting that it is an integral part of the novel as a genre. He writes that mystery 'is essential to a plot ... To appreciate a mystery, part of the mind must be left behind, brooding, while the other part goes marching on' (88). In other words, mysteries are a fundamental part of successful plot structures. Moreover, Frank Kermode argues, texts can take on a secret life of their own. In *The Genesis of Secrecy* he discusses the mysteriousness of texts: '[o]nce a text is credited with high authority it is studied intensely; once it is so studied it acquires mystery or secrecy' (144). This, he suggests, coexists with the 'belief that a text might be an open proclamation, available to all' (144) and is as true of secular texts as it is of sacred books. The more canonical a children's text is, we might then argue, the more mysterious it becomes. Frances Hodgson Burnett anticipates such a claim when she writes in the preface to her novel *A Little Princess*:

> Between the lines of every story there is another story and that is one that is never heard and can only be guessed at by the people who are good at guessing. The person who writes the story may never know all of it. (n. p.)

A word or two should be said about the difference in meaning that the word 'mystery' has in American and British contexts. In American usage the word is often synonymous with detective fiction whereas in British usage it encompasses a wider range of meanings which includes detective fiction but also incorporates the spooky, the uncanny, and the in other ways mysterious. The variance may have something to do with cultural differences and trends in writing. Writing of psychological ghost stories, Peter Penzoldt suggests that 'American authors prefer a natural explanation, while the English do not fear to intimate that there is more in the world than reason can account for' (56). Glen Cavaliero, too, points to 'the repeated tendency of English novelists to write about the supernatural or at any rate about mysterious and inexplicable events' (vi).

Because it is traditionally more open to fantasy and the magical, children's literature perhaps reveals these cultural distinctions as to content less obviously than adult literature, but the distinction in the use of the term 'mystery' is still significant. John G. Cawelti in his examination of the formula of mystery writing uses the term in its narrower, American sense when he states that in

> the true story of imaginary beings, the mystery of the alien is never solved, only somehow dealt with ... This sort of conclusion

is the very antithesis of the mystery story where, once discovered and explained, a secret is no longer capable of disturbing or troubling us. (1976: 44)

In the broader, more British sense in which we use the term here we would class both types of story as mystery, the former as supernatural and the latter as rational detective.

Although perhaps seen most clearly in the 'supernatural' class of mysteries discussed in this collection, most of the essays here reveal a persistent interest in the self-identity which child characters are seeking to establish and which is revealed through mystery. In the 'supernatural' mysteries this also connects closely with issues of subjectivity and agency. Issues of identity are, of course, inherent in children's literature, which generally has as subtext some emphasis on 'growing up', but, as the essays here show, mystery literature provides opportunities for dealing with these issues that are not otherwise available.

The collection begins with a consideration of religious mystery, a type of mystery that is as difficult to grasp as it is to convey. Pat Pinsent's essay, 'so great and beautiful that I cannot write them', examines whether it is possible to create a sense of religious mystery in writing for children. Discussing a wide chronological range of texts, Pinsent considers how successful writers have been in creating a sense of religious awe in child characters and readers. Using Rudolf Otto's ideas on the holy, Jung's concepts of the archetype and the collective unconscious and Northrop Frye's writing on literary archetypes, Pinsent examines the methods writers use to evoke a sense of the Holy. She shows that imagery and symbolism are central to this and that the archetypes of spring and early summer and of comedy rather than tragedy, are used by those writers who most successfully convey religious mystery. Pinsent analyses the effectiveness of the dream vision in Susan Coolidge's *What Katy Did* (1872), of coincidence in Anna Sewell's *Black Beauty* (1877), and of providence in Frances Hodgson Burnett's *The Secret Garden* (1911). Her examination of fantasy includes discussion of C. S. Lewis's Narnia series and Kenneth Grahame's *The Wind in the Willows* (1908), while Susan Cooper's novel *Seaward* (1983) and Ursula Le Guin's *A Wizard of Earthsea* (1968) are used to examine the mystery of evil. Children's books based on the Bible are today largely ineffective as vehicles for religious mystery, Pinsent suggests, whereas poetry might be more effective than prose in describing transcendence. Religious mystery is most effectively communicated in children's literature, she concludes, by works in which the archetypes of literature are left to speak for themselves without over-explanation.

'Nancy's Ancestors', Mary Jeanette Moran's essay on Frances Hodgson Burnett's *A Little Princess* (1888) and *The Secret Garden* (1911) as forerunners to the Nancy Drew series, argues that, in Burnett's work, mystery generally appears as the focus of a 'quest for knowledge', similar to the questing more obviously present in the Nancy Drew novels. The activity of finding a solution in detective narratives is, however, as Moran's essay suggests, more often revealed to be a trope of masculinity than femininity. One of the things that is surprising about Nancy Drew, she reveals, is that Nancy is able to pursue such quests and retain a distinctly feminine persona. Yet, as Moran argues, Nancy Drew did not appear from nowhere, but has her origins in a tradition in which Burnett is an important figure and in which mystery allows female characters to express themselves. Both Sara Crewe in *A Little Princess* and Mary Lennox in *The Secret Garden* find a solution to their disempowerment in the imagination and the authority the imagination provides. Until they learn to understand and use their intellectual and imaginative powers, the mystery faced by both female characters is how to make their voices heard. Mystery here takes the form of a catalyst; the search to find a solution in the respective plots occurs alongside Sara's and Mary's discovery of the secret of how to attain individual authority. Perhaps because of novels such as Burnett's, Moran suggests, the solution to that secret is one that Nancy Drew already knows.

The next three essays in the collection look explicitly at the ways in which detective mystery plots in children's fiction very often overlay a deeper investigation into the adult concerns of class, wealth, and power. Troy Boone's essay, 'The Juvenile Detective and Social Class', compares the treatment of American class relations in Mark Twain's *Tom Sawyer, Detective* (1896), the American girl scout handbook *Scouting for Girls* (1920), and the early Nancy Drew series. Using these three examples the essay charts a development in the juvenile detective. Tom Sawyer's pursuit of the solution to a detective mystery, for example, is paralleled by his implicit pursuit of wealth. *Scouting for Girls* tells scouts how to 'detect' class identity through appearance and behaviour, while at the same time purporting to promote an egalitarian American society. The Nancy Drew series, which begins in the Depression years, is critical, Boone suggests, of America's capitalist system and the dramatic swings in economic fortune it allowed. Basing class identity on social rather

than economic factors, *The Secret of the Old Clock* (1930), the essay
shows, detaches economic well-being from social status. If in the
first novel in the series Nancy shows some inclination towards economic reform, Boone concludes that as the series progresses, this
'hidden' drive becomes lost and Nancy joins Tom Sawyer and the
girl scout handbook in affirming middle-class values.

Christopher Routledge's essay, 'Children's Detective Fiction and the
"Perfect Crime" of Adulthood', also reveals how detective mystery
plots in children's fiction often conceal a more conservative agenda.
Discussing Erich Kästner's novel *Emil and the Detectives* (1928) as well
as Anthony Horowitz's *The Falcon's Malteser* (1986) and Enid Blyton's
Five on a Treasure Island (1942), he argues that behind the detective
plot lies an implicit mystery concerning the relationship between
childhood and adulthood. Childhood is portrayed as anarchic, vigor-
ous and subversive and adulthood as authoritarian and rationalistic,
but also caring and protective. Indeed, in *Emil and the Detectives* childhood is linked with criminality; the thief's criminal act is impulsive
and childlike, while his capture and conviction are due to Emil's adult
application of rationality and logic. The story, Routledge suggests, is
also of Emil's developing understanding of the mysterious, sometimes
frightening adult world, yet the way Emil deals with this fear is to
adopt 'adult' characteristics. In the end, Emil's brief experience as a
detective is seen as a rite of passage from his subversive, criminal,
childish past, to a more responsible, rational, law-abiding adult future.
Kästner's novel describes Emil's development from being a child afraid
of the strangeness of adults, to his becoming a little adult, who views
criminality as child-like and who has discovered that rational and
responsible behaviour leads to what he thinks is power and authority.
Emil's solution to the mystery of adult authority, Routledge's essay
shows, is the erasure or 'murder' of childhood itself.

David Rudd's essay on Enid Blyton, 'Digging up the Family Plot',
explores further the idea of children's mystery fiction as populated by
'subversive' children. Unlike *Emil and the Detectives*, however, Blyton's
detective mysteries often focus on the home and family as the centre
for mystery or at least as a stable, formal structure behind which secrets
lie hidden. In this respect, Rudd's essay poses a challenge to the notion
of Blyton's work as reassuring and comforting. While the formal
mystery of the adventure plot is always solved, Rudd suggests that
more important secrets remain undisturbed. Taking a broadly psychoanalytic approach, Rudd describes here a double-edged Blyton, who
pits the 'imaginary' realm of the children against the 'symbolic' realm

of the adults. Thus, the mysteries investigated by the children in works such as the Famous Five or Secret Seven series involve uncovering secrets created by adults, but not secrets that might be considered strictly 'adult'. Blyton's mystery plots are resolved with the sweep of a torch beam or the sliding back of a secret panel, but these, Rudd shows, operate as a diversion from the darker mysteries of human existence that Blyton hoped would remain unmentioned.

Valerie Krips's essay 'Plotting the Past' also deals with the difference between 'official' and 'unofficial' knowledge and records, but her examination is of the relationship between the present and the past. In particular, she examines the different ways in which the past is remembered by the present. Discussing the 1951 Festival of Britain, at which mention of the Second World War was discouraged, she illustrates how the memory of even recent and cataclysmic events can be altered or erased by an authoritative, 'official' history. By way of illustration of this, Krips examines Philippa Pearce's *Minnow on the Say* (1955) which concerns a search for missing treasure, but the real mystery for the two boys involved in the search is the past itself. The search for the treasure involves reconstructing events and motives and learning how to ascribe meaning. Pearce's mystery plot becomes a vehicle for discussion of changes in the way that history is written, from authoritative history to the folk history of remembered and retold stories and rhymes. In Pearce's later novels, such as *The Way to Sattin Shore* (1983), Krips shows, fewer memories are communal and history is no longer an explicit feature of authority; any secrets the child-historian detective might uncover are things that only he or she need ever know.

Robin Amelia Morris's essay, 'The Secret Development of a Girl Writer', examines Louise Fitzhugh's 1964 mystery *Harriet the Spy*. Morris demonstrates that the intersection of the female *Künstlerroman* and the detective story genres in this novel reveal the subtextual mystery at the heart of this text to centre upon Harriet's personal identity and her development as a writer. Whereas in traditional *Künstlerromane* female protagonists often become entangled in the romance plot and in detective stories the 'external' nature of the mystery offers little scope for personal development and maturation, *Harriet the Spy's* generic hybridity enables its protagonist to achieve her goals. Drawing upon the ideas of Julia Kristeva and considering the position of woman as writer, Morris shows that in order to discover her Self and become independent Harriet must separate from mother figures and learn to 'dwell in the realm of language'. In doing so Harriet operates as a spy: a solitary outsider, who, in secret, collects information and records her observations. The mystery she wants to solve is not the specific mystery a detective like Nancy Drew might face, but is the deeper, less definable mystery of life itself. To Harriet, everyone and everything is a mystery: where she came from, who she is, her female identity, how and why her life differs from those of others, how to balance community with individuality and the artistic self. Morris reveals that Harriet's writing – her account of her unravelling of mysteries through her spying – enables her to detach her self from others and develop her own identity.

Like Morris's essay, Adrienne E. Gavin's 'Apparition and Apprehension' examines mystery in connection with girls' growth into womanhood. Gavin's focus is on the trope of the supernatural or magical that recurs in accounts of emergent womanhood within children's supernatural mysteries by women writers. Discussing Charlotte Brontë's *Jane Eyre* (1847), Emily Brontë's *Wuthering Heights* (1847), and Margaret Mahy's novels *The Changeover* (1984) and *The Tricksters* (1986) as influential and exemplifying novels, she argues that a pattern emerges in which girl characters are initially frightened by the supernatural then take on supernatural powers themselves as they enter into the mysteries of womanhood. The first stage in this pattern, her essay reveals, involves girl characters being frightened both by apparitional visions of themselves in mirrors and by male supernatural figures who appear in their lives. In the second stage of the pattern, girl characters apprehend the supernatural – in the sense of containing it – by taking on supernatural powers themselves and by using those powers to reduce or destroy male supernatural power. The third stage in the pattern occurs when emergent women characters have entered into the mysteries of womanhood and apprehend – in the sense of understand – their own supernatural powers. They now become apparitional to other characters, Gavin argues, demanding recognition of their new form as women, of their secret powers, and of their mystery.

Personal identity and shifts in that identity are also discussed in Clare Bradford's essay, 'Possessed by the Beast', which examines the mysterious nature of metamorphosis from human to animal form. Bradford suggests that narratives of metamorphosis are intertextual in their effect and metaphorical in their nature. Through discussion of the adolescent boy characters in Gillian Cross's *Pictures in the Dark* (1996) and Gillian Rubinstein's *Foxspell* (1994), Bradford shows that metamorphic episodes operate in different ideological ways in these two novels. In both texts, however, metamorphosis is mysterious and connected with issues of subjectivity, agency, sociality, and masculinity. Using Lacan's ideas on subjectivity and the unconscious, Bradford shows that in Cross's novel Peter Luttrell's transformation into an otter is a signifier for his inarticulate 'I' and offers him freedom. In her discussion of *Foxspell* Bradford continues her psychoanalytical reading of metamorphosis and also develops a postcolonialist analysis. Both novels, she points out, centre on families in conflict in which father–son relationships are key, but their settings are different; Cross's novel is set in an English town and Rubinstein's is set in an Australian suburb. Bradford examines the implications in *Foxspell* of Tod Crofton's transformation into a fox, an animal now regarded as a pest in Australia and which has been, like his family and Rubinstein herself, introduced into Australia from England. Bradford argues that the metamorphic episodes in this novel seek to legitimize colonization.

Like Bradford's discussion of Rubinstein, John Stephens and Robyn McCallum's essay 'There are Worse Things than Ghosts' discusses contemporary Australian children's fiction and issues connected with subjectivity and identity. Their focus is on adolescent fiction of the paranormal in which the uncanny irrupts. The uncanny, they suggest, is transformative and suggests mysteries deeper than the transitory mysteries of detective fiction. Given that there is no tradition of mystery or horror writing in Australia, they ask whether hybridic horror stories can have a local Australian nuance. In discussing the stories in Gary Crew's anthology *Dark House* (1995), Isabelle Carmody's novel *The Gathering* (1993), and Judith Clarke's novel *The Lost Day* (1997), they show that the uncanny reveals the 'fissures within everyday lives'. As well as using Mladen Dolar's categorization of uncanny effects and Freud's notion of the uncanny, they discuss the concept of the chronotope. They suggest that the 'present everyday' is the base chronotope of the works they consider and that horror chronotopes in Australian children's fiction are largely absorbed from American sources. In novels such as *The Gathering*, which use conventional horror chronotopes, the uncanny serves to reaffirm culturally dominant ideology, while in works like *The Lost Day* realism is used to 'actualize a local setting' which transforms horror chronotopes and enables social comment. They conclude that modification of chronotopes is a way in which genres hybridized with horror can move forward, but that in Australian horror writing a local discourse has yet to evolve.

In 'The Mysteries of Postmodern Epistemology', Karen Coats examines a change in children's mysteries from the rational, 'sure-footed' and order-restoring nature of Edward Stratemeyer's detective series to the complex, uncertain, and open-ended nature of contemporary mystery written for children. Focusing on the Nancy Drew series and on works by R. L. Stine and Gary Crew, Coats examines cultural context and the postmodernist world view. Nancy Drew, she argues, is 'the prototypic rational individual', representing 'knowingness' and the defensive belief that we can solve mysteries through knowledge. The Nancy Drew novels, she shows, follow familiar plot patterns which move from not knowing to knowing and reflect a modernist stance towards knowledge. Contemporary postmodernist children's mysteries, by contrast, are not predictable in terms of plot and do not conclude in knowingness. Postmodernism, she explains, sees knowledge as 'contingent and subjective', and contemporary novels for children present mystery as an irresolvable part of daily life. She contrasts Nancy Drew novels, including *The Mystery at Lilac Inn* (1931), with postmodernist Stine novels, such as *Escape of the He-Beast* (1998), to demonstrate a movement from modernist epistemological concerns to postmodernist ontological concerns in children's mysteries. In postmodern texts, Coats shows, the abject becomes prevalent, particularly so in more complex works such as Gary Crew's novel *Strange Objects* (1991) in which the body becomes 'a fetishized commodity' and mystery creates more mystery.

The collection is rounded off by two shorter essays which discuss popular contemporary children's mysteries. In the first essay, 'Harry Potter and the Mystery of Ordinary Life', Christopher Routledge examines the much hyped Harry Potter series by J. K. Rowling. In the second essay, 'Enigma's Variation', Adrienne E. Gavin discusses texts by four innovative writers of children's mysteries who are not elsewhere examined in this collection: Avi, Ellen Raskin, Diana Wynne Jones, and Chris Van Allsburg.

Set in a school for witches and wizards, J. K. Rowling's Harry Potter series might at first glance seem to fit our category of 'supernatural mystery'. What Routledge's essay suggests, however, is that the novels are in fact basic detective mysteries and that the magical elements within them are incidental to the detective structure. The effect of this is that ordinary life itself is shown in the novels to be magical and mysterious if lived according to one's instincts, a point that is underlined by Harry's most frequent dilemma: whether to act on his own conscience or go by the rules. Routledge concludes that the Harry Potter novels contain little in the way of supernatural mystery and that the ideological position of their hero remains far from certain.

Gavin's essay discusses the claim sometimes made that we cannot expect the same levels of originality and experimentation in children's literature that we expect from adult texts. In refuting this claim she discusses Avi's *The Man Who Was Poe* (1989), Ellen Raskin's *The Westing Game* (1978), Diana Wynne Jones's *Archer's Goon* (1984), and Chris Van Allsburg's *The Mysteries of Harris Burdick* (1984). She shows that each of these novels, in various ways, avoids the formulaic, provokes puzzling in characters and readers and contains 'enigma' which she argues is essential to innovative children's mysteries. These authors, Gavin reveals, through their use of postmodernist techniques, demonstrate the possibilities of enigmatic and innovative originality in children's mysteries.

Works cited

Aiken, Joan. 'A Thread of Mystery', *Children's Literature in Education*, 2 (1970): 30–47.

Burnett, Frances Hodgson. 'Preface', *A Little Princess: The Story of Sara Crewe* [1905]. London and New York: Frederick Warne & Co., undated.

Cavaliero, Glen. *The Supernatural and English Fiction*. Oxford: Oxford University Press, 1995.

Cawelti, John G. *Adventure, Mystery, and Romance: Formula Stories as Art and Popular Culture*. Chicago: University of Chicago Press, 1976.

Einstein, Albert. 'The World as I See It' [1931], trans and rev. Sonja Bargmann, in *Ideas and Opinions*. [1954]. London: Souvenir Press, 1973.

Forster, E. M. *Aspects of the Novel* [1927], ed. Oliver Stallybrass [1974]. London: Penguin, 1990.

Grossvogel, David I. *Mystery and its Fictions: From Oedipus to Agatha Christie*. Baltimore, MD: Johns Hopkins University Press, 1979.

Inglis, Fred. *The Promise of Happiness: Value and Meaning in Children's Fiction* [1981]. Cambridge: Cambridge University Press, 1982.

Kermode, Frank. *The Genesis of Secrecy: On the Interpretation of Narrative*. Cambridge, MA: Harvard University Press, 1979.

Nikolajeva, Maria. *Children's Literature Comes of Age: Toward a New Aesthetic*. New York and London: Garland, 1996.

Penzoldt, Peter. *The Supernatural in Fiction* [1952]. New York: Humanities Press, 1965.

Stahl, John Daniel. 'The Imaginative Uses of Secrecy in Children's Literature', in Sheila Egoff, Gordon Stubbs, Ralph Ashley, and Wendy Sutton (eds), *Only Connect: Readings on Children's Literature*, 3rd edn. Toronto: Oxford University Press, 1996, pp. 39–47.

Wilde, Oscar. *The Picture of Dorian Gray* [1890], ed. Isobel Murray, Oxford World's Classics. Oxford: Oxford University Press, 1998.

2

'so great and beautiful that I cannot write them': Religious Mystery and Children's Literature

Pat Pinsent

Can religious mystery have any relevance to children's literature? The religious contexts in which the word 'mystery' is found immediately seem to challenge such a possibility. Paul's sublime discourse about resurrection in his Epistle to the Corinthians, for instance, includes such clarion calls as: '[b]ehold I tell you a mystery ... the dead shall be raised incorruptible ... death is swallowed up in victory' (1 Corinthians 15: 51). The author whose implied audience lacks the frame of reference possessed by the adult reader is inevitably deprived of possibilities for intertextual connections with evocative language such as this.

Etymologically the religious sense of the word 'mystery' predates its secular connotations. Nevertheless mystery tends to be defined as a secret beyond human reason, in a religious sense known only by divine revelation. Full initiation into the mysteries of religion is usually reserved for those at least on the threshold of adulthood, and while children's literature has often dealt with religion, its approach has usually been pedagogical and moralistic rather than necessarily inducting readers into the mystery of the power and holiness of God.

Since the texts discussed here have in most cases been written in English, the authors tend be located within a broadly Judaeo-Christian tradition, even when they are by no means traditional in their own beliefs. Some children's literature, like Mary Sherwood's *The History of the Fairchild Family* (1818), is far too explicitly didactic to include mystery. Other less orthodox believers, such as Kenneth Grahame, seem to have fewer reservations about including religious mystery in books addressed to children.

Religious mystery is particularly elusive since so much of the canon of children's literature is prose fiction, whereas by its nature transcendence seems more readily to be the subject of poetry than of novels.

Children's poets, however, tend to exempt themselves from any kind of attempt to deal with sublimity by choosing subject matter which is often explicitly either didactic or comic. Fairy stories, inherently containing mystery and secrets, also use symbolism and the uncanny, features which have made them a useful source for religious writers such as George MacDonald and C. S. Lewis. However, the usual lack of explicit references to religion in such stories make their specific inclusion here too problematic. Instead it is perhaps helpful to start by looking at some of the characteristics specific to religious mystery. Rudolf Otto's seminal study, *The Idea of the Holy* (1917), is concerned with the numinous, defined by its translator, John Harvey, as 'the specific non-rational religious apprehension and its object, at all its levels, from the first dim stirring where religion can hardly yet be said to exist to the most exalted forms of spiritual experience' (xvii). Otto suggests that people experiencing the numinous seem to receive a strong impression of being dependent creatures, feeling awe at something or someone greater than themselves which they sense as both wholly other and fascinating. Otto shows how this sense has been expressed over the ages by the sublime in art, architecture and literature, and frequently is appropriately conveyed by darkness, silence and emptiness, which serve as admissions of the impossibility of conveying the experience to others.

In order successfully to generate a feeling of awe, the writer must make readers aware of their incomprehension, while at the same time creating a sense that what is being conveyed is greater than the understanding of either the characters in the book or its readers. That any evocation of mystery is ever achieved may reflect, as Carl Gustav Jung suggested, the force and universality of symbolism. Jung, unlike Freud, gave religion an important role within his understanding of the human psyche. Anthony Stevens shows how, for Jung, religion's most essential function was to grant access to the numinous (248). It is not possible to summarize here Jung's extensive discussion of symbolism, but the most relevant aspects to religious mystery are his concepts of the archetype and the collective unconscious. Stevens quotes Jung as saying that the term archetype refers to '"an inherited mode of functioning, corresponding to the inborn way in which the chick emerges from the egg ... a "pattern of behaviour"' (37). Stevens goes on to suggest:

Archetypes predispose us to approach life ... according to patterns already laid down in the psyche ... there are as many archetypes as there are typical situations in life. There are archetypal figures (e.g. mother, child, father, God, wise man), archetypal events (e.g. birth, death, separation from parents, courting, marriage, etc.) and archetypal objects (e.g. water, sun, moon, fish, predatory animals, snakes) ... Jung summed it up: 'The collective unconscious is an image of the world that has taken aeons to form. In this image certain features, the archetypes or dominants, have crystallized out in the course of time. They are the ruling power.' (39)

Jung refuses to define the archetype too strictly as any specific kind of mythological image or motif. Rather he claims that the 'archetype is a tendency to form such representations of a motif – representations that can vary a great deal in detail without losing their basic pattern' (58). Such representations can be glimpsed in imaginative literature and in dreams, which both yield access to the collective unconscious; dreams, Jung suggests, contain

collective images ... analogous to the doctrines taught to young people in primitive tribes when they are about to be initiated ... they learn about what God, or the gods, or the 'founding' animals have done, how the world and man were created, how the end of the world will come and the meaning of death. (63)

As these quotations make clear, there will be inevitable variations between the images experienced by members of different cultures, yet enough consistency to show that such images possess 'immense emotional significance' (Storr 41). For Jung, then, it is by means of access to the archetypes of the collective unconscious, largely conveyed through dream and imaginative literature, that human beings become open to religious mystery and the numinous – in effect, to God.

My intention in scrutinizing a range of children's texts is to examine how they convey some of the elements of religious mystery isolated by Otto, whether by means of Jungian archetypal symbolism, or by authorial admissions that mystery cannot adequately be expressed. In these latter cases, readers are made aware that there *is* some quality beyond the ordinary that words cannot express, and furthermore, that this quality needs to be accepted, even if not understood. Authors inevitably vary in the ways they create a sense of something overwhelming and beyond their powers of description. Among the most frequent of these methods are the overarching plot-structure and the portrayal, by means of language and symbol, of the effects of mystery on the characters. It is useful here to consider perspectives such as those of Northrop Frye, the title of whose 'The Archetypes of Literature' (1951) makes explicit its relationship with the work of Jung and reveals Frye's concern with mythology, an area by its nature pertinent to religion. Frye claims that:

> In the solar cycle of the day, the seasonal cycle of the year, and the organic cycle of human life, there is a single pattern of significance, out of which myth constructs a central narrative around a figure who is partly the sun, partly vegetative fertility and partly a god or archetypal human being. (429)

Frye relates these phases in turn to a succession of literary forms: dawn, spring, and birth are linked with romance; zenith, summer, and marriage link with comedy and the pastoral; sunset, autumn, and death link with tragedy; and darkness, winter, and dissolution link with satire. Frye later presents a list of some of the binary oppositions between tragedy and comedy in relation to their appearance in myth and literature (432). He suggests that the terms in which the comic vision represents the human, animal, vegetable, mineral, and unformed worlds tend to be those appropriate respectively to community, pastoral, garden, city, and river. The tragic vision, on the other hand, tends to represent these worlds respectively in terms of anarchy or isolation, animals of prey, wild forests or heaths, deserts and the sea.

Frye's work has rightly been criticized by David Lodge for being 'excessively schematic' (*20th Century*, 21). Frye's framework, however, provides a useful basis for my analysis of religious mystery in children's literature. In the texts I discuss here, which are based on the Christian tradition, the central mystery of Christ's triumph, which provides grounds for the hope of resurrection, is placed, like Easter itself, clearly within the spring season, sometimes accompanied by allusions to an ensuing eternal summer. At the same time, because of this very triumph, the symbolism appropriate to Christian mystery often may be located at Frye's comic (in the sense of Dante's *Divina Comedia*) rather than his tragic pole. Nevertheless, since a full appreciation of the Christian mystery cannot exclude the Cross, it must also embody elements of the tragic vision, which are, however, transmuted by symbolism expressing triumph rather than defeat. In the more successful instances of the creation of a sense of religious mystery, therefore, the authors rely on the archetypes appropriate to spring and early summer, and those of comedy rather than of tragedy.

Imagery and symbolism are central to this process, and an effective instrument for discussing these is what David Lodge terms rhetorical analysis: 'analysing the surface structure of narrative texts to show how the linguistic mediation of a story determines its meaning and effect' (*Structuralism*, 21). Lodge makes use of Roman Jakobson's distinction between metonym and metaphor in order to show 'how the realistic novel contrives to build up a pattern of equivalences without violating its illusion of life' (*Structuralism*, 21). Much of the fiction I propose to examine is realist in mode, but even when it is fantasy it tends to use metonym rather than metaphor, though the process often involves what Lodge terms, 'Metonymic Signified I *metaphorically* evok[ing] Signified II' (*Structuralism*, 22, emphasis mine). This process often results in binary polarities such as life and death, creator and creature, light and dark being used in children's literature to convey a sense of mystery.

While the evocation of mystery may in some cases be a central theme of a novel, in most instances it is to be recognized only within certain heightened moments. Such moments, generally characterized by elevated language, are often to be found near the culmination of the plot, where the reader is made aware that the outcome will be positive. Such moments frequently involve what Tolkien, in his discussion of fairy stories in *Tree and Leaf*, describes as 'eucatastrophe ... a sudden and miraculous grace: never to be counted upon to recur' (68). In children's realist fiction, this eucatastrophic effect is often established through coincidences, which may be used to suggest a merciful and omnipotent creator.

A sense of religious mystery can be created only if the reader realizes that there is no natural explanation for the events which occur, something which presents a different kind of challenge for the author according to whether the mode of the text is realism or fantasy. Within realist fiction, the introduction of a powerful *deus ex machina* figure who can set all to rights is not very common. Even dream, the mode used by Susan Coolidge in *What Katy Did* (1872) for the vision which leads Katy to her change of heart about accepting her illness, may fail to convince:

> She thought she was trying to study a lesson out of a book which wouldn't come quite open ... it was in a language which she did not understand ... Suddenly a hand came over her shoulder and took hold of the book.

It opened at once, and showed the whole page. And then the forefinger of the hand began to point to line after line, and as it moved the words became plain, and Katy could read them easily. She looked up. There, stooping over her, was a great beautiful Face. The eyes met hers. The lips smiled.

'Why didn't you ask Me before, little scholar?' said a voice.

'Why, it is *You*, just as Cousin Helen told me!' cried Katy. (127)

Katy's dream is clearly meant to represent an encounter with the divine: Coolidge is using a means employed by many writers, from the Bible onwards, to communicate insight to characters. Dreams, which can be seen as giving access to Jung's 'collective unconscious', are, as Frye suggests, commonly used in literature to represent divine epiphanies (431). The binary opposition between the great and the little, the scholar and the teacher in Coolidge's dream scene, found by many readers to be over-explicit, nevertheless helps to create the sense of 'creatureliness' which Otto identifies as a sign of encounter with the Holy (21). Coolidge fails to convey a sense of awe of 'beyondness' since very little in the example is left unsaid. Another limitation is that the purpose of the vision is to improve Katy's behaviour, rather than give her access to spiritual experience as such. The initial image of the hand could serve as an effective metonym for the divine, were it not too emphatically reinforced by the ensuing mentions of the face, the voice, the eyes and the finger, all depersonalized by the repeated 'the'. These separate details do not convey the impression that Katy's encounter has been with a whole divine person but convey materiality rather than spirituality. This concreteness is virtually the antithesis of any sense of religious mystery because it seems to leave so little unsaid and may render this passage banal rather than mysterious. Perhaps the use of symbolism from the natural world, which as Frye suggests frequently provides figures for religious visions (432), might have imparted to this scene and to Katy's eventual recovery a greater sense of the miraculous.

An alternative means of indicating a mysterious source of power is coincidence. Writers of children's literature often use fortunate providence as a way of reflecting their personal belief that the universe is governed by Goodness. A notable example of this 'eucatastrophe' is at the end of Anna Sewell's *Black Beauty* (1877), when, after all his troubles, the protagonist, against all odds, is recognized as he is being groomed. The passage perhaps conveys Sewell's personal conviction that God is in charge of the destiny of all his creatures, knowing us as we are known:

> 'White star in the forehead, one white foot on the off side, this little knot just in that place ... It *must* be Black Beauty! Why, Beauty! Beauty! Do you know me! Little Joe Green, that almost killed you?' ...
>
> I could not say that I remembered him, for now he was a fine-grown young fellow, with black whiskers and a man's voice, but I was sure he knew me, and that he was Joe Green, and I was very glad. (216–17)

Here Joe Green, in relation to the horse, serves metonymically as a semi-divine figure, who both recognizes Beauty and will ensure his long-continued ease and happiness, perhaps signifying eternal life. There is in this short passage a binary opposition between the creature and creator figures; both are anatomized, but Beauty's attributes metonymically work to dependence and Joe's to power. For instance, the foot is not described in human terms as 'right' but in terms of the horse's position when ridden, and the 'knot' is that inflicted by human surgery, while Joe's whiskers and voice signify his attainment of man's estate and possession of authority. Creatureliness and dependence rather than awe are predominant here; the reader may also have some scepticism about the likelihood of this meeting. However, the language and attendant symbolism – the star, the recollection of a near fatal experience, the emphasis on the importance of Beauty being known by the divine representative figure – have an archetypal effect, as does the paradisal significance of Beauty's final location: 'I fancy I am still in the orchard at Birtwick, standing with my old friends under the apple trees' (218). As well as providing a reversal of the Fall, the images here are among those identified by Frye as appropriate to the comic vision, involving as they do a pastoral and cultivated world (Frye 432). Black Beauty is now seen to be at the beginning of a new life, to be resurrected into the spring-like surroundings of his youth, but with greater wisdom and experience. Although this book is ostensibly only about a horse, its wider, near-allegorical significance is apparent, especially in light of the Quaker faith of Sewell.

More recent books which make use of coincidence to convey a similar sense of providence include *War Horse* (1982) by Michael Morpurgo, who acknowledges Sewell's influence on his work, and Anne Holm's *I am David* (1963). A sense of God's power and goodness is also communicated in earlier novels such as Frances Hodgson

Burnett's *The Secret Garden* (1911), which provides a clear instance within a generally realist framework of some kind of supernatural power preserving the lives and destinies of the child characters, Mary and Colin. Near the end of the book, Mr Craven has a dream in which he hears the voice of his dead wife, whom he instantly recognizes. She summons him back to Misselthwaite Manor, and when he wakes, her call is reinforced by his reception of a letter from Susan Sowerby. Once home, he witnesses how his young son has been reborn to health, as has the garden so dear to his wife:

> The place was a wilderness of autumn gold and purple and violet and flaming scarlet, and on every side were sheaves of late lilies standing together – lilies which were white or white and ruby ... Late roses climbed and hung and clustered, and the sunshine deepening the hue of the yellowing trees made one feel that one stood in an embowered temple of gold ...
> 'I thought it would be dead,' he said.
> 'Mary thought so at first,' said Colin. 'But it came alive.' (251)

The evocative images of this passage, with their focus on colour (yellow, purple, scarlet, ruby, white, and gold), flowers (lilies and roses), the sunshine, and the 'embowered temple' metonymically combine to create a sense of holiness. The flowers, while literally a part of the scene described, at the same time serve as a metaphor for the divine, thus recalling Lodge's categorization of this type of usage as 'Metonymic Signified I metaphorically evok[ing] Signified II.' The novel generally is marked by the sense of transition from winter to spring, and of resurrection from death to life. At this stage of the novel, these images reinforce a cluster of archetypal nature images which proliferate throughout the book, and are associated with certain characters, notably Dickon and his mother, Susan Sowerby. The cumulative effect of the nature 'Magic', the voice of Colin's dead mother, and the letter from the live 'Earth Mother' create a strong sense of divine power. While little sense of awe is evident in this passage, there is a strong sense of human beings as creatures of Nature, which has been almost personified throughout the book as 'The Magic'. Burnett's approach is not the *via negativa* of claiming that it is impossible to express what she means, but rather one of employing images with an archetypal resonance (starting with the garden itself) in order to build up a sense of mystery both natural and supernatural. As befits someone with a strong belief in Christian

Science (Thwaite 88), Burnett also incorporates a theme of both mental and physical healing.

All the books considered so far could be described as broadly realist, and while Burnett's symbolism more successfully gives the impression of divine intervention than that of the other writers, all are in some way hampered by the need to remain within the limits of what consensus thinking judges to be possible. The situation of the writer of fantasy is perhaps easier, as the creation of characters of more than human power may provide a less problematic mode of representing divine power and mystery.

Probably the best known examples in postwar fiction of the attempt to convey religious mystery in children's fiction are in C. S. Lewis's Narnia series. The location of these books centrally within the Christian divine *comedy* is firmly established by the themes of growth, creation, and restoration from frozen winter which pervade several volumes of the series, notably *The Magician's Nephew* (1955) and *The Lion, the Witch and the Wardrobe* (1950).

Central to all the Narnia books is the lion Aslan, a character who conveys a sense of religious mystery, even awe. Most readers first encounter him in *The Lion, the Witch and the Wardrobe*, where Lewis introduces the character by means of the reaction of other characters. The Beaver refers to Aslan:

> And now a very curious thing happened. None of the children knew who Aslan was any more than you do; but the moment the Beaver had spoken these words everyone felt quite different. Perhaps it has sometimes happened to you in a dream that someone says something which you don't understand but in the dream it feels as if it had some enormous meaning ... a lovely meaning too lovely to put into words, which makes the dream so beautiful that you remember it all your life and are always wishing you could get into that dream again ... Lucy got the feeling you have when you wake up in the morning and realize it is the beginning of the holidays or the beginning of summer. (65)

This represents one of the most deliberate attempts in children's literature to convey religious awe in terms of everyday experiences. Lewis here and elsewhere communicates the sense of fascination, dependence and 'creatureliness' suggested by Otto, though it may be that his use of the 'holiday' analogy and the rather banal repetition of 'lovely' make the passage too explicit. It is interesting that Lewis again uses the comparison with holidays at the end of *The Last Battle* (1956), the final book of the series, to describe the dawn of eternal life: '[t]he term is over: the holidays have begun' (165). The reference to dream in the earlier quotation is consistent with Jung's belief that dreaming provides the easiest access to the collective unconscious, but for some readers the school term and holidays may seem inadequate signifiers of religious mystery.

In *The Lion, the Witch and the Wardrobe*, Lewis goes on to describe Aslan through the words of characters who know him. Mr Beaver tells the children Aslan is 'the great Lion' and when Susan expresses her nervousness about meeting such a dangerous animal, he continues: '[c]ourse he isn't safe. But he's good' (75). It is only after these preliminaries, and a building up of suspense in a chapter entitled, 'Aslan is Nearer', that Lewis actually introduces a description of Aslan himself:

> People who have not been in Narnia sometimes think that a thing cannot be good and terrible at the same time. If the children had ever thought so, they were cured of it now. For when they tried to look at Aslan's face they just caught a glimpse of the golden mane and the great, royal, solemn, overwhelming eyes; and then they found they couldn't look at him and went all trembly. (117)

Here again Lewis is using language which creates a sense of awe. It is interesting to observe the contrast with Coolidge's explicit emphasis on the great 'Face' which Katy sees, as here the children find it impossible to look at Aslan's face; at the same time the words 'golden mane' work to signify power and splendour. The physical reactions of the children involve the reader in the experience, and although 'went all trembly' may be a very apt description of the sensation of religious awe, its colloquial effect is not perhaps wholly appropriate to the register otherwise employed.

Lewis's work suffers from a didactic tendency to ensure that the reader is made aware of Aslan's power and knowledge, an aspect which leads him too frequently to *state* this. Here, for example, the use of four epithets, 'great, royal, solemn, overwhelming', for Aslan's eyes, while it may reflect Lewis's difficulty in describing mystery, at the same time tends to detract from conviction. The symbol of the great Lion is a powerful one, although it might seem to contradict the location of Christian mystery generally with the comic rather than the tragic pole; lions are certainly not domestic animals. However, the intertextual links generated through Biblical associations (the 'Lion of Judah' often being seen as a figure for Christ, the lion lying down with the lamb as a metaphor for peace) tend to override the lion's power as an animal of prey, so that we have in his figure a conflation of the tragic and comic with the latter appearing supreme because of Aslan's goodness and love. Lewis ensures that his descriptions of Aslan's appearance and actions maintain the tension between the good and the terrifying; when Lucy and Susan encounter Aslan after his resurrection, they play with him, and 'whether it was more like playing with a thunderstorm or playing with a kitten Lucy could never make up her mind' (Lion, 149). Lewis has thus, in what is usually read as the first volume of the series, created Aslan as a character who is awesome, all-powerful and yet approachable. This is reinforced throughout the Narnia series in what might be described as the mystical relationship between Aslan and Lucy. The theme of healing is pervasive too, notably in *The Magician's Nephew* (1955), with the sudden restoration to health of Diggory's mother after she eats a piece of apple, symbolically reversing the negative connotations of the apple of the Fall.

Lewis's admiration for George MacDonald is well known (Wilson 45), and his desire to include a character embodying religious mystery may have been influenced by the semi-divine Grandmother in MacDonald's *The Princess and the Goblin* (1872) and *The Princess and Curdie* (1882). She is a figure of immense age – 'more than a hundred' (Goblin, 21) – has instantaneous powers of healing, and spins the very fine thread – associated both with the Fates and the minotaur myth – which enables Irene to rescue Curdie. We also hear about her pigeons – reminiscent of the dove which symbolizes the Holy Spirit – and her lamp, which resembles a moon, with all its goddess associations. MacDonald thus uses archetypal images to suggest the grandmother's possession of supernatural power and to create an aura of mystery about her; the experience of encountering her makes Irene aware of her own creatureliness. The grandmother's numinous qualities differ from those of Aslan, perhaps more obviously associating her with the feminine side of deity, relating to archetypes of wisdom. Place seems to be more important in creating a sense of religious mystery in MacDonald's works than in Lewis's; the grandmother is only 'experienced', when she is prepared to be, within her attic.

While the major world religions have tended to associate mystery with certain sacred places, pantheism, lacking an emphasis on a personal God, perhaps attaches the greatest significance to place. Douglas Davies in his introduction to *Sacred Place* claims that even when a religion 'wishes all life contexts to be sacred', it tends nevertheless to envisage this sacredness as being heightened in certain specific locations (1). Kenneth Grahame, whose orthodox Christian upbringing left him with a hostility to most established religions yet a strong sense of the sacred (Green 36, 83, 188), is described by Peter Green as a 'rural pantheist' (137), and evidence of this may be found throughout his work. Several contributors to *Sacred Place* note that rivers are frequently seen as especially holy locations in, for instance, Christianity, Buddhism, Chinese religions, and particularly Hinduism, so that Grahame's use of the river as a place of vision in his best-known work *The Wind in the Willows* (1908) has many religious precedents. Frye associates rivers with the comic vision, and floods and the sea with the tragic vision (432); the Water Rat's resistance to the temptation to wander provided by the wayfarer Rat in chapter nine could be seen as Grahame's probably unconscious fidelity to his ultimately comic vision. The powerful emotive effect of the novel's springtide opening scene creates a powerful overall impression of comic vision which pervades the whole text.

The major locus of religious mystery in *The Wind in the Willows*, again because of its association with comic vision, is in the chapter 'The Piper at the Gates of *Dawn* [my emphasis]', the quality of which has proved somewhat contentious among critics. W. W. Robson states: '"[h]istorically speaking it was ... an afterthought on the author's part; artistically, it is the reason for which the whole book exists"' (quoted in Hunt 101). Green suggests that Grahame was much affected by some kind of visionary experience which provided the source for the chapter concerned (84), and it was clearly important to Grahame to express this in some way, presumably for himself as much as for any reader. In this chapter, it is impossible to separate the figure of Pan, who makes such an impact on Mole and Rat, from the place in which they hear his music. We have a sense of the scene meaning more than we or the characters understand, and Grahame's technique of conveying the experience through witnesses recalls the biblical narrative of Christ's Transfiguration (Mark 9: 1–9). As in the description of Christ's raiment becoming white as snow and his companions being Moses and Elias, in Grahame's novel the numinous effect is created by the incomprehension and subsequent incoherence of the witnesses. Grahame's description is lengthy, and brief excerpts can hardly convey more than an impression of its effect within the book. Rat and Mole anxiously search for the young otter, Portly, when Rat begins to hear music:

'It's gone!' sighed the Rat ... 'so beautiful and strange and new! Since it was to end so soon, I almost wish I had never heard it. For it has roused a longing in me that is pain, and nothing seems worth while but just to hear that sound once more and go on listening to it for ever. No! There it is again!' he cried, alert once more. Entranced, he was silent for a long space, spellbound ... 'the beauty of it! The merry bubble and joy, the thin, clear happy call of the distant piping!' ... Rapt, transported, trembling, he was possessed in all his senses by this new divine thing that caught up his helpless soul and swung and dandled it, a powerless but happy infant in a strong sustaining grasp. (131–2)

In this and what follows, there is much language which both generates a sense of physical involvement and conveys an impression of divinity, such as 'breathless and transfixed', 'intoxicating melody', 'unsurpassable', and '[h]ere in this holy place, here if anywhere, surely we shall find Him!' The effect is enhanced in particular by the use of exclamations. It is notable that, unlike Lewis, Grahame here is making use of metaphor in addition to metonym. Particularly at the end of the passage quoted above, the cluster of images associated with infancy enhances the sense of the characters' creatureliness. Whatever the nature of Grahame's presumed personal mystical experience, the sense of awe it generated in him could subconsciously have been the origin of his choice of animal, that is, 'creaturely', protagonists. Whether readers share the characters' fascination and incomprehension is a matter for them, yet it is possible that in his endeavour to convey the nature of the experience, Grahame is guilty of over-explicitness:

Then suddenly the Mole felt a great Awe fall upon him, an awe that turned his muscles to water, bowed his head, and rooted his feet to the ground. It was no panic terror – indeed he felt wonderfully at peace and happy – but it was an awe that smote and held him, and without seeing, he knew it could only mean that some august Presence was very, very near ... Then the two animals, crouching to the earth, bowed their heads and did worship. (134–6)

A number of children's writers, notably Tolkien and Lewis, have made use of Judaeo-Christian, classical and Scandinavian myths, which often adds resonance to their fiction for the reader who is familiar with the originals, while providing the child reader with what serves as a pre-text for later readings. Jung regarded myth as a means of getting closer to the 'deeper instinctive strata of the human psyche' than is generally possible 'in the consciousness of modern man' (36) and his ideas have been particularly important to several children's writers who have attempted to include within their works the mystery of evil, an endeavour which might be thought even more intractable than the mystery of encounter with the Holy. Unlike orthodox Christians, Jung considered there to be a dark side to God, and expressed his 'personal indignation with God for His "divine savagery and ruthlessness"' (Stevens 250). The idea of a balance in the universe between goodness and what seems at first to be evil has proved attractive to those who find the concepts of a personal devil, or of utterly evil characters, equally unacceptable.

Susan Cooper's *Seaward* (1983) is the story of Cally and Westerly, both of whom have lost their parents and are on a mysterious symbolic quest over a strange country dominated by Lugan, the figure of light, and Taranis, that of darkness, to the islands of the dead, of Tir n'An Og. Faced upon their arrival with the choice between life and death, they turn towards life. Cooper makes use of figures and places from Celtic mythology to provide a story framework which helps to make the quest accessible to the young reader. As the characters come to terms with the mystery of death, they are also informed of the balance between light and dark; Taranis says to Lugan: '"I have two faces, certainly. But so do you."' She continues, '"I am Death ... But Life rules with me. He is my brother and my father and my son, and all of them are called Lugan. We are one, even in our opposition"' (163). Cooper's ultimate rejection of duality, suggesting that what seemed to be evil forces were really simply the dark side of the good, is similar to the way in which, for instance, Ursula Le Guin in *A Wizard of Earthsea* (1968) shows the sense of balance within the apparently good and evil sides of her central character, Ged. The work of Cooper and Le Guin brings to mind Jung's concept of the Shadow. As Stevens says:

> There is a very understandable tendency ... for desirable traits to be built into the persona, while qualities perceived as undesirable, unacceptable or reprehensible are repressed or hidden from view. These repressed dispositions come to form another complex or sub-personality, which Jung called the *shadow*. (43)

Le Guin's magician, Ged, is pursued by a dark figure whom he has liberated when, in his youthful arrogance, he deals with spells he does not understand. It is only at the end of the novel that Ged realizes the identity of his pursuer and addresses it by his own name, thus taking ownership of his negative as well as his positive qualities. Le Guin's portrayal of evil here, and its association with the human character, perhaps reflects her Taoist belief in the importance of balance in the universe.

This kind of treatment of the mystery of evil, generally making use of images Frye associates with both the comic and the tragic visions (432), works better than some of the attempts by more traditional Christian writers to depict evil. Lewis's White Witch in the Narnia series appears slightly stagey, while Tolkien's depiction of Gollum in *The Hobbit* (1937) evokes too much pathos for him to be seen as absolutely evil. The fact that Lewis and Tolkien were respectively Anglican and Roman Catholic, and relatively 'orthodox' in their beliefs about good and evil, perhaps inclined them to set the mystery of evil within a framework which renders it less convincing to those who do not share their theological interpretations. Both authors presumably believed in a personal and powerful devil; it would thus be difficult for them to have presented evil characters as causing the same degree of awe as that conveyed by a divine figure.

It may be that the direct use of material related to any specific religious communion is less effective today as a vehicle of religious mystery, good or evil, than the more symbolic use made in fantasy. Examination of children's books based on the Bible reinforces this conviction. Historical novels, such as Elizabeth George Speare's *The Bronze Bow* (1961), often present the figure of Jesus in a way which never quite conveys the same sense of mystery as the gospels, while children's versions of Bible stories are frequently little more than edited and illustrated versions of the text. Enid Blyton's many adaptations for children of stories from both the Old and New Testaments tend to play down any mysterious and awe-inspiring aspects; her treatment of Moses encountering God in the Burning Bush, for instance, amplifies the scriptural account and almost attempts to explain it, processes which tend to subtract the mystery from it. The bush loses its supernatural significance and becomes merely a puzzle; Blyton is most successful when closest to the Bible, as in her concluding words, '[t]hen Moses hid his face, for he was afraid to look upon God' (69).

To communicate a sense of mystery, it is probably more effective either to draw back in incomprehension, or to transmute it in some way by the use of symbol. As was suggested at the outset, both of these approaches to transcendence might seem more appropriate to poetry than prose. Much religious verse for children, however, has tended to be strongly moral or instructional, despite the fact that the work of poets such as Henry Vaughan, Thomas Traherne, and William Blake suggests that childhood has a special openness to religious mystery. In 'The Retreate', Vaughan writes: 'Happy those early days! When I / Shin'd in my Angell-infancy,' while Traherne's *Centuries* are replete with recollections of how his perceptions in childhood presented illuminations recaptured only with difficulty in adulthood: '[m]y knowledge was divine: I knew by intuition those things which [later] I collected again, by the highest reason' (III.2). Blake's *Songs of Innocence and Experience* contain attractive images, strong rhythms and simple rhyme, partly because Blake was influenced by the Nonconformist hymn writers, Isaac Watts and Charles Wesley. Such Blake poems as 'The Tyger' are regarded by anthologists as accessible to children, although their full meaning remains beyond the intellectual understanding of adults.

Few other poets get anywhere near achieving Blake's fusion between simple language and mystery. Those who combine depth of religious conviction with the choice of a child audience include Cecil Frances Alexander ('There is a green hill far away') and Christina Rossetti, whose 'Goblin Market', while scarcely a children's poem, has often appeared in anthologies for children. More recently, the work of Charles Causley is characterized by a combination of religious belief and a lack of condescension or didacticism in his poems for children.

It is apparent that some contemporary prose authors, such as Robert Cormier – in *The Chocolate War* (1975), *Darcy* (1990), and *Tunes for Bears to Dance to* (1992) – and Monica Furlong – in *Wise Child* (1987) and *Juniper* (1990) – are not afraid of treating explicitly religious themes, while Michael Morpurgo – in *War Horse* (1982) – does not shirk providential coincidences. Philip Pullman's use of *Paradise Lost* in his trilogy *His Dark Materials* (1995–99) suggests that some authors today are prepared to confront some elements of religious mystery in fiction.

Paradoxically, the more a writer attempts to make religious mystery explicit, the less mysterious it becomes, yet if the approach is too indirect, there is the danger not only that child readers will not understand, but that they may have no awareness of the book involving mystery. This is of course true of all attempts to convey religious mystery in fiction, even for adults. Mystics have been uncertain whether to stand back in silence, in which case they would communicate nothing of their experiences, or to render them in terms which by making them communicable might devalue and make them seem banal. Whether or not the reader possesses a frame of reference which gives symbolism its full resonance, the most successful attempts at creating numinosity seem to be those in which 'the archetypes of literature' make their appearance and are allowed to speak for themselves, rather than being over-explained. Perhaps the most evocative attempts are those which embrace the tragic as well as the comic vision, and which succeed in conveying a sense of the ultimate triumph of good. Lewis perhaps most effectively voices the sentiments of the author who seeks to convey a sense of religious mystery at the end of the concluding volume of his Narnia series, *The Last Battle*, when the narrator voices his inability to describe Aslan's own country at which his protagonists have arrived: '[t]he things that began to happen after that were so great and beautiful that I cannot write them' (165).

Works cited

Blyton, Enid. 'The Burning Bush', in *Tales from the Bible*. London: Methuen, 1944, pp. 65–70.

Burnett, Frances Hodgson. *The Secret Garden* [1911]. Harmondsworth: Penguin, 1951.

Coolidge, Susan. *What Katy Did* [1872]. Harmondsworth: Penguin, 1982.

Cooper, Susan. *Seaward* [1983]. Harmondsworth: Penguin, 1985.

Davies, Douglas. 'Introduction: Raising the Issues', in Jean Holm and John Bowker (eds), *Sacred Place*. London: Pinter, 1994, pp. 1–7.

Frye, Northrop. 'The Archetypes of Literature' [1951] in David Lodge (ed.), *20th Century Literary Criticism* Harlow: Longman, 1972, pp. 422–33.

Grahame, Kenneth. *The Wind in the Willows* [1908]. Harmondsworth: Penguin, 1961.

Green, Peter. *Kenneth Grahame*. London: John Murray, 1959.

Hunt, Peter. *The Wind in the Willows: A Fragmented Arcadia*. New York: Twayne, 1994.

Jung, Carl G. et al. *Man and his Symbols*. London: Picador, 1964.

Le Guin, Ursula. *A Wizard of Earthsea* [1968]. Harmondsworth: Penguin, 1971.

Lewis, C. S. *The Last Battle* [1956]. Harmondsworth: Penguin, 1964.

——. *The Lion, the Witch and the Wardrobe* [1950]. Harmondsworth: Penguin, 1959.

Lodge, David. *Working with Structuralism: Essays and Reviews on Nineteenth- and Twentieth-Century Literature*. London: Routledge & Kegan Paul, 1981.

—— (ed.) *20th Century Literary Criticism*. Harlow: Longman, 1972.

MacDonald, George. *The Princess and the Goblin*. [1872]. London: Collins, 1956.

Otto, Rudolf. *The Idea of the Holy* [1917], 4th edn, trans. John Harvey. Oxford: Oxford University Press, 1926.

Sewell, Anna. *Black Beauty* [1877]. Harmondsworth: Penguin, 1954.

Speare, Elizabeth George. *The Bronze Bow* [1961]. London: Gollancz, 1962.

Stevens, Anthony. *On Jung*. Harmondsworth: Penguin, 1990.

Storr, Anthony. *Jung*. London: Collins, 1973.

Thwaite, Ann. *Waiting for the Party: The Life of Frances Hodgson Burnett* [1974]. London: Faber, 1994.

Tolkien, J. R. R. *Tree and Leaf* [1964]. London: Unwin, 1975.

Traherne, Thomas. 'Centuries', in Alan Bradford (ed.), *Thomas Traherne: Selected Poems and Prose*. Harmondsworth: Penguin, 1991, pp. 187–315.

Vaughan, Henry. 'The Retreate', in French Fogle (ed.), *The Complete Poetry of Henry Vaughan*. New York: Anchor, 1964, p. 169.

Wilson, A. N. *C. S. Lewis: A Biography*. London: Collins, 1990.

3
Nancy's Ancestors: the Mystery of Imaginative Female Power in *The Secret Garden* and *A Little Princess*

Mary Jeanette Moran

When my grandmother gave me *The Secret of the Old Clock* (1930), the first book in the Nancy Drew series, I immediately became addicted to the escapades of the dauntless heroine. From my ten-year-old point of view, it seemed perfectly natural that a woman of the oh-so-mature age of eighteen would have the unlimited independence that Nancy enjoyed. Looking back from an adult perspective, however, it appears a bit bizarre that the young sleuth could gallivant around the world to track villains and right wrongs. As a child, I never suspected that Nancy's freedom might be due to the dearth of authority figures in her life; she had a father, of course, but Carson Drew was always more deeply involved in lawyering than in parenting. Anyone who remembers her Nancy Drew will also recollect Hannah Gruen, the 'mother-substitute' who has cared for Nancy since the detective's toddler days. Interestingly enough, Hannah never seems to have the authority of a mother, although it is debatable whether this is simply due to her servant status, or whether any power she might have is further diminished by Nancy's frequent need to rescue her from various ill-intentioned criminals. The ineffectiveness of Hannah as a mother-substitute, coupled with the absence of Nancy's biological mother, poses a distinct advantage for Nancy's independence. While a mother might encourage her daughter to accept the passive gender role thrust on her by society, the absence of such an authority allows Nancy the freedom to uncover secrets through her sleuthing even as she risks her life to gain that information.

In *The Girl Sleuth*, Bobbie Ann Mason suggests that I am not alone in my fondness for Nancy's freewheeling life. She maintains, 'that [the] heroines of adolescence were teenage detectives with unusual freedom is important to feminist consciousness – for better or worse' (6).

According to patriarchal standards, women develop a bad reputation by 'knowing' too much, whether that knowledge is about sexuality, politics, or science; women are also supposed to remain passive rather than active. By virtue of her profession, however, Nancy breaks both taboos when, as all detectives must, she acts in order to know. In her alliance with knowledge as well as her active self-determination, Nancy represents a distinctly 'unfeminine' lifestyle, which is exactly why she has fascinated female readers for decades.

We can also see this intriguing dynamic of active knowledge at work in two novels which predate Nancy Drew and, arguably, much of children's mystery literature: Frances Hodgson Burnett's *A Little Princess* (1888) and *The Secret Garden* (1911). Although the increasingly liberated Nancy of the 1990s shows less and less danger of succumbing to stereotypes of female passivity, late nineteenth-century heroines had to counteract a much more widespread scepticism about women's capacity to maintain individual autonomy. Female authors encountered a similar distrust of their abilities, leading to what Shirley Foster and Judy Simons have called the 'hybrid nature' of early classics of girls' literature (20). In other words, these books paradoxically seem to reinforce patriarchally sanctioned gender roles even though they also provide scope for feminine self-exploration and self-expression. Despite the patriarchal overtones, however, *A Little Princess* and *The Secret Garden* provide an important backdrop for later novels with more transgressive heroines like Nancy Drew. The commonalties between these two sets of books suggest, first, that Burnett's novels set the stage for later developments in the feminist undertones of girls' literature; second, that they support the possibility that encounters with mystery enable the development of a feminist viewpoint.

Although Burnett's novels focus on the heroines themselves over any discoveries they make, both books have mysteries at their centres. Mary Lennox, the protagonist of *The Secret Garden*, not only solves the mystery of the eerie cries which float through her uncle's house; she also solves the problem behind the mystery – her cousin Colin's illness – with the help of the secret garden's near mystical powers. For Sara Crewe, the 'little princess' referred to in the title, the central mystery is the disappearance of her fortune, which she eventually discovers hidden, in true 'purloined letter' fashion, right next door. The importance of these mysteries, though, lies in the way in which Mary and Sara respond to them: in the process of their discoveries, they grow in self-determination as they investigate different means by which to make their voices heard. Throughout the books, both girls experiment with sources of imperialist, maternal, and creative authority. Although each of these areas allows an expression of feminine autonomy, modern readers may feel that the imperial and maternal sites actually contradict feminist ideals. This essay argues that authority, acquired through imagination, creativity or intellect, remains the most redeeming actualization of power for Burnett's heroines.

If the Nancy Drew mysteries enable the heroine's physical freedom, Sara and Mary take advantage of their mysteries to develop the empowering possibilities of the imagination. As the eventual result of these imaginative acts, mysteries get (re)solved; more significantly, however, the imaginative process models an image of autonomy which may very well be what continues to draw young readers (and especially young female readers) to modern-day mysteries or fantasy stories. This foregrounding of imaginative power reminds us of the ways that more modern girls' books also privilege imaginative exploration; just as Sara and Mary exercise their mental capabilities to counter the problems which face them, Nancy must always use her intellect to anticipate a criminal's next move.

While *The Secret Garden* and *A Little Princess* may not be conventional mysteries, the imaginative power of Burnett's heroines locates them as early figures in the tradition of the many mystery series which represent women as empowered, albeit in often flawed or problematic ways. My approach to the element of mystery in these books, then, is twofold. Finding feminist heroines in early juvenile fiction is always something of a mystery (in the sense of a problem whose solution is unknown and perhaps unknowable), since patriarchal echoes can hinder or discourage the search for an occluded matrix of power. In addition to resembling a mystery, however, this search is also served by mystery. In other words, well before Nancy Drew and her ilk appeared on the scene, their textual predecessors were taking advantage of mysterious circumstances to exercise intellectual and imaginative authority.

In the criticism on Burnett's novels for children, *The Secret Garden* has received the greater share of attention as a novel more psychologically complex than Burnett's other book for girls. Recent criticism, such as the work of Phyllis Bixler and Claudia Marquis, as well as that of Foster and Simons, has emphasized the existence of a nurturing feminine presence in *The Secret Garden* but also stresses the exclusion of that positive element from the novel's conclusion. Bixler states that 'Burnett's masterpiece [is] a celebration of nature's power as a primarily female power ... [a] community of mothers centered in the secret garden' (209, 213).

Marquis, in contrast, argues that this community of mothers needs to be placed in a historical context in order to be understood. She claims that 'the book clearly promotes a conception of motherhood as power of a sort ... ostensibly it honours the mother, but never observes that this is actually a cultural procedure by which women are subordinated and consumed' (184). Similarly, Foster and Simons point out that 'the text constructs a significant opposition between the male establishment and the ability of women to deconstruct that order and invest it with new meaning' (188) but that '[t]he fantasies of female power which the novel projects so powerfully remain ... tantalizingly unresolved' (172). Marquis and Foster and Simons make convincing arguments that the closing chapters of *The Secret Garden* betray the feminist possibilities of the earlier portion of the novel. However, by examining the interplay of authority throughout the book, we can see that many of the positive aspects of Mary Lennox's search for feminine power lie in the search itself. A concurrent discussion of *A Little Princess*, the less studied of the two works, can help us in our attempt to understand the appeal of these books, since Burnett allows Sara Crewe to retain some of the power which is forbidden to Mary Lennox.

The quest for authority and self-expression is inherently imbued with mystery for Burnett's heroines, simply because they are heroines instead of heroes. According to patriarchal assumptions of the time, the idea of agency for girls would be an oxymoron, a mystery without a solution. As Deborah Gorham tells us, Victorian notions of parenting dictated that boys should assert themselves while girls should remain passive (*Victorian Girl*, 75). Gorham also describes the Victorian system of child-rearing as dependent on organization and structure: '[t]he perception of the child as naturally sinful was nearly always accompanied by a belief that the patriarchal model for family organisation was the only correct one. According to that model, a family functions properly only if it possesses a hierarchy of authority' (76). Girls received messages encouraging their subordination from widely differing sources. Female characters in both religious tracts and 'penny dreadfuls' were either

> damsels in distress, pure, innocent models of nineteenth-century femininity ... [or] girls or women who have been led astray by passion or by a desire for wealth or power, and who are invariably punished for their unfeminine behaviour. (Gorham, 'Ideology', 41)

In order for children – especially female children – to be able to exercise authority, then, the figures which usually exert control over them must be removed or made ineffective, and Burnett does this with a vengeance. Both Sara and Mary are orphaned. Even before he dies, Sara's father not only places her in a boarding school at the age of seven, but then apparently does not see her for the next four years. Mary is the lone survivor of an epidemic in India, in which her father and mother have 'died and been carried away in the night' (*Secret Garden*, 6). Although these children seem to be disadvantaged, the lack of parental guidance actually sets the stage for opportunities of autonomy.

Just as the absence of parents leaves Burnett's children to their own devices, the adults who do appear, much like Hannah Gruen, prove to be ineffective as authority figures. In *A Little Princess*, Captain Crewe is a 'rash, innocent young man [who] wanted his little girl to have everything she admired and everything he admired himself' (14). As a result of misguided intentions, Sara's father and her classmates' parents transfer the care of their daughters to Miss Minchin, the cold, selfish, and money-driven headmistress. The children, then, not only lack the supposed benefit of direct parental care, but the parent-substitute fails them as well, leaving them with no adult guidance. This situation directly contradicts prevailing theories of child education in the Victorian era when, as Gorham points out, the 'middle-class mother was encouraged to exhibit an unprecedented amount of concern with the child-rearing process' (*Victorian Girl*, 65) while 'the husband and father … had a God-given responsibility to be head of the family' (76). With no mothers to guide them and fathers who behave in childish or self-centred ways, the girls at Miss Minchin's school suffer from neglect, but their situation also allows the stronger characters among them, such as Sara, the opportunity to exercise authority on their own behalf. Sara, for instance, takes advantage of her destabilized surroundings to reinvent herself as princess, political prisoner, mother, and philanthropist. She solves the mystery of parental neglect by turning to her own imaginative resources.

In *The Secret Garden*, Mary Lennox experiences a similar lack of adult concern for her mental well-being. Even before she is orphaned, her parents abandon her to the care of servants. After her parents fall victim to the plague, Mary is thrust into dependence on relatives who feel no affection for her; her uncle even refuses to see her when she first comes to Misselthwaite Manor (19). Mary's new home at times eerily mirrors her plague-desolated house in India, since she finds Misselthwaite to be a 'queer place [where] one scarcely ever saw any one at all' (46). In fact, Misselthwaite resembles both a haunted house and a gothic mansion with its gloomy atmosphere and disembodied voices. Left to her own devices, Mary gradually finds ways to amuse herself; interestingly, it is precisely because she has never been taught the proper way to behave that she manages to survive in her initially lonely environment. When confronted with a rainy day, she decides to explore the house, never dreaming that she might need the approval of an authority figure to do so: '[s]he had never been taught to ask permission to do things, and she knew nothing at all about authority' – that is, authority which originates anywhere but from herself (47). The neglectful behaviour of Mary's parents may have turned her into the disagreeable child which Burnett portrays; however, it is only through continuing neglect that she is able to recover from the effects of her early upbringing. Mary's disdain for adults benefits her bedridden cousin Colin as well, for as Elizabeth Keyser notes, '[f]rom the first Mary is an independent, self-contained, yet self-assertive child ... she defies adult authority in order to find, befriend, and liberate Colin' (9). Burnett suggests that Mary actually thrives in a vacuum of adult care at this point in her life. Whenever an adult intervenes (an adult who has the ability to control her, as opposed to the servants who give her guidance but who do not have the class sanction to give her orders) she instantly shrinks into a shadow of her healthier, happier self. At the mere thought of encountering her uncle, for instance, '[a]ll the pink left Mary's cheeks. Her heart began to thump and she felt herself changing into a stiff, plain, silent child again' (100). Because she is emotionally scarred by the neglect of her parents, the only environment that allows Mary to recover is one removed from adult control.

Mary and Sara, then, encounter and take advantage of an empowering lack of adult supervision when they travel to England. The 'mystery' surrounding successful feminine independence requires that they find a way to develop their own authority without bringing the forces of patriarchy crashing down on them. Neither heroine lacks experience in giving orders; in fact, both girls have enjoyed an unusual capacity for authority from their earliest years, simply by virtue of their status as white children in colonized India. Colonial power does not provide a lasting source of power for either girl, however, partly because it does not transfer well to English soil. Sara even seems to disregard her history of imperial authority once she becomes a resident of England. Although she has 'been used to seeing many servants who ... called her Missee Sahib and gave her her own way in everything,' she does not condescend to her English servants, and her fantasies of royalty are those of an English princess, not an Indian ranee or an imperial 'Mem Sahib' (*Little Princess*, 8). At the end of the novel, Sara does re-enter a colonialist power dynamic when she accepts it as right that the Indian servant Ram Dass should salaam to her. However, she does not actively choose imperialist power as a way of exercising authority.

In her contrary way, Mary not only takes complete advantage of her unlimited power over native servants while in India – she considers them 'not people' (*Secret Garden*, 24) – she also tries to transfer this type of authority to her life in England:

> Mary had always slapped her Ayah in the face when she was angry. She wondered a little what [Martha] would do if one slapped her in the face ... she had a sturdy way which made Mistress Mary wonder if she might not even slap back – if the person who slapped her was only a little girl. (22)

Mary finds that the new circumstances of her life have changed the way in which people respond to her, and her relations of power will now be dictated not by her supposedly superior race but by her inferior age.

Mary's attempt to control others through imperialist power fails because, as the book implies, although Indian servants might exist to serve one's every whim, English servants, while still comfortingly maintaining their lower-class status, must at least be addressed with respect. On a broader lever, the imperialist authority to which both Sara and Mary have access is a corrupted authority at best, since it attempts to invalidate the agency not just of one child, but of a whole people. In order to be successful either in their fictional worlds or as fictional characters in the world of the reader, Sara and Mary must find a way of exercising authority which is not complicit in the oppression of another marginalized group.

In a traditionally approved feminine manner, both girls turn to maternal authority to take the place of the colonial power they lose upon coming to England. This new site of power does not require an acceptance of outwardly directed oppression, although it may very well lead to internal repression on the part of the girls. By accepting a maternal source of power, the girls risk giving up all other opportunities for self-expression in favour of the limited sphere of a Victorian mother; the mystery of feminine autonomy would then become unsolvable. The redeeming factor in both cases is that the communities which the girls mother are communities of their own creation, families which they dream into existence as the response to the mysteries in their lives. This may still seem an imitation of the experience of an adult mother, who, after all, shares in the creation of her children. However, Mary and Sara, unlike biological mothers, create their 'children' with their minds, not their bodies, and rather than sharing creation with a father, the motivating force is purely their own.

This is not to say that biological motherhood cannot act in an empowering way, or that each girl's imaginative creation of a family structure does not mirror the social reality which contributes to the repression of women. However, the fantasy of motherhood gives Mary and Sara an independent and imaginative power which lends them authority in the intellectual realm, a space traditionally reserved for men. As each girl takes on the role of mother, the act of creation which she performs does not bring another person into being; rather, she re-creates herself by inhabiting a role in which she can justifiably assert power.

Mary Lennox seems an unlikely candidate for the position of a mother in the traditional sense. Not only does her contrariness not fit the picture of a loving, caring mother, but she also recoils from the quintessential training tool of motherhood, reacting to a package from her uncle by 'wondering if he had sent a doll, and also wondering what she should do with it if he had' (*Secret Garden*, 149–50). The famous scene of Mary and Colin's confrontation comes to mind as an example of the ways in which Mary's unusual methods of nurturing transcend the traditional image of calm, gentle motherhood. By this time Mary has solved the mystery of the cries which haunt the house, but the mystery of how to cure Colin – both emotionally and physically – still remains. Rather than trembling in fear before the young master of the household as all his attendants do, Mary gives his tantrum the response it deserves, chastising him for his selfishness and in the process diverting his attention from the self-pity which has helped to cripple him.

Although Mary has more class privilege than the nurse who cannot control Colin, she still owes her livelihood to the Cravens, almost as much as the servants in their employ. However, because she does not recognize this economic authority over her, she can help to cure Colin. In addition to benefiting Colin, this confrontation allows Mary the opportunity to assert her independence and control her own actions in the face of Colin's blatant display of his authority. She says:

'If you send Dickon away, I'll never come into this room again!'
'You'll have to if I want you,' said Colin.

'I won't!' said Mary.

'I'll make you,' said Colin. 'They shall drag you in.' ...

'They may drag me in but they can't make me talk when they get me here. I'll sit and clench my teeth and never tell you one thing. I won't even look at you. I'll stare at the floor!' (146–7)

In this scene, Colin confronts Mary with all the weapons in his power: his status as invalid, young master, and spoiled child, and with every expectation that he will be obeyed as always. Threatened with the loss of autonomy and even with violence, Mary makes it quite clear that she still has control over, at the very least, her gaze and her speech, and that she will not allow anyone to transgress these limits of her personal authority. This scene may seem a strange example to demonstrate Mary's nurturing capabilities; however, it proves her skill at mothering Colin without losing a sense of her own identity. Paradoxical as it may seem, Mary's temper tantrums actually represent an adept negotiation: through them she can help Colin as the adults cannot, while refusing to succumb to his authority and in fact even strengthening her own.

Just as Mary mothers the family she constructs from other children and the animals in the garden, Sara Crewe invents families, and invents herself as mother, throughout *A Little Princess*. She becomes a surrogate mother for the smallest children of the school, and regards her doll Emily as her child, saying in a curious acknowledgment of societal expectations, 'I should like [Emily] always to look as if she was a child with a good mother' (16). In addition, this girl who feels 'as if she had lived a long, long time' (7) fills the place of a mother and wife for both her own father, Captain Crewe, and her adoptive father, Mr Carrisford. As Sara's reward for growing up in England, Captain Crewe promises that she will 'keep the house ... ride with him, and sit at the head of the table when he had dinner-parties ... talk to him and read his books' (9). This adult-sanctioned future as society matron seems like a stultifying life for an intelligent girl; in contrast, the mothering that Sara does on her own terms, once her father disappears from the picture, offers her more opportunity to use her unique gifts as a way of achieving authority. In a scene prescient of Mary's confrontation with Colin, Sara is presented with the spectacle of Lottie, a screaming child over whom adults have no influence. Sara then takes control of the situation, but unlike Mary, who uses her temper and threatens to withhold stories in order to fight Colin's rage, Sara employs storytelling as a means of reaching the spoiled, self-pitying Lottie. Sara is similar to

Mary, however, in that her success with the recalcitrant child stems from the novel, even imaginative strategy she uses to interrupt Lottie's display of frustrated rage. Her statement that she, like the younger child, has no mother is 'so unexpected [as to be] astounding' to the little girl (42). Again, the lack of a parent produces the possibility for authority on the part of the child; while Mary's motherless status empowers her because no one has taught her to restrict or confine herself, Sara takes the fact of her mother's death and incorporates it into her treasury of stories, which she uses to pacify Lottie.

Although both Sara and Mary find new ways of mothering that exercise their own talents or personality traits – creating a locus of power in a traditionally feminine role – the danger inherent in their occupation of this role is that they will shrink to fit its limits, that they will nurture not because they do it particularly well but because it is the only possibility open to them. Maternity is not a sufficient 'solution' to the mystery of potential sources for feminine power. Carol Dyhouse reminds us that women who find power in a maternal function succeed according to public opinion because 'the maternal role was (and still is) the most publicly acceptable kind of role for women in authority. And yet [this role] is a very limited one' (29). As Dyhouse notes, motherhood does offer girls a certain autonomy, and yet their role still confines them, since it is bounded by an ideology of 'proper' behaviour for women. Consequently, Mary and Sara need to turn their search elsewhere. They must find a source of authority which allows them the possibility of threatening the male establishment, a source of authority which indicates to readers of Burnett's time and those of today that women can hold power even when transgressing the boundaries of traditionally feminine roles.

The source of this power is present in Sara's control over Lottie, where Sara simultaneously solves the mystery of the screaming child and the dilemma over feminine authority. Both Mary and Sara find agency in their imagination and intellect, in the way they create fantasy and bring it to life with words. Mary demonstrates her intellectual and reflective abilities as she learns from the things the servants tell her. Although many of Martha's statements contradict the world as Mary knows it, and she rebels at first at the thought of changing her behaviour, she also continues to ponder over what she has heard. When, for example, an exasperated Martha compares Mary unfavourably with her four-year-old sister, Mary shows 'her contrary scowl for an hour after that, but it made her think several entirely new things' (*Secret Garden*, 47).

Perhaps as a result of her active mind, Mary feels drawn to books and reading, although here again she prefers to find her own way rather than submitting to the guidance of adults. Her bad temper drives away governess after governess, and she learns only because she has 'chosen to really want to know how to read books' (1). In her affinity for reading, coupled with her inability to knit or sew, Mary represents a satisfying contradiction to the advice of *The Mother's Home Book* of 1879, which gave the opinion that '"[n]othing can be more pitiable than to see a female ... unable to ply her needle, her case being somewhat similar to that of a male ... who does not know how to read"' (quoted in Gorham, *Victorian Girl*, 74).

As Keyser has argued, part of Mary's appeal comes from her 'contrariness'. Keyser here refers to the girl's bad temper, but Mistress Mary is also contrary in the ways in which she defies expectation; Mary's intelligence and love of reading constitute another large part of her appeal to readers. Indeed, her control over narrative endears her to the other characters in the story as well. One of Colin's first commands to her is, '[t]ell me about Rajahs' (131), while Martha assures her that stories about 'riding on elephants and camels, and about the officers going to hunt tigers' would send her brothers and sisters 'clean off their heads' (61).

Unfortunately, as critics such as Keyser, and Foster and Simons, have remarked, despite the positive and creative opportunities for Mary in the early parts of the novel, the conclusion silences her quite effectively. There the focus of the narration moves from Mary to Colin and Archibald Craven, and she does not speak a word in the entire final chapter. This disappointing development indicates the extremely vexed nature of the 'mystery' of feminine authority; to find an ending with greater possibility, we will have to return to *A Little Princess*.

If Mary Lennox feels drawn to books, Sara Crewe's engagement with learning and imagination is almost mystical in its intensity. Burnett introduces her as a child who is 'always dreaming and thinking odd things' (*Little Princess*, 7), and as a result of this active imagination, she has the ability to empathize with those whose experience she cannot understand. She can thus take pity on Mr Carrisford's loneliness as well as servant girl Becky's victimization. Although Sara accepts the class difference between herself and Becky, and maintains that separation even after her accession to wealth, her imagination reveals to her the arbitrary nature of the difference, when she tells Becky, '"we are just the same – I am only a little girl like you. It's just an accident that I am not you, and you are not me!"' (53). Sara's imagination endears her to other children, but adults find her intelligence disconcerting, perhaps because of the authority it gives her, perhaps because in exerting her intelligence she threatens the boundaries of proper feminine behaviour. Even Sara's doting father reveals an uneasiness over Sara's behaving against feminine type with her love of reading. In his instructions to Miss Minchin, he stipulates that Sara should be encouraged to play outside, rather than reading all the time, that '[s]he ought to play more with dolls' (13).

The authority Sara derives from her imaginative intelligence particularly offends Miss Minchin, who attempts to stifle creativity wherever she encounters it. In trying to account for this facet of the story, Bixler claims that if Burnett 'suggests any motive for Miss Minchin's malignancy towards Sara, it is her jealousy of Sara's class and wealth,' demonstrated in a scene where Sara reveals her proficiency at French (216). I would point to the same scene to uncover the reason for the headmistress's hostility; however, I take the view that it is Sara's intelligence, rather than her money, which inspires Miss Minchin's envy. Burnett tells us that one of Miss Minchin's 'chief annoyances was that she did not speak French herself, and was desirous of concealing the irritating fact' (22–3). Once again, Sara's intelligence discomfits those who want her to behave according to their expectations.

Sara repeatedly demonstrates that although Miss Minchin may control reality, her own imagination is more powerful: it can even make the headmistress lose control, as when she forces Sara to tell her thoughts, only to find that she is imagining herself a princess. Sara comes so close to creating a reality with her words that it 'seemed for the moment to [Miss Minchin's] narrow, unimaginative mind that there must be some *real* power hidden behind this candid daring' (139, emphasis added). Sara's fantasies even have the power to transform her; she seems possessed, even fevered by her stories as she sits 'rather huddled up ... her green eyes [shining] and her cheeks flushed' (32). Finally, the force of her words stands her in good stead when she loses her material wealth; as Phyllis Bixler Koppes states, Sara's 'ability to see with the imagination is also a power – it helps Sara to endure her physical hardships and to maintain her sense of self-worth' (194–5). By creating stories about herself and Becky, the rats and the sparrows, and the people she sees in the street, Sara keeps her mind working amid the degradation of her daily life. The authority she demonstrates while wealthy, since it is predicated on her mental abilities rather than on her money, remains with her in poverty and allows her to maintain a sense of control over her life.

Imagination carries Sara a long way, but it does finally have its limits, as does the ending of the novel. With the intervention of Mr Carrisford, Sara regains her wealth, though at a price, for she also becomes reinserted into imperialist and patriarchal structures. Despite these shortcomings, the novel still allows Sara to maintain the opportunity for empowerment, especially when compared with the dismal ending of *The Secret Garden*. Unlike Mary, Sara retains her power over words, mesmerizing the Carmichael children with her stories, although now she tells stories about herself rather than imagined histories. In addition, we can see her as imagining her happy ending into existence, since she has created tales about her new friends and Mr Carrisford which eventually prove to be true. She comes to know the Carmichaels in all the detail she had previously imagined about them, and she attains her wish to bring comfort to Mr Carrisford. Finally, she engages in charity work which is not prompted by her new wealth or position; rather, her money becomes a means through which she can expand the generosity already demonstrated in the midst of her poverty.

After experimenting with several different manifestations of authority, among them discourses of imperialism and maternity, Mary and Sara come to rest on an expression of power which is particularly appropriate to their status as literary heroines. Through the use of words and imagination, they are able to acquire agency in a way which neither marginalizes an oppressed group nor threatens to restrict them to the traditionally domestic feminine sphere. While the conclusions of both books falter to some extent in the presentation of their heroines, weakening a possible critique of either imperialism or patriarchy, Mary's and Sara's roles as feminist protagonists are not invalidated by the slippage of power. The fact remains that they do search for and employ authority throughout their respective stories. And perhaps the search itself is as important as its outcome, in its implication that girls too have the right and the ability to discover a voice for themselves, a way of actively participating in their world.

The secrets and confusion running through *The Secret Garden* and *A Little Princess* point to a more far-reaching mystery; we might title it, 'The Search for the Missing Source of Authority'. Embedded in a culture which presents only partial and temporary sources for female power, Sara and Mary nevertheless discover a path to individual agency. And it is their destabilized surroundings which provide the medium for this discovery, a destabilization not unlike that of a more traditional mystery, where even truth and goodness are constantly in doubt. Given the feminist repercussions of these encounters with mystery, the freedom demonstrated by female sleuths such as Nancy Drew may derive not so much from a textual vacuum of parental authority, but from an intertextual source: the rich imaginative tradition of heroines like Mary Lennox and Sara Crewe.

Works cited

Bixler, Phyllis. 'Gardens, Houses, and Nurturant Power in *The Secret Garden'*, in James Holt McGavran Jr (ed.), *Romanticism and Children's Literature in Nineteenth-Century England*. Athens, GA: University of Georgia Press, 1991, pp. 208–24.

Burnett, Frances Hodgson. *A Little Princess* [1888]. New York: Dell, 1979.

——. *The Secret Garden* [1911]. New York: Dell, 1979.

Dyhouse, Carol. 'Miss Buss and Miss Beale: Gender and Authority in the History of Education', in Felicity Hunt (ed.), *Lessons for Life. The Schooling of Girls and Women, 1850–1950*. New York. Basil Blackwell, 1987, pp. 22–38.

Foster, Shirley and Judy Simons. *What Katy Read: Feminist Re-Readings of 'Classic' Stories for Girls*. Iowa City: University of Iowa Press, 1995.

Gorham, Deborah. 'The Ideology of Femininity and Reading for Girls, 1850–1914', in Felicity Hunt (ed.), *Lessons for Life. The Schooling of Girls and Women, 1850–1950*. New York: Basil Blackwell, 1987, pp. 39–59.

——. *The Victorian Girl and the Feminine Ideal*. London: Croom Helm, 1982.

Hunt, Felicity (ed.) *Lessons for Life: The Schooling of Girls and Women, 1850–1950*. New York: Basil Blackwell, 1987.

Keyser, Elizabeth Lennox. 'Quite Contrary: Frances Hodgson Burnett's *The Secret Garden'*, *Children's Literature*, 11 (1983): 1–13.

Koppes, Phyllis Bixler. 'Tradition and the Individual Talent of Frances Hodgson Burnett: A Generic Analysis of *Little Lord Fauntleroy*, *A Little Princess*, and *The Secret Garden'*, *Children's Literature*, 7 (1978): 191–207.

Marquis, Claudia. 'The Power of Speech: Life in *The Secret Garden'*, *AUMLA: Journal of the Australasian Universities Language and Literature Association*, 68 (1987): 163–87.

Mason, Bobbie Ann. *The Girl Sleuth: A Feminist Guide*. Old Westbury, NY: Feminist Press, 1975.

4
The Juvenile Detective and Social Class: Mark Twain, *Scouting for Girls*, and the Nancy Drew Mysteries

Troy Boone

What literary figure could be more perverse than the child detective? In *The Case of Peter Pan*, Jacqueline Rose provocatively argues that juvenile literature, in order to maintain a notion of childhood innocence, 'carries with it a plea that certain psychic barriers should go undisturbed, the most important of which is the barrier between adult and child' (70). In these terms, the union of children's fiction and detective fiction should be most disturbing, impossible even: detective mysteries require the lurid display of exactly the deceptions, instabilities, and corruptions of the adult world that children's fiction supposedly seeks to keep from the young. Yet this union of literary forms, wherein juvenile investigators discover and probe the illicit doings of their elders, has proven to be one of the most popular, and resilient of generic innovations. The phenomenal success of the children's mystery series produced by Edward Stratemeyer's syndicate of ghost-writers (see Billman 1–35; Johnson 1–17), particularly the Nancy Drew novels, is only the most striking index of the widespread pleasure taken in challenging such deeply held beliefs about the necessary segregation of child and adult, mystery and certainty, innocence and experience.

In what follows I offer a genealogy of the juvenile detective in American literature, tracking this figure through three texts: Mark Twain's *Tom Sawyer, Detective: As Told by Huck Finn* (1896); *Scouting for Girls: Official Handbook of the Girl Scouts* (1920); and the Nancy Drew mysteries, represented by the inaugural novel in the series, *The Secret of the Old Clock* (1930). These texts reveal a contradiction that dominates juvenile detective fiction: like classical detective fiction for adults, such works suggest that the pursuit of knowledge through the solution of mysteries is never innocent of the desire to accumulate wealth and power. The involvement of the juvenile in this process risks contaminating the very notion of innocence and its primary representative in Western culture, the figure of the child itself. These works also seek to stave off this contamination, and resolve the contradiction central to the generic experiment of juvenile detective fiction, by equating the pursuit of knowledge through the solution of mysteries with the natural curiosity of youth. This equation seeks only not to preserve the notion of youthful innocence but also to confer innocence upon the acquisition of wealth and power, thereby mystifying the class issues represented in these narratives. Twain's 1896 novel is an early instance of the process by which juvenile detective fiction, in resolving its own generic contradictions, performs a rewriting of American class relations. This ideological work is influentially carried on by early Girl Scout literature and achieves its most resonant form in the genre of juvenile detective fiction in the 1930s adventures of Nancy Drew, adolescent sleuth *par excellence*. The Nancy Drew novels represent the economic divisions resulting from 1920s capitalism as an unnerving mystification of American class identity. As the solution to this mystery, the novels – which first appeared and achieved their great popularity during the Depression years – fantasize a redistribution of wealth resulting not from a radical transformation of the economic system but from exactly the social coalescence of middle-class identity and disavowal of working-class consciousness that has become the dominant feature of American ideological life in the second half of the twentieth century.

Trust in Tom Sawyer

It seems perfectly natural that Tom Sawyer, the very personification of youthful shrewdness, should be a pioneer among juvenile sleuths. Yet, as a result of this career move, the title character of Mark Twain's *Tom Sawyer, Detective: As Told by Huck Finn* (1896) is a good deal more worldly, adult even, than that of *The Adventures of Tom Sawyer* (1876). The preface to *The Adventures* declares that it 'is intended mainly for the entertainment of boys and girls,' although Twain hopes that

> it will not be shunned by men and women on that account, for part of my plan has been to try to pleasantly remind adults of what they once were themselves, and of how they felt and thought and talked, and what queer enterprises they sometimes engaged in. (33)

By contrast, Twain notes in a 23 January 1895 letter to Henry Huttleston Rogers that *Tom Sawyer, Detective* 'is really written for grown folk, though I expect young folk to read it, too' (*Correspondence*, 122). Twain's preface to the 1876 novel thus confirms Rose's observation that juvenile literature presents its youthful protagonists as able to restore to adult readers 'a primitive or lost state to which the child has special access ... with a facility or directness which ensures' that the adult reader's relation to the world represented in the text 'is, finally, safe' (9). However, Twain's concern that the two novels be read differently – the earlier as a more juvenile and the later as a more adult book – echoes a crucial change in their protagonist. What most distinguishes Tom Sawyer, innocent adventurer, from Tom Sawyer, detective, is the latter character's mature awareness of *money*. Chapter 27 of *The Adventures of Tom Sawyer*, 'Doubts to be Settled – The Young Detectives', informs us that Tom

> was like all boys of his age and station in life, in that he imagined that all references to 'hundreds' and 'thousands' were mere fanciful forms of speech, and that no such sums really existed ... If his notions of hidden treasure had been analyzed, they would have been found to consist of a handful of real dimes and a bushel of vague, splendid, ungraspable dollars. (188)

By contrast, the title character of *Tom Sawyer, Detective* correctly calculates that the reward for twelve thousand dollars' worth of diamonds will be at least '"a thousand dollars, sure"' (379). As if to reinforce that such a modest speculation can accrue interest, the reward Tom actually receives at novel's end has grown to '"two thousand dollars"' (414). Thus, the narrative exposes Tom's awareness of the relationship between his interest in solving mysteries and the financial reward for this investment of time and talent.

Tom's best-known talent – the ability to deceive not so much by lying as by misleading others regarding his interests – is a skill necessary to detection. As Sherlock Holmes observes in Doyle's *The Sign of Four* (1890), one must never let informants '"think that their information can be of the slightest importance to you. If you do, they will instantly shut up like an oyster. If you listen to them under protest, as it were, you are very likely to get what you want"' (63). Regarding their interview with the criminal, Jake Dunlap, Tom gives Huck nearly identical advice:

> We was in a sweat to find out what his secret was, but Tom said the best way was not to seem anxious, then likely he would drop into it

himself ... but if we got to asking questions he would get suspicious and shet up his shell. It turned out just so. (*Detective*, 366)

Tom Sawyer, Detective initially proposes that this talent for deception is identical to the craftiness Tom displays in *The Adventures*. At the beginning of the later novel, when Aunt Polly orders the boys to Arkansas, Tom pretends that such a journey is a most distasteful proposition: '"Huck Finn, do you want me to let her *see* how bad I want to go? ... I reckon I know how to work her"' (*Detective*, 358). Fooling Aunt Polly here is a reversal of the psychological trick involved in convincing one's chums that whitewashing a fence is a thrilling occupation. In that famous scene from *The Adventures of Tom Sawyer*, Tom avoids doing the work himself and manages to make some money into the bargain, yet he also remains innocent of the implications of his ruse, as the narrator of *The Adventures* suggests:

> If he had been a great and wise philosopher, like the writer of this book, he would now have comprehended that Work consists of whatever a body is *obliged* to do and that Play consists of whatever a body is not obliged to do. (50)

In *Tom Sawyer, Detective*, Tom's involvement with jewel thieves and murderers results in a much more adult understanding of the way in which this ability to deceive others can be turned to financial advantage. Although Tom's motive for solving the mystery appears to be 'the glory of being' the one 'that knows a lot more about it than anybody else' (378), this participation in what Audrey Jaffe describes as the 'fantasy of knowledge' that is detective fiction (97) is not merely a result, as Huck claims, of Tom's childlike wish '"to be a ... hero, as he calls it' (410). If, as Huck wryly observes, it is '"more heroic to keep mum, there warn't two boys in a million could do it"' (391), Tom's manipulation and retention of knowledge is motivated by desire for financial reward. Thus, Tom instructs Huck:

> 'there'll be a big reward offered for [the diamonds] – a thousand dollars, sure. That's our money! Now we'll trot in and see the folks. And mind you we don't know anything about any murder, or any di'monds, or any thieves – don't you forget that.' (379)

The seemingly innocent desire for glory and the child's pretence that he is innocent of adult goings-on are here mere cover stories, behind which lurk unnervingly mature calculations. Paradoxically, Tom uses the apparent incompatibility of childishness and the ability to solve mysteries actually to assist him in solving the mystery. When Tom undertakes Silas's courtroom defence, '"just the same as a regular lawyer, nearly"' (403), Tom's apparently selfless motives would seem to redeem his innocence: Tom proclaims that solving the mystery and discovering the true murderer '"won't only be an honor to us, but it'll be an honor to uncle Silas"' (394). In turn, the judge declares that '"it will be a real pleasure ... to hand"' Tom the reward money, for he has '"earned the deepest and most sincerest thanks of this community"' (414). However, even as the 'laws bless' Tom thus (395), the fact that lawyering might, like detecting, be an unsuitable job for a child is none too subtly suggested by one of Huck's funnier malapropisms, his reference to Tom's opponent as the '"lawyer for the prostitution"' (401).

Twain's novel expresses anxiety about the child's involvement in adult mysteries and seeks to soothe this anxiety by presenting detection as a form of the curiosity natural to childhood. As Tom demurely tells the judge, solving the case was '"just an ordinary little bit of detective work; anybody could 'a' done it"' (412). Early in the novel Huck presents attraction to sleuthing as a quality innate to Tom:

> It was always nuts for Tom Sawyer – a mystery was. If you'd lay out a mystery and a pie before me and him, you wouldn't have to say take your choice, it was a thing that would regulate itself. Because in my nature I have always run to pie, whilst in his nature he has always run to mystery. People are made different. And it is the best way. (362)

Huck contrasts Tom's attraction to mysteries with his own more childlike love of sweet things. He claims that each attraction is a matter of the individual child's essential 'nature' and implies that these qualities, as providential dispensations, are beyond critique. Moreover, in spite of Huck's many comments regarding his friend's unfathomable smarts – 'I never see such a head as that boy had' (379) – the novel often depicts Tom's relation to mysteries not as one of adult intellectual mastery but as childlike physical surrender. Thus, Tom 'didn't sleep much, he was in such a sweat to get in there and find out the mystery' (363). The bedtime conferences between detective and narrator yield not the solution of recondite puzzles but, rather, typically juvenile sensations: '[w]e talked the murder and the ghost over and over again, and got so creepy and crawly we couldn't get sleepy no how and no way ...

so at last we was tuckered out and went to sleep and had nightmares, a million of them' (384–5). Indeed, both the novel and its narrative of detection begin with the boys' ordinary desire 'to go wandering far away to strange countries where everything is mysterious and wonderful and romantic' (358), which desire itself results from 'spring fever' (357). In this way, Huck divorces detective fever from adult actions and depicts the former as a natural, childlike, urge.

This naturalization of the juvenile detective's inquiry into the adult mysteries of money – and the ideological motivations for this naturalization – are nowhere more evident than in Twain's use of Huck Finn as narrator. Unlike *The Adventures of Tom Sawyer*, with its ironic adult narrator, *Tom Sawyer, Detective* comes to us 'as told by Huck Finn' and thereby both seeks to obscure Twain's presence as author and asks us to trust the observations of Huck, who consistently appears more innocent than Tom regarding the financial implications of the detective's pursuit of knowledge. Moreover, because Huck narrates the story in dialect, the text appears to be the unrevised, unsophisticated testimony of youth. After the diamonds disappear, the fact that 'Tom didn't feel no more intrust in' the murder mystery – although he did feel 'ever so bothered and put out and disappointed and swindled' (386) – suggests that Tom is motivated by desire for money more than any natural 'interest' in mystery. Indeed, 'Tom [is] so cut up he couldn't take any intrust in' the bloodhound he and Huck are using to unearth the corpse (395). The frequent repetition of 'intrust' in such passages asserts that detection results from mere childlike curiosity; yet the word 'interest' always threatens to become a pun identifying the bond, which the novel works so hard to obscure, between this curiosity and economic speculation. Twain almost uniformly renders the word in dialect, as 'intrust', and textual evidence suggests that he rigorously corrected his typist's mistranscription of 'intrust' as 'intrest' (see Twain, *Works*, 692). In revisions Twain deleted an opening passage in which Huck makes explicit the relation between the child's curiosity and the other, economic meaning of 'intrust': 'our bag of gold that we had smouched from where the robbers hid it had been out at intrust in Judge Thatcher's hands, and there was six hundred dollars apiece for us coming due' (quoted in Twain, *Works*, 697). As we will see in considering Girl Scout literature and the Nancy Drew mysteries, juvenile mystery fiction tends to place on its readers – whether 'grown folk' or 'young folk' – a considerable ideological demand: to trust not only in Tom Sawyer but in the naturalness, purity and innocence of the child's 'intrust' in mysteries, and thus to disavow the economic inequalities imposed in the interest of capitalist accumulation.

Scouting for Girls

This naturalization of the interest which the child invests in mysteries, such that it appears an innocent inquisitiveness, rather than an adult acquisitiveness, is perhaps most influentially dispersed by Scouting literature. Robert Baden-Powell's *Scouting for Boys: A Handbook for Instruction in Good Citizenship* (1908), the bestseller that launched the Boy Scout organization in Britain, suggests that solving murder mysteries might be an everyday part of boyhood:

> It may happen to some of you that one day you will be the first to find the dead body of a man, in which case you will remember that it is your duty to examine and note down the smallest signs that are to be seen on and near the body before it is moved. (123)

Moreover, the handbook suggests that, if the British boy's play area does not happen to be littered with corpses, such observational skills can be instilled in young people by directing their reading habits. The lists of recommended books with which each chapter of *Scouting for Boys* concludes have done much to incorporate adult detective fiction – particularly the works of Doyle – into the juvenile canon. Indeed, Baden-Powell naturalizes the child's interest in mystery by equating it with the normative attainment of literacy itself: '[d]eduction is exactly like reading a book' (142). Furthermore, the processes of both reading Scout literature and solving mysteries have, in the handbook, a crucial class component. Although Baden-Powell intends for the organization to unite a Britain fractured along class lines – '[s]couting appeals to boys of every class' (viii) – the instructions regarding how to solve mysteries in fact reinforce the notion of essential class differences. Baden-Powell tells Scouts that they should, when observing people, 'try and make out from their appearance and behaviour whether they are rich or poor' (121). *Scouting for Boys* recommends that Scoutmasters employ a game called 'Telling Character': '[s]end scouts out for half an hour to look for, say, a brutish character, or a case of genteel poverty, etc.' (127).

The importation of Scouting into America in 1912–13 (see Tedesco 19–39) involves a similar proposal that solving mysteries is a natural activity for the juvenile reader. As Laureen Tedesco notes, early hand-books for American Girl Scouts (like those for British Girl Guides) bor-rowed much material from *Scouting for Boys* (27–8). *Scouting for Girls: Official Handbook of the Girl Scouts* (1920) offers the following instruc-tions regarding observation:

> *Using your Eyes* – Let nothing be too small for your notice – a button, a match, a hair, a cigar ash, a feather, or a leaf might be of great importance, even a fingerprint which is almost invisible to the naked eye has often been the means of detecting a crime.
>
> With a little practice in observation you can tell pretty accurately a man's character from his dress. (42)

Sherrie A. Inness claims that Girl Scout literature was 'actively engaged in convincing women that domesticity was the *sine qua non* for feminine happiness' (*Girl Scouts*, 237). However, the mention of finger-prints and crime suggests that the world inhabited by the Girl Scout is no less mysterious than that of her male equivalent. Moreover, although the items listed in this passage (buttons, matches, and the like) might suggest that 'using your eyes' is a matter of domestic tidying, the sort of minutiae in question (particularly 'a cigar ash') often figures in the solution of, for instance, Sherlock Holmes's cases. If Girl Scout literature commonly reinforces normative notions of femininity, the treatment of detection as integral to the activities of even the most domesticated girl is – given that Western culture has historically valued feminine innocence even more than masculine – a powerful reinforce-ment of the naturalization of the child's interest in mysteries. Indeed, like *Scouting for Boys*, *Scouting for Girls* offers a list of recommended readings in which crime fiction is prominent. It, too, insists that the observational skills necessary for detection are identical to literacy: 'the great reason for looking for signs and tracks is that from these you can read a meaning. It is exactly like reading a book' (40).

In fact, the most striking differences between *Scouting for Boys and Scouting for Girls* are not the revisions necessary to make Girl Scouting accord with normative notions of femininity but, rather, those neces-sary to make the organization promote the notion that economic class differences in no way impede the social equality of Americans. The handbook explicitly presents Girl Scouting as a model of American democracy: 'the Patrol System ... by which eight girls of about the same age and interests elect their Patrol Leader and practice local self-government in every meeting, carries out American ideals in practical detail' (4). In this way, the Patrol System represents a 'broad democracy' that, based on mutual rather than competing interests, 'is American in every sense of the word' (4). The mutuality of interests that all Americans supposedly share even transcends age difference and renders the girl equal to the adult: '[f]rom the youngest Lone Scout up to the National Director, the organization is democratic, self-governing and flexible, adjusting itself everywhere and always to local circumstances and the habits and preferences of the different groups' (16). Although the handbook here briefly acknowledges the existence of 'different groups', they are distinguished not by competing class interests but (as is common in American political discourse) by regional variation in 'habits and preferences'. Thus, 'the world looks to great organizations like the Girl Scouts to break down their petty barriers of ... class and make our sex a great power for democracy in the days to come' (6–7).

Promoting this fantasy that American democracy could, indeed, result in a classless society is, in turn, crucial to the establishment of the nation as a world power. The first version of the Girl Scout handbook, *How Girls Can Help Their Country* (1913), clearly indicates this goal: '[i]n all that you do think of your country first. We are all twigs in the same fagot, and every little girl even goes to make up some part or parcel of our great whole nation' (Hoxie, 17). If Inness is correct that Girl Scout literature 'helped perpetuate the idea that the "true" American girl was ... bourgeois' ('Girl Scouts', 237), this literature does so by treating middle-class identity as an effect of social behaviour rather than economic status, and therefore as an identity all patriotic and hard-working Americans possess.

The American *Scouting for Girls* presents the relation between detection and social class very differently from the British *Scouting for Boys*. Baden-Powell argues that observation largely involves reading the outward signs of essential class identity – such that 'appearance and behaviour' are an index not only of a person's economic status but also of their inner 'character', whether 'genteel' or 'brutish' (127). By contrast, the parallel passage in *Scouting for Girls* observes: 'you can tell pretty accurately a man's character from his dress' (42). The examples that follow offer no evidence that poverty exists in America, much less that it is a determinant of character. A girl can 'recognize that a gentleman was fond of fishing' by noting a torn 'thread or two of the cloth' in his headgear, because when a fisherman 'takes his flies off the line he will ... stick them into his cap to dry' (42). It should be noted that 'cap' is generally a signifier of working-class status, as opposed to the more lofty 'hat', yet this cap-wearing fisherman is 'a gentleman'. Similarly, whereas Baden-Powell glosses one of the Scout Laws, 'A Scout is Loyal', by noting that Boy Scouts must stick to their employers through 'thick and thin' (48), *Scouting for Girls* interprets the same law as meaning that the Girl Scout 'is true to ... those for whom she may work, or who may work for her' (5). Significantly, when *Scouting for Girls* acknowledges class differences, they appear as 'petty barriers' to 'break down':

> Good breeding means first of all thoughtfulness of others, and nothing shows lack of breeding so quickly as a lack of such politeness to those who happen to be serving us in hotels, at home, in shops, or when travelling, or anywhere else.
>
> When acting as waitress, stand at the left of the person to be served, so that the portion may be taken with the right hand. (131)

If the first paragraph presumes a middle-class Scout, the second suggests that, in her usual domestic duties, she takes up different class positions. Although the phrase 'acting as' seems to segregate the middle-class Scout from any *real* experience of wage-labour, *Scouting for Girls* offers a rather sinister warning to the opposite effect: the Girl Scout 'feels, too, a special responsibility ... toward the very poor and the unfortunate, either of which she may be any day' (7).

Even as *Scouting for Girls*, like *Tom Sawyer, Detective*, naturalizes the interest that the child invests in mysteries, the handbook admits, even if obliquely, adult economic issues – including the threat of downward economic mobility – that are central to the Nancy Drew detective mysteries, and the particular fantasies of American egalitarianism they promote.

Nancy Drew's New Deal

> Money is a very useful thing to have. (*Scouting for Girls*, 10)

Nancy Drew, the quintessential adolescent detective of juvenile series fiction, is the apotheosis of the Girl Scout, and she arrives just in time, at the beginning of the Great Depression, to aid those who have suddenly and unexpectedly found themselves among the ranks of 'the very poor and the unfortunate'. The inaugural novel in the Nancy Drew series, *The Secret of the Old Clock* (1930), involves Nancy's discovery of a missing will that disinherits her arrogant *nouveau-riche* neighbours, the Tophams, and enriches poor but deserving relations of the deceased. In succeeding volumes, Nancy rights economic wrongs by exposing real estate swindles, defeating counterfeiters, and restoring stolen goods. Given that early plots in the series so prominently feature the loss of money, it seems odd to conclude, as many critics have, that the Depression 'passed unnoticed in Midwestern, suburban River Heights' (Prager 76), with Nancy 'serenely ignoring the world crashing all around' (Mason 49). According to such readings, the mysteries celebrate an upper-middle-class Neverland and effectively repress the contemporary economic circumstances of their composition and consumption. By contrast, as Deborah L. Siegel remarks, since the heroine works to

> restore the financially downtrodden to their rightful state of ownership during a historical moment in which the financial order was radically and unexplainably upset, the question of what Nancy Drew emerged as a figure for becomes of increasing interest. (160)

Siegel's succeeding analysis focuses on gender rather than class. But although her argument – that 'Nancy Drew in the 1930s "solved" the contradiction of competing discourses about American womanhood by entertaining them all' (171) – is persuasive, the sleuth's role in figuring class relations in Depression-era culture is allowed to remain a mystery.

Yet the Nancy Drew novels represent the most extensive articulation of the process, revealed in Twain's work and *Scouting for Girls*, whereby the juvenile detective's interest in solving mysteries resolves American class differences. Nancy Drew embodies the public discourse on social and economic class that characterizes responses to the Great Depression, on the level of both popular culture and government policy, from the last years of the Hoover Administration to the Second New Deal, and beyond. The early novels in the series condemn unregulated capitalist speculation as the cause of unequal distribution of the nation's wealth and, by implication, of the economic disasters of 1929. Although the solutions to Nancy's cases involve a selective redistribution of wealth, this economic engineering does not challenge the capitalist order but, rather, seeks to obscure the class divisions inherent within it by fantasizing a capitalist culture in which all citizens are united by middle-class social, if not economic, status. The apparent conservatism of the Nancy Drew novels (or the apparent radicalism of Roosevelt's New Deal policies) should not lead us to conclude, as James

P. Jones does, that 'Nancy Drew's authors ... opposed the New Deal and its welfare policies' (714). Rather, the Nancy Drew mysteries are one particularly influential example of a popular discourse that promotes a powerful American fantasy in which capitalism destroys class barriers and thus enables rather than inhibits social equality. Roosevelt drew heavily on this discourse to popularize the New Deal and the Nancy Drew mysteries accord with his argument that practical cooperation – 'fair play or a square deal' – is the solution to 'most of our problems' which 'have arisen because of greed and selfishness' ('Roosevelt Says', 7). The fact that, in the Nancy Drew novels, New Deal ideologies are presented as the rational *solution* to economic *mysteries* naturalizes, even more potently than does Roosevelt's common-sense discourse, the notion that American capitalism promotes American egalitarianism. The tidy opposition of 'liberal' and 'conservative' in discussions of the Nancy Drew mysteries, Depression-era public discourse, and American culture more generally, obscures the way in which the two cooperate. This is a point that Roosevelt made with unusual explicitness in his 29 September 1936 address to the Democratic State Convention in Syracuse, New York: the 'true conservative seeks to protect the system of private property and free enterprise by correcting such injustices and inequalities as arise from it. ... Liberalism becomes the protection for the far-sighted conservative' (5: 389).

Nancy Drew's long career as a detective begins with the well-to-do lawyer's daughter condemning unregulated capitalist speculation and the unequal distribution of wealth. *The Secret of the Old Clock* opens with Nancy's exclamation: '"[i]t would be a shame if all that money went to the Tophams! They will fly higher than ever!"' (1). Nancy initially 'turns sleuth' (59) because the Tophams get richer while more deserving relations of the deceased are living in poverty. The desire to solve mysteries is seamlessly integrated with the desire to right economic wrongs. '"A mystery always interests me, I guess, and it does seem to me that someone ought to help those poor relatives"' (9), Nancy reflects, while the omniscient narrator confirms that the sleuth 'delighted in a battle of wits when championing a worthy cause' (61). Nancy's animosity towards the Tophams has everything to do with the fact that Richard Topham '"is an old skinflint who made his money by gambling on the stock exchange"' (3). Although the terms with which Nancy condemns Topham – 'gambling' and 'skinflint' – appear contradictory, they are at the heart of denunciations of both the unregulated capitalist speculation of the 1920s, and the failure of either big business or the Hoover Administration to enact effective relief measures and deal with the resulting economic disaster. Thus, in his fireside chat of 28 June 1934, Roosevelt lamented that the 1920s had been an 'unfortunate decade characterized by a mad chase for unearned riches, and an unwillingness of leaders in almost every walk of life to look beyond their own schemes and speculations' (3: 313).

Just as 'gambling on the stock exchange' summarizes the popular view of the wild speculation with capital that leads to Black Tuesdays and Thursdays, Nancy's observation that 'skinflint' behaviour is just as bad parallels the argument of the most prominent economist of the 1930s, John Maynard Keynes. Keynes remarks in *The General Theory of Employment, Interest and Money* (1936) that economic growth under capitalism and 'the removal of very great disparities of wealth and income', rather than 'being dependent on the abstinence of the rich, as is commonly supposed, is more likely to be impeded by it' (372–3). Far from being a celebration of 'the paternal benevolence of the businesses, institutions, and laws of the reigning upper classes' (Mason 68), *The Secret of the Old Clock*, which was published in April 1930, just six months after the national trauma of October 1929, vilifies unregulated capitalist speculation as the crooked source of the social wrongs that the sleuth works to right. Moreover, this critique extends to the institutions that support big business, including the law, and is seconded even by noted attorney Carson Drew, who observes that the will benefiting the Tophams and disinheriting Josiah Crowley's poor relations '"isn't fair. But it is legal"' (6).

Therefore, it is difficult to credit Sally E. Parry's claim that Nancy 'aligns her sense of good with wealth, believing, like the Puritans, that those who succeed in a material sense are inherently better people' (153). Although Parry is correct that the solution of Nancy's cases typically involves the restoration of 'goods to the right person' who 'usually comes from a "good" family' (146), the narratives do not merely work 'to restore the status quo, with all that implies about ideological, economic, social ... relations' (145). Rather, *The Secret of the Old Clock* explicitly objects to the governing ideology of capitalism, that class inequality is natural, and instead validates an ideology of longer duration in American culture: that the natural state of affairs is equality among the hard-working and therefore deserving. In *The Secret of the Old Clock*, the result of Nancy's investigation of the crime of capitalist greed is a most remarkable transformation of the economic standing of Josiah Crowley's relatives. The Tophams get their come-uppance, of course, and in a manner particularly resonant in 1930: Richard '"has been losing steadily on the stock market of late"'

(205). With the loss of the inheritance, on which he has been depending '"to pull him through a tight place"' (182), he is '"practically in bankruptcy"' (205). More ironically, Crowley's poor relations are the beneficiaries of an estate made up of '"stocks, bonds, and notes"' that amounted to '"well over three hundred thousand dollars"' (178–9).

Unlike the juvenile fiction of Horatio Alger, which Michael Moon argues tends to reinforce the 'modest-demand, modest-reward ethos of the rapidly expanding corporate/clerical workplace' (88–9), *The Secret of the Old Clock* seems shameless in its promotion of the 'rags to riches' myth. Thus Allie Horner notes that, if their '"luck doesn't change soon,"' she and her sister Grace will '"be mistaken for rag pickers"' (69), whereas their inheritance of '"seventy-five thousand dollars each"' (198) should certainly place them at the top of the economic ladder in early 1930s River Heights. However, these radical transformations of *economic* circumstances resulting from Nancy's detections in fact leave *social* relations unchanged. In spite of Nancy's rather malicious statement that it '"would serve the Tophams right if they lose everything"' (182), the nearly bankrupt villains do not go begging but are merely '"forced to give up"' their luxury home and move '"into a small house,"' from which '"they'll not be able to carry themselves so high"' (205). Yet the social elevation of the Tophams was insecure in the first place, in that their riches never really conferred respectability: 'Carson Drew and his daughter were cordially welcomed in River Heights homes which merely tolerated the Tophams or, in a few cases, barred them' (97). Similarly, the Horner sisters are relatively unaffected by their sudden wealth: it does not grant respectability, which they have all along, but merely allows them to go about '"putting in incubators"' and generally sprucing up their chicken farm (207). Indeed, the novel gives no indication that the sisters' poverty would have prevented Nancy from befriending them beforehand. As Carson Drew comments upon first meeting them, '"[c]harming girls ... and undoubtedly deserving"' (49). Moreover, the Horner sisters' 'charms' are of the middle-class variety: Allie has a 'cultured voice and manner' (31), and Grace 'poured the tea and served the cake with as much poise as though she were gracing an elegant drawing room' (38). As the unsubtle pun on Grace's name suggests, the sisters possess charm and social respectability regardless of poverty or wealth. Thus Allie 'did not appear to be the daughter of a farmer who would live on this poor land, yet she seemed to fit into her background' (31). All that is needed to make the picture right is for the land to be less poor, a windfall provided by Nancy's solution of the economic mystery of the Crowley will.

The differences between a novel such as Alger's *Ragged Dick; or, Street Life in New York* (1867) and *The Secret of the Old Clock* reveal a significant ideological shift. Published in a period when apparent national prosperity testified to the virtues of capitalism, Alger's novel depicts a society in which the hero's industriousness results in working-class social respectability but in which his economic status is fixed and not subject to radical transformation. Published, by contrast, in a period characterized by the most shocking reversals of economic fortune, the first Nancy Drew mystery novel depicts a society in which no amount of hard work can prevent poverty, but in which sudden wealth is also, mysteriously, possible, and in which the only constant is a middle-class identity defined not in economic but in social terms. Writing in 1954, the historian David M. Potter admits that 'the American class structure is in reality very unlike the classless society which we imagine' (102). Nevertheless, he claims that 'American social distinctions, however real they may be and however difficult to break down, are not based upon or supported by great disparities in wealth, in education, in speech, in dress' (101–2). Like Potter's views, the Nancy Drew mysteries are exemplary participants in the ideological process whereby the concept of 'class' has been flattened out in American culture, such that labourers identify as 'middle-class' and the middle-class as 'hard working'. For example, in the second novel in the Nancy Drew series, *The Hidden Staircase* (1930), we are told that Grace is '"fairly rolling in wealth"' (16) – not because she has inherited an astronomical sum but because her dressmaking business '"has picked up tremendously and she has more orders than she can fill"' (16). Similarly, at the end of *The Secret of the Old Clock*, '"the thing that pleased [Nancy] the most was the realization that Allie and Grace were happy in their work"' (207).

Nancy here embodies an economic engineering that displaces the invisible hand of classical economics, and her refusal to let a mystery alone is certainly in opposition to a *laissez-faire* notion of economic change: '[t]here was something about a mystery which aroused Nancy's interest, and she was never content until it was solved' (7). Yet the resulting fantasy of a society in which everyone's interests are those of the middle class in no way opposes – and has indeed been a crucial ideological support for – twentieth-century American capitalism. The Nancy Drew mystery novels thus influentially disperse what Michael Kazin calls the language of populism, whose 'speakers conceive of ordinary people as a noble assemblage not bounded narrowly by class, view their elite opponents as self-serving and undemocratic, and seek to mobilize the former against the latter' (1). As Kazin eloquently argues, populism has enabled Americans 'to protest social and economic inequalities without calling the entire system into question' and to maintain that 'most citizens – whatever their occupation or income – are moral, hardworking people' (2). In other words, 'class barriers, according to the national creed, are not supposed to exist in the United States' (2). In order to defuse any suggestion that the economic order of things demands radical political transformation, the Nancy Drew series represents economic change as innocent of politics. Reform comes simply as a result of the juvenile heroine's natural interest in mysteries: 'Nancy Drew had a natural talent for unearthing interesting stories, and now a sixth sense seemed to tell her that she had encountered something unusual' (32).

The Secret of the Old Clock begins the series provocatively, with the gumshoe's criticism of capitalist speculation and her conviction that the economic inequalities of River Heights demand investigation and reform. However, the gothic mystery of *The Hidden Staircase*, which is much more typical of the series as a whole, represents Nancy's return to sleuthing as the result of a physical urge. Feeling 'nervous and uneasy' for 'no apparent reason' (1), Nancy solves this psychological puzzle with her usual ease: '"I know what's the matter with me," she told herself. "I'm aching for another adventure"' (2). At the conclusion of the novel Nancy again describes the desire for the next escapade in similarly bodily terms: '"[n]ow that ... the mystery is solved, I'm aching for another one"' (205). In spite of Nancy's much-vaunted ratiocination skills, the detective urge that keeps the heroine in action (and readers eagerly buying) is rendered somatic: a 'zest for adventure' (148). The signs of this are the detective's physical reactions: 'Her heart began to beat faster as she contemplated the adventure before her' (129). The desire for economic change that initiates Nancy's detections becomes, by the second novel, no more than the bodily excitement normal to a curious youth. In this the series confirms its primary theme, which is also the theme of works representing juvenile detectives from *Tom Sawyer, Detective* to *Scouting for Girls* and that of twentieth-century America itself. The homogenization of middle-class social identity, and the disavowal of working-class consciousness, seem to be so natural a part of American culture, even a child could see it.

I thank two outstanding Americanists, Christopher Breu and Pamela Lougheed, whose advice greatly enabled the writing of this essay. Of course, they remain innocent of any errors of fact or interpretation and of any stylistic infelicities that appear herein.

Works cited

Baden-Powell, Robert. *Scouting for Boys: A Handbook for Instruction in Good Citizenship* [1908], 7th edn. London: C. Arthur Pearson, 1915.

Billman, Carol. *The Secret of the Stratemeyer Syndicate: Nancy Drew, the Hardy Boys, and the Million Dollar Fiction Factory.* New York: Ungar, 1986.

Doyle, Arthur Conan. *The Sign of the Four* [1890], ed. Christopher Roden. Oxford: Oxford University Press, 1994.

Hoxie, W. J. *How Girls Can Help Their Country.* New York: Knickerbocker Press, 1913.

Inness, Sherrie A. 'Girl Scouts, Camp Fire Girls, and Woodcraft Girls: The Ideology of Girls' Scouting Novels, 1910–1935', in Ray B. Browne and Ronald J. Ambrosetti (eds), *Continuities in Popular Culture: The Present in the Past and the Past in the Present and Future.* Bowling Green, OH: Bowling Green State University Popular Press, 1993, pp. 229–40.

—— (ed.) *Nancy Drew and Company: Culture, Gender, and Girls' Series.* Bowling Green, OH: Bowling Green State University Popular Press, 1997.

Jaffe, Audrey. 'Detecting the Beggar: Arthur Conan Doyle, Henry Mayhew, and "The Man with the Twisted Lip"', *Representations*, 31 (1990): 96–117.

Johnson, Deidre. *Edward Stratemeyer and the Stratemeyer Syndicate.* Boston, MA: Twayne, 1993.

Jones, James P. 'Nancy Drew, WASP Super Girl of the 1930's, *Journal of Popular Culture*, 6 (1973): 707–17.

Kazin, Michael. *The Populist Persuasion: An American History.* New York: Basic-HarperCollins, 1995.

Keene, Carolyn. *The Hidden Staircase* [1930]. Bedford, MA: Applewood, 1991.

——. *The Secret of the Old Clock* [1930]. Bedford, MA: Applewood, 1991.

Keynes, John Maynard. *The General Theory of Employment, Interest and Money* [1936]. Volume 7 of *The Collected Writings of John Maynard Keynes.* London: Royal Economic Society / Macmillan / Cambridge University Press, 1973.

Mason, Bobbie Ann. *The Girl Sleuth: A Feminist Guide.* Old Westbury, NY: Feminist Press, 1975.

Moon, Michael. '"The Gentle Boy from the Dangerous Classes": Pederasty, Domesticity, and Capitalism in Horatio Alger', *Representations*, 19 (1987): 87–110.

Parry, Sally E. 'The Secret of the Feminist Heroine: The Search for Values in Nancy Drew and Judy Bolton', in Sherrie A. Inness (ed.), *Nancy Drew and Company: Culture, Gender, and Girls' Series.* Bowling Green OH: Bowling Green State University Popular Press 1997, pp. 145–58.

Potter, David M. *People of Plenty: Economic Abundance and the American Character.* Chicago: University of Chicago Press, 1954.

Prager, Arthur. *Rascals at Large, or, The Clue in the Old Nostalgia.* Garden City, NY: Doubleday, 1971.

Roosevelt, Franklin D. *The Public Papers and Addresses of Franklin D. Roosevelt,* ed. Samuel I. Rosenman, 13 vols. New York: Random / Macmillan / Harper, 1938–50.

'Roosevelt Says Fair Play by Every Citizen Would End Most of America's Problems', *Times* (New York), 13 February 1934: 7.

Rose, Jacqueline. *The Case of Peter Pan or The Impossibility of Children's Fiction* [1984], rev. edn. Philadelphia: University of Pennsylvania Press, 1993.

Scouting for Girls: Official Handbook of the Girl Scouts [1920], 6th rpt. New York: Girl Scouts, 1925.

Siegel, Deborah L. 'Nancy Drew as New Girl Wonder: Solving It All for the 1930s', in Sherrie A. Inness (ed.), *Nancy Drew and Company: Culture, Gender, and Girls' Series*. Bowling Green, OH: Bowling Green State University Popular Press, 1997, pp. 159–82.

Tedesco, Laureen. 'Making a Girl into a Scout: Americanizing Scouting for Girls', in Sherrie A. Inness (ed.), *Delinquents and Debutantes: Twentieth-Century American Girls' Cultures*. New York: New York University Press, 1998, pp. 19–39.

Twain, Mark. *The Adventures of Tom Sawyer* [1876], in Twain, *Works*, pp. 31–237.

——. *Mark Twain's Correspondence with Henry Huttleston Rogers 1893–1909*, ed. Lewis Leary. Berkeley: University of California Press, 1969.

——. *Tom Sawyer, Detective: As Told by Huck Finn* [1896], in Twain, *Works*, pp. 357–415.

——. *The Works of Mark Twain*, vol. 4, eds John C. Gerber, Paul Baender and Terry Firkins. Iowa City: Iowa Center for Textual Studies; Berkeley: University of California Press, 1980.

5
Children's Detective Fiction and the 'Perfect Crime' of Adulthood

Christopher Routledge

As one of the most popular of literary types, detective fiction is also one of the most common forms of mystery in children's literature. But the mysteries investigated in children's detective fiction rarely, if ever, only deal with the immediate problem on which the formal plot is based. Perhaps even more than in its adult incarnation, the formal problem of 'whodunit' in children's detective fiction allows the investigation of other kinds of mystery – mysteries that become apparent during childhood itself and concerning issues such as identity, economic power, and social status. More specifically, detective fiction for children often explores the differences and tensions between adulthood and childhood.

Taking Erich Kästner's 1928 novel *Emil and the Detectives* as its primary text, this essay will consider the relationship between childhood and adulthood, and in particular how, in detective fiction for children, the discourse of adulthood attempts to overwhelm and eradicate the discourse of childhood. This attempt, if successful, amounts to the 'perfect crime' since it leaves behind no victim, and no blame can be attributed. In children's literature, the interplay and frequent antagonism between children and adults may be seen as the interaction and competition between two distinct discourses, two distinct agendas. In children's detective fiction, children and childhood are threatened not only by adult criminals, but also by the rational process of detection itself, which serves adult authority's need for order and conformity.

Yet childhood can also be seen as a 'radical' discourse: child detectives often pose a challenge to adult hierarchical structures. Like the archetypal 'great detective', whose success often rests on finding significance in things overlooked by the police, child detectives attend to things overlooked by, or invisible to, the adult gaze. A staple of children's detective stories such as those in Enid Blyton's Famous Five series, for example, is the child detective's continuing interest in a problem or danger the adults have long since disregarded. This attention to details outside the adult gaze, and indeed the absence of childhood and children from adult discourses more generally, might actually assist the child detective in a radical interrogation of the mysteries of both adulthood and childhood.

The child detective, then, can be seen as operating in a unique position between the two discourses, combining childish playfulness and adult rational method to solve the mystery. Detective fiction, however, often unsettles the distinction between detectives and criminals. The character of Flambeau, in G. K. Chesterton's detective stories, for example, first appears as an arch-criminal, and later becomes Father Brown's friend and assistant, while the genius of Sherlock Holmes is mirrored in the intellectual abilities of his enemy Professor Moriarty. In children's detective fiction, this distinction becomes still more uncertain, since the child detective must behave in rational, adult ways, while adult criminals and criminality are often presented as irrational and childish. The child-adult detective's efforts to uncover and capture the adult-child criminal point still more decisively towards a tendency to expose, punish and finally remove childhood and childish behaviour from society at large.

In detective fiction for adults, the 'perfect crime', of childhood's 'murder' by adulthood, has already been successfully attempted; children and childhood are almost entirely absent from the adult forms. Detectives as diverse as Raymond Chandler's Philip Marlowe and Agatha Christie's Hercule Poirot, for example, rarely, if ever, mention the past; their childhoods, in particular, remain a mystery. Where children do appear in adult detective narratives they tend to be presented as falling into two types. They are either needful of sympathy, perhaps victims of crime or disease, or else they occupy a similar, marginal, space as the detective. Like the detective, they are told lies, denied access to certain things, and their opinions are ignored, although, interestingly, less often by the detective than by other adults.

Lawrence Block's *A Walk Among the Tombstones* (1994) is unusual in this respect in that it contains children of both the 'requiring sympathy' and 'marginalized detective' types. One child character, for example, is kidnapped and mutilated before she can be rescued by private detective Matt Scudder. More interesting for us here, however, is a street kid called TJ, who spends most of the novel trying to convince Scudder that he too can operate as a detective. TJ is proud of his ability to remain invisible in the face of danger:

'I couldn't [call right away], man. I had to follow the dude.'
'You followed him?'
'What you think I do, run away when I seen him comin'? I don't walk arm in arm with the man, but he walk out an' I give him a minute an' I slip out after him.'
'That's dangerous, TJ. The man's a killer.'
'Man, am I supposed to be impressed? I'm on the Deuce 'bout every day of my life. Can't walk down the street without you're fol-lowin' some killer or other.' (249)

The ability to be inconspicuous makes TJ a useful assistant for Matt Scudder; as a child TJ is better able than Scudder to do things such as follow a criminal without arousing suspicion.

Rather than playing a secondary role, like TJ in Block's novel, in children's detective fiction child detectives are usually at the centre of the narrative. In addition, child detectives must frequently compete with adult sleuths or the police in solving mysteries. In Anthony Horowitz's *The Falcon's Malteser* (1986), for example, the thirteen-year-old brother of Herbert Simple, aka Tim Diamond, an extraordinarily incompetent adult private eye, manages to solve the mystery while his older brother is in custody on suspicion of murder. The child detective in this case at first competes with his brother and later with the police in solving the crime. Rather than playing a subordinate role to the adult processes of law, justice and detection, child detectives work hard to show that they, too, have a contribution to make. For Nicolas Simple, aka Nicky Diamond, it is the fact that he is a child that allows him to pursue the case, since he is too young to be locked up like his brother.

In children's detective fiction the exclusion or elimination of child-hood is more subtly attempted than in detective fiction for adults, since it is very often perpetrated by the child at its centre who, in order to find success as a detective, must behave in adult ways. In Horowitz's clever parody of the American hard-boiled detective novel, for example, the child detective Nicky Diamond takes more physical pun-ishment than Sam Spade in the Dashiell Hammett novel on which *The Falcon's Malteser* bases its name. In fact the young sleuth behaves so much like an adult that Horowitz places comic reminders that he is a child:

This was the perfume hall. They stocked all the perfumes in the world – and you could smell them all at once.

'Do you want to try this one?'

A pretty girl leaned over the counter, holding a bottle of after-shave towards me. I shook my head. She had a nice face. But she was a couple of years early. (159)

A little later, Nicky is chased into the Christmas grotto in Selfridges, where he is forced to sit on Father Christmas's knee. The full extent of this disjuncture between Nicky's childishness and his adult role becomes clear when the gunman who is chasing him shoots Father Christmas dead. Nicky struggles to be accepted as an adult, and it is achieving such acceptance, and the rejection or 'murder' of childhood it implies, that may be considered the real goal of the child detective.

Emil and the Detectives is usually considered to be the first children's book featuring a child detective. It tells the story of Emil Tischbein, a boy who travels alone to Berlin to visit relatives, and is robbed while sleeping on the train. Knowing the police will not believe him, and afraid of being arrested himself, Emil sets out to apprehend the thief, a 'man in a bowler hat', and recover his money. Although the story is one of crime and detection, Emil, and the friends he makes on the streets of the city, do not have to detect the identity of a criminal. The criminal, Mr Grundeis, is known to them from the start, and instead their detection involves following, and finally entrapping, the thief.

While such detection requires little in the way of ratiocination – that is, the observation and elimination of possible clues – it does involve organization, planning, and a reasoned understanding of the world. As such, the 'mystery' Emil and his friends investigate is to do with the world itself, and the most effective way of understanding and explaining events in it. The type of detection practised by Emil and the other 'detectives' is that which allows for the most profound examination of the world and its mysteries since it combines theorizing with a testing of those theories on reality. Rational detective method alone may solve specific puzzles or mysteries, but it depends on particular theories about reality always holding true. The combination of rational method and physical engagement with the world in Emil's detection allows prior, theoretical knowledge to be tested against reality and revised when it is found wanting. Emil's initial distrust of strangers, for example, turns out to demand complex revision; he discovers that while Mr Grundeis is not to be trusted, other strangers offer him kindness and support.

Besides telling the story of Emil's capture of Mr Grundeis, then, Kästner's novel also relates Emil's detecting of the world, and his first taste of adulthood. The mystery of what lies beyond his home in the town of Neustadt makes Emil cautious and uncertain at the novel's opening; by its end, that mystery has been solved through the rational and physical confrontation of his fears. Yet he does not 'grow up' in the novel; as Walter de la Mare points out in his introduction to the 1959 English translation, Emil is as much a child at the end of the novel as he is at the beginning. Rather, Emil and his detectives bring to their rational pursuit of the thief a childish enthusiasm and vigour that spills over, at the end of the story, into a chaotic celebration party.

It is the ability of child detectives to go unnoticed by the adults around them that is perhaps their most important asset when solving mysteries. For readers at the start of the twenty-first century, perhaps one of the strangest features of Kästner's novel is its description of large groups of children wandering freely about the streets of Berlin. Emil and his friends seem to be passed over by adults as insignificant; they are not thought capable of posing a threat. In this respect, detective fiction for children, like detective fiction in general, describes, legit-imizes, even privileges marginal existences. While the actions of indi-vidual detectives often may be seen as affirming the validity of conservative or bourgeois ideologies, in general detectives are also mar-ginal figures, whose status as 'outsiders' in relation to the society in which the crime takes place, assists them in their detecting.

The issue of marginality, and the need to reassess the relationships between discourses is also problematic for the status of children's detective fiction as a genre. Children's literature itself has, until com-paratively recently, been considered a marginal area of study for schol-ars of literature. Peter Hunt makes the unhappy claim that:

> Children's books ... are rarely acknowledged by the literary estab-lishment. [They are] invisible in the literary worlds in much the same way as women writers have been – and still are – invisible in the eighteenth-century novel. (7)

This exclusion of children's books from adult academic literary dis-course may be seen as analogous to the exclusion of childhood from the discourse of adulthood in children's detective fiction. The relatively recent and continuing reassessment of the place of children's literature in the academy, like similar reconsideration of the eighteenth-century women writers Hunt mentions, also provokes reassessments of the writers, works, and genres that have so far dominated literary studies. The child detective, in a similar way, is able to interrogate adulthood and childhood more effectively by observing them from a new perspective.

In what follows, the conflict between the discourses of adulthood and childhood will be explored in more detail in relation to detective fiction as a literary type, and especially in its manifestation for children. In particular, *Emil and the Detectives* provides examples both of attempts by adulthood to suppress or eradicate the discourse of childhood, and the ways in which childhood itself is complicit in its own eradication. It is this collaboration of the victim with the perpetrator that makes the crime perfect. Kästner's story reveals the importance of the child-detective's position in between adulthood and childhood. Success for Emil depends not on his remaining bound to one discourse or the other but in shifting between them; his success as a detective depends on his ability to behave in rational 'adult' ways while retaining his 'childish' qualities of imagination and unworldliness.

Before going on to discuss the ways in which childhood and adulthood confront one another in children's detective fiction, it is worth considering briefly the function of marginality as a tool for solving mysteries in detective fiction generally. An indication of how central the figure of the marginal detective is in the structure of detective stories can be seen in the example of two very different adult detectives, Hercule Poirot and Philip Marlowe.

While Poirot participates in middle-class social events, and helps to retain order in them, his marginal status is signalled by his foreignness and, particularly significant in England, perhaps, his self-confessed status as an intellectual. Poirot's Belgian nationality, combined with what – despite his reputation as a sleuth – are seen by criminals as his intellectual pretensions, render him unworthy of consideration by wrongdoers. Poirot achieves much of his success in solving mysteries through being considered 'harmless', even childlike, by witnesses and conspirators alike. During his investigations Poirot's concern seems to be with the peripheral detail, rather than the case itself. As Julian Symons points out in *Bloody Murder*, 'Poirot, in the best Holmesian style asks obscure questions that turn out to be meaningful, like his concern [in *The Murder of Roger Akroyd*] with the colour of the suspect's boots' (98).

In another type of detective fiction, Raymond Chandler's Philip Marlowe operates, in class terms, from a position of alienation from any one grouping; his marginal status enables him to have contact with a wide range of social types. Fredric Jameson, among others, com-ments on the episodic and 'synoptic' nature of Chandler's novels: Marlowe moves from one part of Los Angeles to another, crossing boundaries of class and wealth as well as geographical markers. Yet, although he is able to operate in a range of social and geographical set-tings, Marlowe himself is unable fully to engage with any of them and remains committed to a solitary life.

Both Poirot and Marlowe, in their different ways, occupy a position that is both a part of and challenging to the societies in which they operate, Poirot because of his intellectual abilities and his foreignness and Marlowe because of his romantic individualism. As such, their marginality is positively applied; it is part of their respective identities, but it is also, to varying degrees, self-imposed. By contrast, child detec-tives begin from a marginal position in relation to adulthood that is not of their own choosing and from which they usually hope to escape. The adventures of Enid Blyton's Famous Five, for example, take place not because the children choose a marginal position from which to observe the adult world – on the contrary, the Five seem determined to behave in as grown-up a way as possible – but because they have been marginalized by adults. Where adult detectives use and retain the characteristics that make them positive marginal figures, child detec-tives use the process of detection to overcome their marginalization, to become 'visible' in the adult discourse. Paradoxically, like their adult counterparts, child detectives also depend on that marginality in the process of detection; the child detective operates in a space between childhood and adulthood. In other words, the marginal position of the child detective, and the link she or he provides between adulthood and childhood, is intrinsically unstable; the relationship between the two discourses must continually be reassessed through their adventures.

An example of this process of reassessment may be found in Blyton's first Famous Five novel, *Five on a Treasure Island* (1942), the plot of which depends on the children's enforced estrangement from the con-cerns of adults. Julian, Anne, and Dick are sent to stay with their cousin, George, by parents who want a holiday without them, and they are largely ignored by George's parents because the difficulties experienced by the adults are not ones with which they think the chil-dren can help. In their view, the childish discourse of play, of summer holidays, boat trips, and picnics, can contribute nothing to adult con-cerns of finance and academic life. The incompatibility of the two dis-courses can be seen in Uncle Quentin's refusal at the end of the adventure to believe that the Five have found the treasure:

'Do you know why [the men] wanted to buy the island and the castle? Not because they really wanted to build an hotel or anything like that – but because they knew the lost gold was hidden there!'

'What nonsense are you talking?' said [Julian's] uncle.

'It isn't nonsense, Father!' cried George indignantly ...

George's father looked amazed and annoyed. He simply didn't believe a word! (149)

A more dangerous and irreconcilable rift between the children and adults in the novel, however, takes place earlier in the story when the Famous Five, who attempt to prevent the criminals from making off with the gold ingots, are held captive and are threatened with a gun. This physical threat from adults towards the child detectives in the novel is a manifestation of a more general threat in children's detective fiction to eradicate or, at the very least, exclude childhood itself from the lives of adults and adult discourses. More benignly, Uncle Quentin's acceptance of the truth of the story at the conclusion of the novel represents his own reassessment of his relationship with his daughter, and perhaps with children in general. The hint at other Famous Five adventures to come, with which the novel ends, is also a hint that this reassessment of the relationship between adulthood and childhood is an ongoing process.

In order to examine this process of reassessment more closely, it is worth comparing the antagonism between adulthood and childhood with the notional conflict between what I. A. Richards, in *Principles of Literary Criticism*, calls 'scientific' and 'emotive' language. Both Richards's general approach to linguistics and his descriptive style now seem rather dated, but his ideas are worth considering here because what he describes taking place in terms of language may be seen as roughly analogous to the experiences of child detectives as they negotiate between adulthood and childhood.

The 'scientific' and the 'emotive', Richards explains, are the 'two uses' of language. 'Scientific' use can be described as referential language, that is a form of language use in which references are 'true'. As Richards explains it:

A reference is true when the things to which it refers are actually together in the way in which it refers to them. Otherwise it is false. This sense is one very little involved by any of the arts. (269)

In contrast, he argues, for poetic or 'emotive' language 'the widest differences in reference are of no importance' (268). In other words, 'scientific' language is utilitarian. It might describe a glass of wine, for example, as 'a fermented alcoholic drink made from grape juice'. In comparison, Keats's language is more 'emotive', describing the same glass as 'a beaker full of the warm South', in his 'Ode to a Nightingale'.

J. M. Barrie's presentation of the conflict between adulthood and childhood in *Peter and Wendy* is also comparable with the views about 'scientific' and 'emotive' language expressed by Richards. Peter Pan explicitly makes the connection between his 'emotive' imaginative life, and the solemn, 'referential' (or 'scientific') concerns of adults. At the end of the novel Peter Pan explains his own refusal to grow up as an evasion of adulthood's repressive tendencies:

> 'Would you send me to a school?' he inquired craftily.
> 'Yes.'
> 'And then to an office?'
> 'I suppose so.'
> 'Soon I should be a man?'
> 'Very soon.'
> 'I don't want to go to school and learn solemn things,' he told her passionately. 'I don't want to be a man ... no one is going to catch me and make me a man.' (216–17).

Peter's fear is that adulthood will eradicate from him the qualities of childhood he enjoys; as Mr Darling knows only too well, being 'gay and innocent and heartless' (221) is incompatible with the world of schools and offices and social position. Unlike Peter, the Darling children must learn to curb their childish impulses in order to thrive as adults, yet it is her faded memories of Neverland that will later make Wendy a caring and sympathetic mother. Similarly, Richards attempts to propose poetry, which he calls 'the supreme form of *emotive* language' (273), as the best method of organizing emotional responses. In *Literary Theory*, Terry Eagleton exposes an ideological thread running through Richards's approach that is perhaps also present in Barrie's novel:

> Organizing the lawless lower impulses more effectively will ensure the survival of the higher, finer ones; it is not far from the Victorian belief that organizing the lower classes will ensure the survival of the upper ones, and indeed is significantly related to it. (46)

Peter Pan, then, embodies the childish, non-referential, impulses which, although suppressed, continue to exist in all the adults in

Barrie's book. Like the Victorian lower classes, while Peter cannot be adapted to 'respectable', rational, middle-class adult life, he can be partially controlled through understanding and acceptance. Ultimately, however, Peter Pan can only be resisted by closing the nursery window. Just as Richards argues for an acceptance of the emotive as a way of balancing the necessity of the referential, Barrie foregrounds the playfulness of Peter Pan as a counterweight, although for most children not an alternative, to the 'solemn things' with which adults must engage.

While Richards worried that social cohesion might be threatened by a failure to address people's emotional needs through poetry, more recently, Jean Baudrillard, in *The Perfect Crime*, has expressed the opposite view that in fact referentiality or 'reality' is at risk from a surfeit of non-referential linguistic structures. For our purposes here, then, the discourse of childhood may be roughly equated with emotive language (what Baudrillard calls the 'structural play of value') while adulthood may be viewed as equivalent to the referential or 'scientific'. While children's detective narratives depend on a conflict between the two discourses, they do not attempt to balance one with the other in the name of stability, as Richards suggests should be the case with 'emotive' and 'scientific' language. Rather, children's detective fiction, as we have seen, describes the child detective operating in between the discourses of adulthood and childhood. The child detective, in this system, is the point of engagement between the two, and, crucially, is able to interrogate them both.

In contrast to the simple opposition of adulthood and childhood on which Barrie's novel depends, child detectives must learn to combine elements from both discourses in their detection. In detective fiction for adults and for children, the child is usually invisible to adults, who would prefer him or her to stay that way. The child ceases to be invisible only when her or his actions disrupt or otherwise impinge upon adult discourses. For example, at the beginning of Kästner's novel, Emil is worried that he might be recognized by the policeman, Jeschke, as being one of the boys who had, in an act of Dadaesque playfulness, defaced a statue of Grand Duke Charles. While Emil had certainly been highly visible to Jeshke as he ran away from the scene, when he and his mother later meet the policeman, Emil is hardly noticed:

> as Emil was good at drawing, he had been lifted up by the others to chalk a red nose and a black moustache on the duke's face. He was just adding the finishing touches when sergeant Jeschke turned the

corner of the square, and although they had all raced off at top speed, they were awfully afraid he had recognized them.

However, Jeschke made no reference to that now. He merely wished Emil a pleasant journey, and asked his mother how she was, and hoped business was good. (28)

The realization that as long as they do nothing to challenge the rules of the adult discourse they go almost unnoticed by adults is useful to Emil and the other 'detectives' later in the novel when they spy on the man in the bowler hat who has stolen Emil's money. While they realize they must be careful not to be seen to be following the man, they also become aware that, as children, their usual invisibility to adults makes their occasional appearance in an adult's field of vision all the more dramatic. For example, Mr Grundeis is dismissive of the boys he sees gathering outside his hotel when he looks out of an upstairs window. Although they disgust him, he is unable to see how they might impinge upon him:

Quite a crowd of boys [was] playing football on the grass, and more boys were standing in small groups at the corner of Kleist street and outside the entrance to the underground station. 'I suppose it's holiday-time,' he thought in disgust. (145)

However, it is this very crowd which, in a different context, becomes threatening and assists in his capture:

very soon Mr Grundeis found himself completely surrounded.

He looked about in amazement. Boys swarmed round him, all laughing and talking among themselves, jostling each other, yet somehow always keeping up with him. Some of them stared at him so hard that he hardly knew where to look. (151–2)

The imposition of the crowd, and in particular the way in which individuals within it make themselves visible by staring at him, makes Grundeis suddenly aware of the children's presence. Grundeis comes to the obscene realization that the anonymous crowd is composed of individuals and that children can pose a threat to him as an adult. Taking the view that detective fiction generally may be read as an evocation of attempts to 'fill in' the gaps in knowledge, that is to solve mysteries, this detection of the adult criminal by the child may be seen as the detection not only of the specific criminal, but of adulthood itself.

Adulthood is presented in *Emil and the Detectives* as a dominant, if mysterious, discourse. Adults appear to be in control of everything – including what passes for the truth – to the extent that Emil decides not to go to the police after he is robbed because he knows he will not be believed. Although Emil begins the novel fearful of adults and the ways in which he might be punished or exploited by them, the point at which he decides not to go to the police but to follow the thief himself is a moment of existential clarity. From that point onwards Emil and the other detectives appear to reject adult authority and control and set about exercising self-will.

While this approach can be expressed, for the individuals them-selves, as an act of self-definition and rebellion, it is also significant in assessing the conflict between the discourses of adulthood and child-hood. The challenge posed to the adult criminal by the child detectives may be compared with the radical challenge posed to the art establish-ment by the avant-garde. In the terms of Ihab Hassan's 1967 view of postmodern or 'anti-literature' expressed in 'The Literature of Silence', the child detective challenges the dominant discourse of adulthood just as 'anti-literature', in Hassan's view, challenges the 'ancient excel-lence of literary discourse' (11). In attempting to evade capture, Grundeis appeals to the 'ancient excellence' of his status as an adult in order to dismiss Emil's improvised objections. Having admitted that he has no proof that the money is his, Emil seems for a moment to be beaten:

> 'Gentlemen,' said the thief, 'I give you my word of honour that the money is mine. Do I look like the kind of man who would steal from a child?'
> Emil suddenly gave a jump.
> 'Wait a bit,' he cried, enormous relief in his voice, 'I've thought of something. In the train I pinned the envelope with the money to the inside of my pocket, so there ought to be holes pricked through all three notes.' (163–4)

Having implied that the detection of the adult criminal by the child detective demonstrates the radical nature of childhood as a discourse, it is worth noting here that the process of detection itself, even in chil-dren's detective fiction, seems peculiarly adult. Emil's realization that the pin-holes in the money might 'mean' something appeals to the adult authorities' predilection for rational methods and referentiality. Indeed, it is perhaps Emil's earlier challenge to adult authority – the defacing of the statue – that seems the more subversive, since the actions of child detectives such as Emil are ultimately pleasing to responsible, law-abiding adults.

This apparent reversal in our view of the child detective can be explained in terms of the earlier brief consideration of Richards and Baudrillard. In their own ways, both are concerned with shifts in the balance between emotive and referential language, in other words between the use value and referential value of the sign. The rational process of detection in this formulation would seem to be more akin to the 'scientific' language Richards identifies while, by contrast, the playfulness of Emil's defacing of the statue could be described as 'emotive'. Indeed, the similarity between Emil's addition of a moustache to a public statue and Marcel Duchamp's reworking of the *Mona Lisa* suggests that Emil's own Dadaist project might also have the effect of problematizing through ridicule the relationship between signs and their referents. At the very least, Emil's act of vandalism might appear to render the statue, and its cultural 'meaning', absurd.

This challenge to referential systems of value is suggestive of what Baudrillard describes as the 'structural play' of signs. For Richards, the benefit of emotive uses of language, such as poetry, is that they need have no political purpose or relationship to a reality beyond their own structural boundaries. For Baudrillard, however, such a lack of functional or referential systems of linguistic exchange makes protest impossible. Thus, the addition of the moustache to the statue proves to be, as Emil himself later discovers, no threat at all to the dominant adult discourse, since Emil's 'critique' involves nothing more than the benign juxtaposition of statue and moustache.

In becoming a detective, then, Emil shifts away from a discourse of interchangeable meaning and the relative value of signs to one another that characterizes childish behaviour in the novel. As we have seen, the discourse of childhood, while appearing subversive, in fact leaves him powerless to protest his marginalization. The 'functional' system he adopts as a detective, in which value relations purport to be absolute and comparable and signs have referential value, allows him no more freedom, however, than 'play' since in detecting in this way he must subscribe to a value system that is independent of him and preordained. Unfortunately, the apparent freedom Emil gains through solving the mystery is bought at the cost of his accepting the place of the statue (which glorifies a militant, imperialistic aristocracy) within a referential system that places political power elsewhere.

As a detective story, *Emil and the Detectives* is closer to the American 'hard-boiled' form than the deductive 'scientific' model of, say, Doyle or Christie. It is difficult to describe Emil's and the other detectives' method as 'scientific', since, like hard-boiled detectives, their detection is more to do with following the thief, watching, and finally apprehending him than it is with interpreting clues. The mystery that Emil and other detectives like him investigate is more to do with the mystery of their identity and their place in the world than with who committed the crime. In particular, they learn adult modes of behaviour such as patience and organization, but along the way they also reveal the secret of the link between criminality and childishness.

Kästner's novel, like other detective novels for children in which child detectives solve crimes committed by adults, privileges a referential system of exchange by equating childhood with criminality. Criminals tend to be characters who operate outside of this 'adult' discourse of referentiality. For example, Grundeis's theft is wrong in the absolute terms of the prevailing moral and legal structures, but also because it subverts the referential adult exchange system of work and pay which those structures serve to protect. Grundeis's irresponsible theft of money that Emil's mother had to work hard to earn can be compared here with Peter Pan's refusal to work in an office. Like Peter Pan, Grundeis behaves 'childishly'. He rejects the 'solemn' existence of most adults who work for a living; he eats well, travels by taxi, and stays in hotels. Just as Peter Pan's decision not to grow up means he must stay in Neverland with the 'Lost Boys', Grundeis's decision to become a thief rather than earn his living leads to his arrest and imprisonment. Rather than radically challenging adulthood, then, the child detective in such a formulation detects and punishes, if not childhood itself, then at least its impulse to relative value and structural exchange. A further example is that Emil later confesses his 'crime' against the statue in Neustadt and expects, but does not receive, punishment for his 'emotive' act of playfulness. The child detective's responsible handing over of the adult criminal to adult authorities is a betrayal of his or her own radical and subversive discourse of childhood.

Far from directly challenging the discourses of adulthood, then, child detectives seek to eradicate or at least abandon their defining characteristics as children. Following the success of his detective work, Emil explicitly rejects his earlier childish behaviour and seeks absolution for his 'sin':

Emil took the plunge. 'I chalked a red nose and moustache on the statue of Grand Duke Charles in Neustadt,' he confessed. 'So you'd better arrest me sir.'

To his surprise the five men burst out laughing, instead of looking grave as he expected.

'Bless me!' exclaimed the big man, 'we can't go arresting one of our best detectives!' (179–80)

Emil's surprise that he is not punished for his 'crime' suggests he is, up to this point, unaware of the full significance of his detecting; he is being rewarded not only for apprehending the thief, but for rejecting the childish exchange system that the act of vandalism represents. Emil further shows his participation in adult discourses and systems of exchange when he offers to treat 'Mr. Kästner', a journalist who paid his tram fare during the pursuit of the criminal, to cream cakes in a café. His willingness to participate in adult economic activity is seen as a sign of independence by 'Kästner' and the other adults, when it might also be seen as a capitulation to the dominant referential adult discourse. The fact that Emil offers to buy cream cakes rather than any other kind of food might suggest that he remains childish in his tastes despite having 'solved' the mystery of adulthood.

The success of a child detective, then, lies not so much in apprehending a criminal as escaping childhood and achieving the right to self-determination that Peter Pan so flamboyantly and paradoxically rejects. Furthermore, that attainment of the freedom of self-determination is expressed in the awarding of the privilege of participating in economic, that is referential, exchanges. For example, at the end of *Emil and the Detectives*, part of Emil's reward is in being allowed to buy his mother a coat: to participate in a 'referential' or 'functional' exchange of money for goods. Similarly, at the end of *The Falcon's Malteser*, the two brothers receive one of the missing diamonds and are able to settle their debts, while at the end of *Five on a Treasure Island*, George explains that she will divide up the treasure between the four children. As we have seen, however, since a refusal to participate in such a system is considered childish or even criminal, the extent of the freedom on offer is rather more limited than it might seem.

In Kästner's novel, Emil's decision to purchase his mother a coat is not only indicative of his participation in the discourse of adulthood, however, but is also a reversal of the economic power relationship between the male child and his mother with which the novel begins:

Emil's father was dead, so Mrs. Tischbein had to work to keep herself and him ... She had not only to earn enough to pay the rent, the gas and coal bills, but there were Emil's school fees as well, and the cost of his books. There were also times when she was not well, and had to have a doctor ... Emil used to look after her at such times, and even did the cooking. (23)

Emil begins the novel playing the 'feminine' role in the relationship and ends having earned the right to play the 'masculine'. This is presented not as conflict but compromise. Emil can do housework and be 'masculine', and we are told not to laugh at Emil 'for being rather a good boy to his mother' (23–4). However, it is significant that Emil's temporary transition from child to adult behaviour and exchange systems should occur alongside this shift from what is presented as the feminine to the masculine in terms of the acquisition of economic power.

Although the novel is conservative in its privileging of the referential over the emotive, with all the implications outlined above, Emil himself does not, during the period covered by the plot, make a permanent move from childhood to adulthood, or from the 'emotive' to the 'referential.' Because of his age he must return to the position of the child. One 'lesson' Emil's mother learns from his adventure, for example, is that 'children shouldn't be allowed to travel alone' (217). As we have seen, however, Emil seems less at risk from the actual thief than from adulthood itself which lures him into behaving in an adult way, and it is perhaps of this 'growing up' that his mother is most afraid. As Bobbie Ann Mason points out in relation to the (female) Bobbsey Twins, 'from the cradle the girl is oriented backward, to prevent her blossoming and awakening, her growth' (27). Similarly, while Emil's success is rewarded, and his future adult status confirmed (one possible difference between male and female child detectives), there is relief among his adult relatives that he remains a child, although a rather more worldly one than before.

Children's detective fiction, then, appears not as a radical detection of adulthood by the child, or childlike, detective, but rather a struggle for participation in adult discourse. The temporary participation in adult discourse that makes possible the child detective's success depends on the child detective being able to move between adulthood and childhood, to operate, in a sense, between the two. As has been noted by Mason, however, girl detectives are prevented from developing into women within their fictional framework. In contrast, Emil is given some temporary access to adult male power, although the final transition he will make from childhood to adulthood – outside the boundaries of the novel – will be controlled by his mother and other adult relatives.

Such an ability to operate from a position between competing discourses is characteristic of many detective narratives. What makes this interesting in terms of children's detective fiction is that the process of detection involves the detective's interrogation of the mystery of what he or she is or has been (a child), and what she or he will become (an adult). Furthermore, the perceived 'childishness' of the criminal's behaviour suggests that the child detective in some way attempts not only to capture the adult criminal, but to make sure that childhood itself is apprehended and locked away. What distinguishes the child-adult detective and the adult-child criminal from others in the novel is their ability easily to shift between the two competing discourses, each of which is absent to the other. For example, as we have seen, for many of the adults in Kästner's novel, including at times the thief himself, children and childhood are practically invisible; it is such invisibility to the eyes of adults that makes it possible for them to operate covertly as detectives.

We are talking here, perhaps, about a third, marginal discourse of the child-adult detective and the adult-child criminal. It is a discourse founded on absence, which emerges as subversive not only of the dominant adult discourse but of the very notion of competing discourses itself. It is the child detective's marginal position that enables him or her to make the transition from the 'invisible' to the 'visible'. In terms of Mr Grundeis's experience in *Emil*, the child detective shifts from being part of a meaningless crowd, to being an intimidating, staring face – the face of the victim refusing to be victimized.

Works cited

Barrie, J. M. *Peter and Wendy* [1911]. Oxford: Oxford University Press, 1991.

Baudrillard, Jean. *The Perfect Crime* [1995], trans. Chris Turner. London: Verso, 1996.

Block, Lawrence. *A Walk Among the Tombstones*. London: Phoenix Books, 1994.

Blyton, Enid. *Five on a Treasure Island* [1942]. London: Hodder Children's Books, 1991.

de la Mare, Walter. 'Introduction' [1959], in Erich Kästner. *Emil and the Detectives*. London: Red Fox, 1995, pp. 9–12.

Eagleton, Terry. *Literary Theory: An Introduction*. Oxford: Blackwell, 1983.

Hassan, Ihab. 'The Literature of Silence' [1967], in *The Postmodern Turn: Essays in Postmodern Theory and Culture*. Columbus, OH: Ohio State University Press, 1987, pp. 3–22.

Horowitz, Anthony. *The Falcon's Malteser* [1986]. London: Walker Books, 1995.

Hunt, Peter. *An Introduction to Children's Literature*. Oxford: Oxford University Press, 1994.

Jameson, Fredric. 'The Synoptic Chandler', in Joan Copjec (ed.), *Shades of Noir*. London: Verso, 1993, pp. 33–56.

Kästner, Erich. *Emil and the Detectives* [1928], trans. Eileen Hall. London: Red Fox, 1995.

Mason, Bobbie Ann. *The Girl Sleuth: A Feminist Guide*. Athens, GA: University of Georgia Press, 1995.

Richards, I. A. *Principles of Literary Criticism* [1924]. London: Kegan Paul, Trench, Trubner & Co., 1938.

Symons, Julian. *Bloody Murder: From the Detective Story to the Crime Novel*. Harmondsworth: Viking, 1985.

6
Digging up the Family Plot: Secrets, Mystery, and the Blytonesque

David Rudd

Introduction

Enid Blyton's name is synonymous with mystery. She used the word, together with the almost equivalent term 'secret', in some fifty titles, and the concept in a good many more. Blyton wrote a number of individual mystery titles in addition to her famous series: the Famous Five (21 titles), the Secret Seven (15 titles), Five Find-Outers (15 titles), the Adventure series (eight titles), the Barney series (six titles), Secrets (five titles) and the Adventurous Four (two titles). Sheila Ray in *The Blyton Phenomenon* differentiates 'holiday' stories from 'mysteries', equating the latter term with detective fiction (specifically the Secret Seven and Find-Outers) (152–77). However, I do not find this division useful. Most of Blyton's plots, as I shall argue, are set in holiday time and are also centrally concerned with uncovering secrets of some sort. Although it could be argued that this use of the word 'mystery' was mere commercial expediency, I shall suggest in this essay that a sense of mystery in Blyton's work runs deeper, and I shall endeavour to lead us down its dark passages towards some sort of illumination. Let me begin by looking at Blyton's conception of story, and her closely associated views of home – as expressed not only in her mysteries, but in her autobiographical writing, too.

Mystery/my story

Middle-class ideas of homeliness are central to Blyton; more than almost any other writer, she celebrates home. Her own (Elfin Cottage, Old Thatch, and most famously Green Hedges) even feature in her fiction, providing inviting and secure titles such as *Tales of Old Thatch*

(1938) and *A Story Party at Green Hedges* (1949). These titles lead us to see her homes as the originary sites of stories, to which children are openly invited (the latter even includes an invitation card and map). Yet, in running these two together – home and story – there is also the suggestion that home is associated with untruths, that the fabric of home is built on fabrication.

This notion is compounded in Blyton's autobiography, *The Story of My Life* (1952), which also plays on 'story' as simultaneously revealing and concealing; in telling one version of events others are immediately submerged, hidden: *my-story* simultaneously generates *my-stery*. Almost half this book is about her writing self. In fact, Blyton hardly seems to exist before this, with the chapter 'How I began' solely relating her coming to be an author. *The Story of My Life* suggests, then, that she storied herself into existence; topics that she does not wish to story are simply glossed over – or, in Freudian terminology, repressed. As an example, we are presented in the book with a supposedly happy family unit, but no mention is made of the fact that the man pictured at Green Hedges is not the father of the two daughters who sit dutifully alongside him. And although we do see pictures of Old Thatch, where Blyton had lived with her first husband – her daughters' biological father – he is not in them. This man left the family after their marriage broke down, just as Blyton's own father had walked out of the family home when she was 12 years old. However, as a child she was forced to conceal this fact outside the home, just as she later hid her own divorce, making her 'happy family' image always something of a fictional construction (see Stoney).

Home, then, is a site of ambivalence in Blyton's writings, both fictional and autobiographical. It is a place of great familiarity but also one that can suddenly be defamiliarized (or perhaps defamily-ized), becoming strange. This brings to mind Freud's notion of the *Unheimlich*, or 'uncanny,' which, as Freud notes, has at its root the word *heimlich* – 'homely'. Freud quotes Schelling's definition of the uncanny as 'the name for everything that ought to have remained secret and hidden but has come to light' ('The Uncanny', 345). In many ways, this is the paradigm of Blyton's mysteries – secrets being brought to light – except that, in Blyton, the secrets frequently turn out to be less consequential than we might have expected, given the prior sense of mystery generated. So, in Blyton, everything that ought to remain secret and hidden remains so, while more tractable and material secrets are brought to light.

The homes that feature in the mysteries, then, seem to be secure structures, but they are frequently revealed to have subterranean

depths, openings that lead from the realm of culture into more primitive, natural spaces: tunnels, caves, seashores, and islands. Again, the
play on presence and absence is apparent, as these hidden areas
depend for their existence on the visible fabric; in other words, for a
secret passage to exist there must be occluding but tangible walls, the
presence of one concealing the other. Such occlusion is common in
Blyton. Despite being seen as a writer of plain prose, whose words seem
utterly transparent, it is often worth tapping them, to see what unsaid
lies behind the said – what signifieds slide unsuspected beneath the
seemingly transparent signifiers, just as they do for her adventurers:
'[s]uddenly ... the panel slid silently back ... The children stared at the
space behind, thrilled' (*Five Go Adventuring Again*, 149).

In turning to the series themselves, we can begin to see many frac-
tures in home life and the adults that constitute it. In Blyton's first full-
length mystery, *The Secret Island* (1938), the children are physically
abused by their guardians, their parents being presumed dead. (Since
writing this, a much earlier, previously unknown text of Blyton's has
been discovered: *The Wonderful Adventure*, published by Birn Bros in
1927.) As a consequence the children run away, setting up home for
themselves on an island. In the 'Adventure' series, one pair of siblings,
Jack and Lucy-Ann, are orphans who are looked after in their school
vacations by an unsympathetic uncle and a housekeeper who, as Jack
puts it, '"hates us to go home for the holidays"' (*The Island of
Adventure*, 17). The other two siblings, Dinah and Philip, have no
father and their mother does not live with them: '"[s]he's a very good
business woman – but we don't see much of her,"' the latter says
(*Island*, 18). The 'Barney' series features two children without parents –
Barney himself, who is also homeless, and Snubby, who '"gets kicked
about from one aunt to another, poor kid"' (*The Rockingdown Mystery*,
11). Even when more loving parents are featured they often seem more
concerned with each other than with their progeny. Thus, at the
beginning of the first 'Five' story, the children's father, with inklings of
the Oedipal triangle, suddenly announces that the children will be
holidaying apart from their parents:

'Mother and I won't be able to go with you this year. Has mother
told you?'
   'No!' said Anne. 'Oh, Mother – is it true? Can't you really come
with us on our holidays? You always do.'
   'Well, this time Daddy wants me to go to Scotland with him,' said
Mother. 'All by ourselves!' (*Five on a Treasure Island*, 7)

Even more peculiarly, they are taken off to stay with a cousin whom they have never met – a cousin whose parents, as Julian later notes, frequently go away without letting the children know where: '"it's so like them not to give us an address!"' (*Five Have Plenty of Fun*, 117). This said, he elsewhere states, '"[w]e don't tell tales about our parents in public"' (*Five Go to Demon's Rocks*, 51). Family secrets should be contained, it seems, whether it be in Blyton's own home – of her Beckenham childhood, at Old Thatch or Green Hedges – or in the more fictionalized Craggy-Tops (Adventure series) and Kirrin Cottage (Famous Five). All turn out to be places of secrecy: homes with passages worming beneath, linking them to indistinct pasts.

As I have already mentioned, in Blyton home is a slippery signifier, concealing as much as it reveals. But it is the children who frequently uncover its secrets, children who show the flimsiness of the walls, the fact that the fabric lacks solidity, and who reveal openings, gaps, and flaws. The adults, on the other hand, are the ones shown to be wanting – the ones responsible for the secrets. Although I have generally talked about parents and guardians so far, it is worth emphasizing that adults in general are suspect in Blyton mysteries. They try to shut children out, to exclude them from the grown-up world. In the Find-Outer series the village policeman is contemptibly known as 'Clear-Orf' because that is what he is always saying to the children, telling them not to meddle in adult concerns. But, of course, this is just what the children must do. Only in this way can they find out about the mysteries of the adult world.

Criminals are most interesting in this respect. There is a famous and frequently misquoted comment by the librarian Eileen Colwell, which captures what for many adults is both the essence and the fatuity of Blyton's mysteries: '"what hope has a band of desperate men against four children?"' (quoted in Ray 52). It is an unlikely reversal, but, like the folk-hero Jack battling against the Giant, this is surely the point: that adversaries are more powerful, but abusive of their power. More importantly in Blyton, these criminals, frequently parents or guardians themselves, are shown to be abusive of children and animals. In fact, this is often a key factor in identifying their criminal tendencies. Thus there is the crook, Uncle Dan, who physically abuses his young charge, Nobby, the latter appearing with 'a tear-stained face, bruised and swollen.' The boy is told '"we'll show you what a real beating is! And if you can walk down to the camp after it, I'll be surprised"' (*Five Go Off in a Caravan*, 134–5). The 'baddies', then, are frequently more than crooks, their crookedness being metonymic of adult duplicity and abuse of power. They attempt to shut the children out of their grown-up world, doing things behind closed doors:

> 'What about the kids?'
> 'We'll leave them locked up here ... Teach you to come poking your noses into what's no business of yours!' (*The Secret Seven*, 96–7)

However, Blyton shows that though powerless in the order of things – '[i]t wasn't a bit of good fighting grown-ups. They could do exactly as they liked' (*Five on a Treasure Island*, 108) – children can accrue power through knowledge. Foucault's equation of *power/knowledge* is relevant here, for he argues that the two are inextricably linked, that power inheres in having things to say, which means giving voice to discourses (knowledge) that have institutional support. As Foucault puts it, '[d]iscourse transmits and produces power; it reinforces it, but also undermines it and exposes it, renders it fragile and makes it possible to thwart it' (101). In other words, power is not simply repressive, something imposed from above, but is part of the fabric of society, in which all are involved. Thus, through power, bodies are organized and regimented. So a discourse which constructs children as knowing their place, as being marginalized, simultaneously gives them the latitude to exploit these margins, to eavesdrop and peek through keyholes – in short, to inhabit the interstices of the homely fabric.

Through gaining knowledge – clues and the like – the protagonists in Blyton's books seek to make a space in which children can be heard among adults: '"let's hope we ... understand the boys and girls that are growing up when *we're* men and women"' as Dinah puts it in *The Island of Adventure* (192–3). This said, the children generally only share their knowledge with adults when they have plumbed the mystery, knowing that otherwise they are likely to be dismissed, as 'Clear-Orf' dismisses the Find-Outers all the time, or as another anonymous functionary of the law tells the children: '"[y]ou go away, all of you ... I shan't report you this time. But don't you go spreading silly stories like that or you'll get into trouble"' (*Five on a Hike Together*, 85). Before they reveal the truth to adults the children know that they must be in a position of mastery where the various clues cohere, that is when they feel that they have uncovered the plot and that they are party to the adult secrets, as in this example from *The Secret Seven*:

> 'Ought we to tell our parents?' asked Pam.
> 'Or the police?' said Jack.

'Well – not till we know a little bit more,' said Peter. (74)

The Secret Seven, like other Blyton collectives, forms its own elect society in order to explore mysteries. Their initiations, passwords, ritual meals, and home-building activities all mirror and mimic adult exclusiveness:

> Janet looked round the clean shed, pleased with their work. Boxes to sit on – mugs on the little shelf, ready for any drinks that were brought ... and an old, rather raggedy rug on the earth floor ...
> 'Nice!' said Janet ... 'I've put the S. S. on the door.' (*Look out Secret Seven*, 17–18)

In doing this the children develop a corporate identity – as the 'S.S.' or 'Famous Five' – the five even using the epithet 'Famous Five-ish' to describe themselves (*Five on a Secret Trail*, 74). It is significant that Blyton's heroes are almost always groups of children, too, not lone detectives, and that their corporate identity is usually forged as a result of their marginalization by adults. In other words, it is adult put-downs, such as: '"[y]ou're only a child ... You surely don't think you can keep us from getting our way?"' (*Five on a Treasure Island*, 148) that cause children to challenge the definition of childhood imposed on them. As a result the children take advantage of the licence permitted them – to 'run off and play' – generally by exploiting times when they are beyond the gaze of officialdom. Most obviously, this is the holiday period, about which much fuss is made in the novels. Holiday is the time of freedom – a carnivalesque period when normal prohibitions are relaxed. Dick of the Famous Five describes the word 'holidays' as '"the nicest ... in the English language"' (*Five Have a Mystery to Solve*, 9) and elsewhere is the narratorial comment:

> How lovely to wake in a strange place at the beginning of a holiday – to think of bathing and biking and picnicking and eating and drinking – forgetting all about exams and rules and punishments! (*Five Go Down to the Sea*, 37)

The paratactic construction of this passage is worth noting, the 'ands' levelling out life's pleasures, simultaneously undoing the hierarchical ordering of school life. This latter world of the symbolic, where the Law of the Father obtains, is in abeyance, and any reminder of it is unwelcome: '"[l]et's not talk of school,"' says Anne in *Five Go to*

Demon's Rocks (111) when the subject is raised. Typically, in the one Five story in which a holiday tutor is imposed on them (*Five Go Adventuring Again*), he is subsequently found to be a crook. Such inversions are common in this period of licence. Thus Kiki, the parrot in the Adventure series, is excellent at mimicking the rule-bound interdictions of the symbolic, telling all and sundry, but especially adults, to wipe their feet, shut doors, use their handkerchiefs, and he is especially effective at mocking the world of school: '"[a]ttention, please," said Kiki sternly. "Open your books at page 6"' (*The Castle of Adventure*, 17). Holiday is not a time for such rules; instead, it is a time of indulgence – of sensual pleasures, like food and drink, staying up late and going to fairs and circuses:

> 'I can't think of anything nicer than lying down on hot sand with the sun on every part of my body, eating an ice-cream, and knowing there are still three weeks' holiday in front of us.' (*Five Have Plenty of Fun*, 9)

This 'time-out' period (similar to what Barthes refers to variously as 'mythic time' and 'dilatory space') is important in the stories. For, although some critics maintain that Blyton plunges straight into mystery, this is not, in fact, usually the case. There is often quite an extended period of preparation during which this space is created, when the adventurers come together and celebrate their unity. It is in this more leisurely, dreamlike space that the possibility of adventure is envisaged: '"I have a kind of feeling there might be an adventure somewhere about"' (*Five Go to Smuggler's Top*, 47). There is a suggestion that during the time when the symbolic reigns, mystery is not a possibility. As one Find-Outer comments on their return from boarding school, '"[n]othing at all seems to have happened in Peterswood since we left to go to school"' (*The Mystery of the Disappearing Cat*, 4). Once in the period of 'mythic time', however, mysterious events are not only a prospect, but a plausible fantasy – albeit their fantastic, dreamlike quality is never lost sight of:

> 'This is a most peculiar adventure to have.'
> 'It's probably a dream,' said Julian, and laughed. 'No – not even a dream could be so mad.' (*Five Go to Mystery Moor*, 130)

And there is the fancy that, being in this state, anything adventurous might materialize; thus Julian comments on their travelling in a boat called *Adventure*: '"[w]e might have *known* something would happen!"' (*Five Have a Mystery to Solve*, 94).

Wish-fulfilment is never far from the surface. So, in *The Mystery that Never Was*, when the narrator expresses the protagonist's wish: '[n]ow then – a smashing mystery was what he wanted – complete with clues, strange goings-on, and all the rest of it' (47), sure enough, one materializes: '"[g]osh, this mystery has come true in every detail in a most remarkable way! I'm never going to make up any more!"' (141).

During the early stages of this time-out Blyton teases readers in what Freud calls 'fore-pleasure', tentatively probing the terrain for adventure, sometimes even toying with the idea of withholding it. Thus, in *Five Go Off in a Caravan*, Anne's wish to have '"an *ordinary* holiday ... not *too* exciting"' (32) is honoured, with the other members of the Five continually declining to pick up on adventurous elements. Eventually, however, as another title has it, the 'Five fall into adventure'. This phrase is significant, a fall suggesting a lack of control as they are caught up in things beyond their power (generally adult things), but things that can be mastered. In moving into this time of adventure the protagonists also move, in Freud's phrase, 'beyond the pleasure principle', that is beyond the instant gratification of their desires into a time of lack, when the hardships of tunnelling, being imprisoned, and manhandled (as it usually is) have to be endured.

Mystery/mastery

I have suggested above that the sense of mystery in Blyton is frequently connected with adult secrets – particularly troubles at home – which the protagonists, in solving the mystery, think they can overcome. For instance, in the first Five adventure, after they have found the family treasure, Uncle Quentin assures George and the others that things will be different in future; speaking on behalf of them all in responding to a question about their wealth, he says he'll be

> 'Rich enough to give you and your mother all the things I've longed to give you for so many years and couldn't. I've worked hard enough for you – but it's not the kind of work that brings in a lot of money, and so I've become irritable and bad-tempered.' (*Five on a Treasure Island*, 184–6)

He is described as 'quite different now. It seemed as if a great weight had been lifted off his shoulders' (187). In the first Adventure book, the results are even more dramatic, with Philip's comment on his friends' mother realized:

> 'She's a mother, and she ought to live like a mother, and have a nice home of her own and you and Dinah with her.'
> 'We're going to,' said Dinah ... 'There's enough money now for Mother to make a home for us herself, and stop her hard work ... And what about you and Lucy-Ann coming to live with us, Freckles? You don't want to go back to your old uncle and horrid old house-keeper, do you?' (*The Island of Adventure*, 324)

This notion of everything being righted is, of course, an illusion, but the solving of the mystery provides a sense of mastery, a feeling that all will now be well and, most importantly, that children can be effective agents in this process. In Freudian terms there is a sense of plenitude, of coherence, and of fulfilling the 'family romance'. This romance, or story, as Freud elaborates, involves children moving from a position where they see their parents as all-knowing paragons to seeing them as faulted, so 'that other parents are in some respects preferable' to their own ('Family', 221). Consequently, children entertain the wish that their own carers be replaced in some way. Versions of this, as in fairy tales, are a common narrative outcome in Blyton.

The mystery itself then (the catching of crooks, the finding of trea-sure) is of less importance than its effectivity – its ability to empower children and right some aspect of the adult world – as in the cases quoted above. This is not to deny the magical sense of mystery that pervades her books, and the suspense generated therein. However, at the end, the unveiling of mystery is summarily dealt with; the torch beams of the heroes quickly throw light on the situation, and all is log-ically explained. The mystery is also inveterately physical, both in terms of its materiality – treasure, maps and so on, and in its Newtonian rationality; thus Blyton's famous secret openings are always found to be worked by some mechanism, some 'hidden spring or lever' (*Five Go Adventuring Again*, 149). Here is a characteristic, if somewhat edited, example:

> she went to an enormous tapestry picture over the mantelpiece ... [and] reached up to the dim face in the old picture. The face wore a helmet ... The woman pressed a stud in the helmet ... The great picture slid silently to one side ... enough to show a small panel of wood that looked just a little different from the others.

The woman put her hand firmly on the small panel and pressed it to one side. It slid along under her hand, leaving a tiny space ... [with] a knob in the space behind ... Roger ... pressed the knob hard and it yielded suddenly beneath his hand. At the same moment something rattled softly behind the panelling not far off.

'That knob releases a lever which in turn enables us to press back a bigger panel' ... She pressed her hand against a big panel, and it gradually slid inside into the wall, sliding neatly behind the panel next to it. A hole yawned there at last. (*Ring o'Bells Mystery*, 44–5).

At last, indeed! This is prosaically mechanical. There is no sense of the inexplicable here, and definitely nothing supernatural. In general, then, the resultant mystery turns out to be something that rational knowledge can bring to light; for Blyton, all the mysteries that she sets in motion are solvable.

But in solving them so readily, there is a sense that, although the physical mystery has been cunningly solved, adult secrets remain and, like the repressed, will return. Indeed, the prospect of subsequent adventure is often flagged up before the ending of the last (a useful marketing ploy too). Being *in* adventure is therefore important – the dilatory space in the middle: the period of delays, postponements, captivity and so on. In her most popular series, the Famous Five, Blyton captures this in the titles, many of which are concerned with movement rather than stasis, for example: *Five Run Away Together* (1944), *Five on a Secret Trail* (1956).

What, then, are the underlying mysteries? These, of course, are never explicit, which is why the lesser mysteries stand in place of them. They are an 'absent' core around which the texts are organized. It is precisely by writing about these lesser mysteries that other secrets can remain hidden, unsaid. For Blyton these other things were matters that should not be storied and, probably, she herself would have been unable to make explicit. They involve matters centred round our common Oedipal inheritance, that is sex, castration, a sense of lack, death, and non-existence. Blyton is generally silent on such matters, although they do get occasional voicing in order not to be spoken of again. For instance, she expressed a dislike of Grimm's fairy tales for being too 'cruel and frightening', whereas:

Ordinary, normal children don't like reading cruel or too-sad tales, and I was very normal ... I hated anything cruel or miserable. I

didn't like reading about frightening things ... any more than you
do. (*The Story of My Life*, 49)

What Blyton found particularly distressing was her inability to control
or 'story' such material. She disliked 'sad stories' for this reason, that
they gave her a 'feeling of impotence' because she couldn't 'help to put
things right' ('Things I Don't Like', 193).

For Blyton, such intractable material typified life rather than story,
hence she sought sanctuary in the latter. Following Freud, Peter Brooks
argues in *Reading for the Plot*, that storying is a very successful way of
dealing with the anxieties of life. It offers containment, a solution, a
happy ending (that is, a repeatable one), whereas life itself only has an
ending – a coherence – in death. In story we can safely enjoy the end-
point of mastery having experienced the dangers, delays, and desires of
plot. Indeed, we can participate in story time and again, just as
Scheherazade warded off death nightly in her tales (Blyton, inciden-
tally, retold some of these in her *Tales from the Arabian Nights* (1930)).
This seems to be what is at the heart of Blyton's mystery writing: a narcissistic ego seeking to preserve its wholeness in the face of forces that
would destroy it (Freud speaks of these forces as unbound energies
which the ego therefore seeks to bind).

So behind the mysteries that children are allowed to uncover stands
a range of matters that are simply not discussed, that are repressed.
However, as suggested above, the repressed will return, as Freud argued
in *Beyond the Pleasure Principle* (1920), erupting into consciousness if
not dealt with. The story realm will therefore need to be revisited,
repeatedly, in an attempt to gain control of the repressed material.
Freud calls such behaviour a 'repetition compulsion', wherein certain
actions are replayed incessantly, despite the fact that they are not
pleasurable, in an attempt to gain mastery. He cites examples of trau-
matized war victims reliving disturbing material, and the famous
instance of his grandson coming to terms with his mother's absence by
symbolically reliving the experience in the 'fort-da' game. That is, the
boy repeatedly cast a cotton-reel out of his cot, to which some thread
was tied. Each time the reel disappeared from view the child said a
sound like 'fort', or 'gone'; he would then pull the reel back into view
(though he did this less often) saying 'da', or 'there'. Freud argues that in
doing this the child is gaining a sense of mastery over his environment:
he becomes an active agent, not simply a passive being. He is also rehears-
ing, symbolically, the absence of his mother: her absence is replaced by
the presence of the signifier 'fort'. It is a poor substitute, however,

leaving a gap which language can never fulfil, albeit there is a repeated attempt to recreate that initial sense of oneness.

This non-recoverable object of desire is termed the *objet a* by Jacques Lacan – literally, the (m)other (the *a* is for 'autre') object, although Lacan argues against the term's translation. It is that which mobilizes desire, though it itself can never be attained; it simply plugs a gap, a hole in existence. So, despite retrieving countless wonderful objects from the underworld (treasure, jewels, medals, even family members), Blyton's heroes will always have to return to the realm of mystery for more. The sense of completeness, of a perfect family romance, can never be fully realized.

Even though they might feel wonderfully 'Five-ish' or have the security of the S.S. complete with identification badges, the adult world with its darker mysteries will continue to turn their heads. They cannot be protected forever from that larger world where nastier things than 'mugs and raggedy rugs' are to be found in the woodshed, where, perhaps, a more vicious and ugly S.S. lurks. And yet, Blyton somehow manages to divert the children from such matters into more tractable secrets, putting her heroes once more through the machinations of plot, the ritual cleansing of the landscape, to achieve the magical resolution of yet another mystery. Moreover, it will be clear to the children as they emerge victorious that they have done so *because* of their status as children. They will forever be beaching their coracles on those magic island shores (to paraphrase *Peter Pan*), celebrated by their audience precisely because they remain obdurately on the lee-side of puberty: successful against the adult world, yet distinct from it.

Let me now pull these elements together and spell this argument out more comprehensively. A group of children escapes the confines of the symbolic, an escape usually marked by their return home from boarding school. They return home to celebrate a carnivalesque holiday period in which they can indulge their senses – striving to recreate the sensuousness of what Kristeva calls the semiotic, or Lacan the imaginary, that is a state of wholeness. However, there are problems that inhibit this, often in terms of parents or guardians, but sometimes with the adult world in general. Adults show that all is not right with the world and normal relations are disrupted.

Childhood, despite its freedoms, is shown by these adults to be a marginal state, children being defined in terms of lack, that is as incomplete, incompetent beings, terms that are conventionally used to construct childhood. The children, of course, are all too aware of this marginal status and seek to challenge it – which they do by taking on the adult world and proving themselves within it by solving the mystery, something, it is emphasized, that the adult world in general has been unable to do. The adults then join in singing the praises of the children *as children* – whereas earlier the children had only narcissistically revelled in their own sense of being. In other words, the children receive the approbation of significant Others (of parents and the law). They experience a sense of mastery, of having bound the destructive energies (often literally, with the criminals tied up in ropes), thus keeping the narcissistic ego intact. They attain what Freud regarded as the basic motive of storying: the victory of 'His Majesty the Ego, the hero alike of every day-dream and of every story' ('Writers', 150).

But although the process of solving the mystery is itself satisfying, what the protagonists bring to light can only hint at the *objet a*, the lost object, that is at the cause of desire. At the very moment when their state of wholeness is celebrated, with a new order instated ('improved' parents, rewards and so forth), there remains a sense of lack, which cannot help but persist. This is because recognition of their enhanced status – their identity as collective heroes – demands the affirmative look of the Other, that is a deferring to adults and the Law. This is an alienating experience in that their identity only has validity in the eyes of Others; moreover, these Others are the very beings that the children define themselves against, George being perhaps the most uncompromising in this:

> 'I don't want to grow up,' she thought. 'There can't be anything nicer in the world than this – being with the others, having fun with them. No – I don't want to grow up!' (*Five Go to Billycock Hill*, 46)

Adults, in this schema, are, after all, representatives of the symbolic, of the Law that so oppresses the protagonists, and which they managed to elude to a certain extent at the beginning of the tale. But the only way to allay this after-taste of compromise is to engage in another adventure, to move once again from being passive, marginal beings into the realm of active agency.

Blyton's mysteries, then, are fairly straightforward wish-fulfilment fantasies – which is not necessarily to denigrate them. Their status as fantasy is something that Blyton herself seemed keen to stress, in part because this itself sets them against an everyday world where children are seen as secondary, dependent beings. By storying them in this daydream-like manner Blyton reverses the children's dependence, putting the child reader closer to a position of mastery. There are a number of ways in which she achieves this, but I shall mention just two here: her commentary on the action and her use of metafictional devices. In the former we find Blyton intruding in a manner similar to a Greek chorus; for instance, here she is, apostrophizing Julian:

> If danger was about, [Julian] could deal with it better than George could. After all, she was only a *girl*!
> Yes, Julian, she is – but, as you've often said, she's just as brave as a boy. Don't be too sure about tonight! (*Five Are Together Again*, 135)

This style of writing makes us aware of the presence of the narrator. But the use of metafictional elements makes it more overt:

> 'How did you find out all this?' said the sergeant.
> 'It's too long to tell you now!' said Dick. 'We'll write it all down in a book, and send you a copy. We'll call it – er – we'll call it – what shall we call it, you others?' ...
> 'Shall we really send the sergeant a book about this adventure?' said Anne. 'Did you really mean it, Dick?'
> 'Rather!' said Dick. 'Our fourteenth adventure – and may we have many more! What shall we call the book?'
> 'I know!' said George, at once. 'I know! Let's call it "FIVE HAVE PLENTY OF FUN"!'
> Well, they did – and they hope you like it!   (*Five Have Plenty of Fun*, 181, 183)

Drawing attention to the fictional status of the narrative might seem to undermine readers' identification, but I would suggest that this is not the case. As I have argued elsewhere Blyton deliberately uses the style of an oral storyteller to help her implied readers see themselves as an audience, specifically as a tribe of children, sitting round the hearth (of Green Hedges, or whatever other home) while the tales of the tribe's heroes are regaled (Rudd).

The sense of both mystery and mastery comes through in a number of ways. First, the 'oral style' lends a feeling of immediacy to the story, as though it were unfolding 'before your very eyes' in the 'here and now'. Secondly, an omniscient narrator adds to the sense of control and authority. Thirdly, in flagging up the constructedness of the tale, the paradox of presence and absence in signification is foregrounded (in the same way that 'fort' stands for an absent mother). Fourthly, and related to this, is the fact that the reader is the one that constructs the tale in her or his head; without the reader, the whole fantasy would be meaningless. In other words, the reader is made to feel important and central to the whole enterprise, with a resultant boost to his or her ego.

Some readers of the above paragraph might notice hints here of Christian Metz's Lacanian argument about primary identification in the cinema, and I would like to finish this section by adding to these by making explicit one more parallel with Metz's comments on the cinematic apparatus. In *The Imaginary Signifier* Metz argues that the spectator, or viewer (both words privileging the sense of vision), experiences a feeling of omniscience in her or his own knowing look, which is enhanced by the technology itself. Blyton, I would suggest, also indulges the pleasure and power of looking, though she achieves the effect more simply through print. This 'scopophilia' is especially effective when the gaze is fixed on adults, often with a view to gaining knowledge of their activities, and it is enhanced by the frequent use of technology that helps focus the gaze: binoculars, for instance, are often used, as is the camera, which is central, for instance, to *The Castle of Adventure*, while both these pieces of equipment are used for surveillance in *The Adventurous Four* (1941). More than anything else, however, it is the torch that is metonymic of the children's power of vision: '[t]he beam was strong, and the boys could well imagine how the dark secret passage would be lighted up, once they turned on their torches' (*The Island of Adventure*, 122).

Conclusion

This essay has suggested that the seeming transparency of Blyton's mysteries is built on certain absences. Whereas some children's writers have more openly probed the darker recesses of story – I'm thinking of such issues as lack of control, identity, death, sex, castration, Oedipal struggle, existence, and of such writers as Lewis Carroll, J. M. Barrie, and Russell Hoban – Blyton creates the atmosphere and framework for such mysterious openings only to conceal them in more evanescent secrets. However, the hints are there, in the fractured adult relationships and in the way the children repeatedly draw attention to their problematic nature, often inverting homeliness to explore subterranean depths where less scrupulous adult activities are being conducted.

I am not, let us be clear, suggesting that these issues are hidden in Blyton's mysteries in some coded form; they are, and must remain, absent, for Blyton to succeed on her own terms as an author on the children's side. Blyton ruthlessly seeks to shut out any disturbing, 'gasping-for-breath' issues because it is on these that she thinks the opposition of adult and child worlds turns. To maintain their integrity, and their identity, the children need a separate space, one that openly marks its standing as marginal, and outside the symbolic. Only from this vantage point can they eavesdrop on adults, exploring their secrets. Were they to unearth the real secrets of adulthood, they would then become part of that world – and no longer be children. Then there could be only one story, a *rite of passage* from which there would be no return, rather than a passage that compulsively returns them to childhood, locking them in its mythic time. As a result, the children's secrets can only ever be evasions, although they still provide emotional sustenance in the experience and re-enactment of the mystery-solving process. In this way, the children's perspicacity, their ability to uncover knowledge, is rewarded, and their standing as children is celebrated – all with minimal contamination. Adult secrets, accordingly, remain to haunt the children on another day.

Let me not finish, however, without a brief look at one final secret. I'm referring to that which is all too frequently hidden behind the text – especially the Blyton text – namely, the child reader. Though the focus of this essay has been on the former, the writing, it should not be forgotten that Blyton's books are, more than most children's works, almost exclusively for children. In E. Nesbit's book about an earlier 'Five' – *Five Children and It* – she says that she is not going to write about 'ordinary things' just so that 'aunts would perhaps write in the margin of the story with a pencil, "How true!" or "How like life!"'; instead, she will only relate 'the really astonishing things', so that 'you may leave the book about quite safely' (22).

Certainly, there is little chance of any grown-up endorsement of Blyton mysteries, which are fairly adult-proof. Like the Secret Seven clubhouse, the books exude notions of 'Privacy'. Even the way into her books depends on knowing the initiation rites, the signs and secret knowledge (for example, the meaning of Timmy wagging his tail, or of George's frown). Moreover, as Janice Radway notes of the women romance readers she studied in *Reading the Romance*, the pleasure they derived from the texts came only indirectly from the content. Much of their pleasure came explicitly from the fact that the books allowed the women to create a space within a patriarchal world. By sitting down to read these books they were making a place for themselves as women, declining to prioritize the surrounding domestic chores. Likewise,

Blyton readers, from the moment they open her books, can share in that time-out, a period that decries school and study. As they read about childhood being a separate realm they are simultaneously indulging themselves in it, while entertaining the possibility that they have the measure of the adult world.

In past years this sense of mystery and secrecy would have been heightened, in that Blyton was herself seen as a forbidden and danger-ous author by the adult world. Hence she had to be read behind closed doors or under bedclothes, with the inevitable torch. Not only did the children celebrate their subversive childhood status in this way, but they also learned about adult duplicity, though not, of course, about Blyton's own.

Works cited

Blyton, Enid. *The Castle of Adventure*. London: Macmillan, 1946.
——. *Five Are Together Again*. London: Hodder & Stoughton, 1963.
——. *Five Go Adventuring Again*. London: Hodder & Stoughton, 1943.
——. *Five Go Down to the Sea*. London: Hodder & Stoughton, 1953.
——. *Five Go Off in a Caravan*. London: Hodder & Stoughton, 1946.
——. *Five Go to Billycock Hill*. London: Hodder & Stoughton, 1957.
——. *Five Go to Demon's Rocks*. London: Hodder & Stoughton, 1961.
——. *Five Go to Mystery Moor*. London: Hodder & Stoughton, 1954.
——. *Five Go to Smuggler's Top*. London: Hodder & Stoughton, 1945.
——. *Five Have a Mystery to Solve*. London: Hodder & Stoughton, 1962.
——. *Five Have Plenty of Fun*. London: Hodder & Stoughton, 1955.
——. *Five on a Hike Together*. London: Hodder & Stoughton, 1951.
——. *Five on a Secret Trail*. London: Hodder & Stoughton, 1956.
——. *Five on a Treasure Island*. London: Hodder & Stoughton, 1942.
——. *The Island of Adventure*. London: Macmillan, 1944.
——. *Look out Secret Seven*. Leicester: Brockhampton, 1962.
——. *The Mystery of the Disappearing Cat*. London: Methuen, 1944.
——. *The Mystery that Never Was*. London: Collins, 1961.
——. *Ring o'Bells Mystery*. London: Collins, 1955.
——. *The Rockingdown Mystery*. London: Collins, 1949.
——. *The Secret Island*. Oxford: Blackwell, 1938.
——. *The Secret Seven*. Leicester: Brockhampton, 1962.
——. *The Story of My Life*. London: Pitkins, 1952.
——. 'Things I Don't Like' [1926], in Barbara Stoney, *Enid Blyton: a Biography*. London Hodder & Stoughton, 1974, pp. 192–3.
Brooks, Peter. *Reading for the Plot: Design and Intention in Narrative*. Oxford: Clarendon, 1984.
Foucault, Michel. *The History of Sexuality: An Introduction*. Harmondsworth: Penguin, 1981.
Freud, Sigmund. *Beyond the Pleasure Principle* [1920]. New York: Norton, 1961.

——. 'Family Romances' [1909], in *On Sexuality: Three Essays on the Theory of Sexuality, and Other Works*. Harmondsworth: Penguin, 1977, pp. 221–5.

——. 'The Uncanny' [1915], in *Art and Literature: Jensen's Gradiva, Leonardo da Vinci and Other Works*. Harmondsworth: Penguin, 1985, pp. 339–76.

——. 'Writers and Day-Dreaming' [1908], in *The Standard Edition of the Complete Psychoanalytical Works of Sigmund Freud*, Vol. IX. London: Hogarth Press, 1959, pp. 143–53.

Lacan, Jacques. *Écrits: A Selection*, trans. Alan Sheridan. London: Tavistock/Routledge, 1977.

Metz, Christian. *The Imaginary Signifier*. Bloomington: Indiana University Press, 1982.

Nesbit, E. *Five Children and It* [1902]. Harmondsworth: Penguin, 1959.

Radway, Janice A. *Reading the Romance: Women, Patriarchy and Popular Culture*. London: Verso, 1987.

Ray, Sheila G. *The Blyton Phenomenon: the Controversy Surrounding the World's Most Successful Children's Author*. London: André Deutsch, 1982.

Rudd, David. 'Why the Ephemeral Blyton Won't Go Away', in Nicholas Tucker and Kimberley Reynolds (eds), *Enid Blyton: a Celebration and Reappraisal*. London: National Centre for Research in Children's Literature, 1997, pp. 36–50.

Stoney, Barbara. *Enid Blyton: a Biography*. London: Hodder & Stoughton, 1974.

7
Plotting the Past: the Detective as Historian in the Novels of Philippa Pearce

Valerie Krips

Upon the face of a long-case clock in Philippa Pearce's *Tom's Midnight Garden* (1958) the legend 'Time no more' is engraved. The clock chimes thirteen and, measuring a time out of time, transports a boy into the past. Pearce's novel tells the story of Tom Long, who spends a summer with a girl who, in a remarkable simultaneity, is both the young woman and child she was, and the old woman she has become. Through her Tom experiences the past in the present: he lives the time of her memory, a mysterious realm in which, so it seems, anything can happen.

A fantasy, *Tom's Midnight Garden* is also a mystery, but not one which invites the reader to attempt a solution. Instead, in a return to an older and less secular concept, the appropriate response to Pearce's mystery is wonder. Read alone the novel remains the beautiful and powerful story it was understood to be from its first publication; it has often been thought of as one of the finest books written for children since the Second World War. John Rowe Townsend, for example, declares that: '[i]f I were asked to name a single masterpiece of English children's literature since the last war – and one masterpiece in thirty years is a fair ration – it would be this outstandingly beautiful and absorbing book' (247). However, when it is read in conjunction with two other of Pearce's novels – *Minnow on the Say* (1955) and *The Way to Sattin Shore* (1983) – in which the past is also her subject, its themes can be situated within a trajectory which reveals the particular ideological charge of Pearce's fantasy, and brings the mystery inherent in it into sharper focus.

Many commentators have pointed to the period between 1950 and 1980 as one in which the past became a 'foreign country'; it is also one in which history, the discipline whose subject is the past, was itself transformed. Pearce's three novels respond to these changes, and in particular to certain key aspects of them. Firstly, and most importantly, the novels are concerned to negotiate difficulties arising when different versions of the past become apparent. To put it crudely, history had, until the war, been generally written from what Raphael Samuel calls an 'official' stance (114). Authoritative history generally told the story of the nation and its leaders, or the culture and those who formed it. The stories of women, children, the family, the working-class, immigrants and so on were, by and large, subsumed if not rendered invisible by such history. Postwar, these previously invisible stories came to the forefront of attention with the development of social and oral history. Yet the chasm between past and present grew deeper and wider, as critics such as Eric Hobsbawm argued. Explanations for this phenomenon came from scholars in many disciplines, and some of them pointed to a problem with memory, the living link to the past. As I discuss later, memory was seen to have failed.

In turning to history and memory as the subject of these three novels, then, Pearce rehearses and attempts to resolve problems that concerned the culture at the time she was writing. Her meditations begin with detective fiction, a genre which had its beginnings in a period which was as much marked by a disturbance in past–present relations as was her own.

It was in the late eighteenth and early nineteenth centuries that, according to Richard Terdiman, the social and cultural situation which gave rise to detective fiction developed. During that period, which was one of transition from the traditional social structures of family and village to those of urbanization, 'the problem of the past and of the relation to it through memory came to preoccupy social and psychological thinking' (5). In Terdiman's argument the 'problem' of the past found its focus in human behaviour. In traditional societies 'objects and people could be said to carry their pasts and meanings openly' whereas in

the more complex society of the post-Revolutionary cities and proto-capitalist economies, the interpretation of behaviour became notoriously problematic. Whole literary plots – quintessentially those of the detective stories ... represent the furthest development of the theme of hermeneutic difficulty in fictions from the period – [and] turn on this newly disquieting lack of transparency. (6)

Some of the force of this change can be registered by comparing the novel of detection with the early crime stories which preceded them.

In *Form and Ideology in Crime Fiction* Stephen Knight discusses *The Newgate Calendar*, a collection which, containing accounts of the crimes and punishments of major criminals, first appeared in 1773, and was republished in various editions until the late nineteenth century. The collection's presumptions about audience and world-view differ markedly from those of detective fiction, particularly in the *Calendar's* conception of society as unified and organic, and its further assumption that 'events occur beyond human control' (Knight 17).

The detective, whose first appearance Knight locates in the work of Edgar Allan Poe, reduces the mysteries of the *Calendar* to the level of a solvable puzzle: 'larded with expressions of amazement and an aura of mystery ... great powers are expounded in terms we ourselves can match, richness is found in simple techniques – just as in a game of draughts' (42). Thus Poe's work marks the passage of mystery into the secular and scientific realm, and indicates a growing belief in the efficacy of techniques of observation and the application of method. By the mid-nineteenth century, mysteries, once by definition occult, secret, and insoluble, had become puzzles capable of yielding to the application of intellect. The development of the scientific method, and its increasingly broad application, began to dissolve mysteries of all kinds.

The problem for Pearce's period was not, however, primarily that of interpreting the behaviour of others. The idea that people's motivations were in essence hidden and mysterious had become an accepted part of life, finding its theorization in psychoanalysis. Instead interest focused on the present's relationship to the past, which Pearce poses in terms of the relation of memory to history. This is a relation which the historian Pierre Nora would later analyse in *Realms of Memory*, his work on the construction of French national memory.

Nora argues that from the mid-twentieth century – Pearce's first novel appeared in 1955 – history and memory, which, until then, were mutually interdependent formations, became distinct and even opposed. History, associated with the archive and record, with facts and evidence, became concerned with a past which existed only in terms of its residues and remains. Memory, by contrast, as a function of the human mind and as a cultural construct, in its ubiquity and cognitive status transforms the past it recalls into a feature and function of the present. Nora makes the point that in the gradual separation of history, the official record of the past, from memory, the unofficial record, a sense of the present's connection to the past has been lost. This loss, he argues, transforms both public and private life; as traditions of thought and practice fall into disuse and are forgotten, the need and desire to remember finds its outlet in increasingly individualized and psychologized forms.

When Pearce began to write for children in the 1950s, the differentiation of history from memory had already found a public embodiment. The decade began on a high note, with the Festival of Britain of 1951. The Festival was primarily a showcase for the nation's architects and technocrats: it was to provide a venue in which Britain, reeling still from the effects of winning a war, would show to its people and the world at large that in technology and mind-set it was at the forefront of development. While this positive message about British inventiveness and industry was being prepared, however, Britons themselves were still struggling with rationing and shortages of goods as disparate as building materials and children's sweets. The Festival thus provided some relief from the round of managing and coping which still, six years after the end of the war, was the lot of most people.

According to Barham and Hillier, whose account of the Festival is among the most detailed, in developing the overall plan of the Festival one of the few absolute determinants was a decision to leave aside any reference to 'war like achievements'. The organizers wanted to offer something really different to visitors, a vision splendid of what the future, just around the corner, could and would be. This perhaps understandable decision had far-reaching effects. The most extraordinary event in the recent life of the nation, the war, was practically a forbidden subject for an exhibition which, in large part, purported to celebrate and tell the nation's story: this was an erasure of memory on a grand scale.

The omission of reference to the war's achievements posed a series of problems, particularly in that part of the exhibit representing the story of the British people. That had been a story often told by propagandists at the War Office and elsewhere – in the media (radio, newspapers) and by novelists, dramatists, and so on – during the conflict. British traditions were understood both to have their outcome in the way in which Britons handled themselves, whether on the home front or in theatres of war, and to provide a longed-for destination. In the stories which supported the war effort much was made of the British spirit, famously exhibited at Dunkirk and in the Blitz. Such spirit was the result, as Winston Churchill's speeches made plain, of a tradition long in the making. Britain's contemporary heroes were eulogized in Shakespeare's words, likened to great historical figures; in them the entire history of the British nation had its outcome. The victorious troops would come home to a Britain which embodied that spirit, in which history and memory, past and present, were joined.

The Festival of Britain hoped to show the British people in a different light. Its attempt to play down the recent past typified a more general development of the 1950s and 1960s, a period of modernization, in which much of the past was being repudiated. The will to start afresh, to make a new society in which war was less likely, and in which old inequalities could be addressed, is scarcely to be denounced. While the Festival repudiated various 'official' stories of the past, particularly those concerned with grandiloquence and war, it did not entirely turn its back on tradition. British life was represented through a series of typical and symbolic scenes such as ubiquitous pubs and village greens. These gestured towards a past which could not be pinned down in historical terms, but existed in the glow of 'pastness', relying neither on memory (the pubs were generic) nor on history (they were reconstructions of a 'typical' pub). The result was a peculiarly unspecific account which seemed unable to connect past to present except through nostalgia. On a limited scale, the Festival's organizers had achieved what few others managed: they rewrote the past while it was still fresh in collective and individual memory, and rendered the connection between past and present mysterious and hidden.

It is the mysteriousness of the connection of past to present that engages the main characters in Philippa Pearce's *Minnow on the Say* in which two boys go in search of a treasure, lost at the time of the Armada. Their clue is a rhyme, whose meaning had been forgotten: '"no-one knows / none but my daughter"' (31). The daughter had failed in memory even as her father taught her the rhyme by heart: but this failure of memory is of a particular kind. She remembered the rhyme, but not what it signified.

It is the loss of the signified which motivates the boys' detection. Their search for treasure is represented as an attempt to find much more than the purely material; when the boys eventually see the jewels they have sought, that which seemed the referent slips away into a cascade of barely differentiated material:

> a skein of delicately worked silver and gold ensnaring precious stones fell like a snake by the jam pot, a huge unpierced pearl rolled until it was brought to a stop by the butter dish, brooches and rings, chains and earrings came to rest where they could. (*Minnow*, 239)

Yet this imprecision is an essential element in recovering the referent. The jewels remain a 'treasure', but one reworked: no longer simply the possession of the Codling family, they have become part of a wider heritage to which they refer metonymically. It is this transformation which the boys' detection plots as they move from clue to clue, metaphor to metaphor.

The story of the past that Adam and David recover is, on the face of it, just about hiding and finding a treasure. But as readers of detective stories are well aware, the obvious is only part of the story, and not even the most important part. Questions about what is obscured and what revealed, of what meaning can be ascribed to others, of the culprit's motivations and so on, constitute the story's mystery. Why did Adam's ancestor hide his treasure and why, when it was later found – as it turns out it was – did Adam's grandfather hide it again? A further and equally important question revolves around the detective himself: why did the detective take the case in the first place?

The answers to some of these questions appear simple: in this, as in many children's books, motives are frequently clear, and cause and effect held in stable relation. Adam's grandfather was waiting for his son, Adam's father, to come back from the war to disclose the secret. But Adam's father is dead, and his grandfather does not remember this vital fact. So the old man waits. And as he waits his family's fortune continues to decline. Without the treasure, Adam must leave his family home. However, the true complications of Pearce's plot become apparent only when the last question is put: why does the detective take the case?

David Moss is not invited to help by the Codling family in any simple sense, as in the way Sherlock Holmes might have been approached by someone seeking his skills. Nor does solving mysteries fall to him professionally, as it might to Inspector Dalgleish. Instead his commitment is secured in such a way that the detection he undertakes ensures that the plot or history he uncovers becomes his, too. David is the child of villagers, a couple who have reared three children in a terraced house. His friendship with Adam Codling, the only son of a family who were once the largest landowners in the district, is unremarkable within the sociality of the period. But as David uncovers the plot of the past the differences that once separated the families, and to some extent still do so, threaten. It is the uncertainty of this relationship that helps secure his commitment to the Codlings in general and their mystery in particular.

David approaches Adam's house with some misgiving, expecting to experience a lifestyle very different from his own, one in which rare and precious things are in everyday use and so on. But he finds a house

in disrepair and a family struggling with shortages: the two great lev-
ellers of the postwar period. And he finds kindness and acceptance. As
he becomes more and more closely entwined in the family's affairs, he
takes on the role of detective for them: he will collect clues, follow up
leads, bring the story of the past into focus.

What Adam's ancestor forgot, David will try to recall. However, his
detection, while it makes good a loss of memory, serves also to accen-
tuate the loss of both the past and memory. David's is a task of cogni-
tion, of a piecing together of evidence which has much in common
with history, the analytical discourse whose first presupposition is that
its object – the past – is gone. Memory, by distinction, links past and
present, and insists upon synchronicity rather than the diachrony of
history. In this sense David does not, cannot 'remember' the Codling's
past. But he can write their history.

The story of the past that David uncovers does not, however, remain
separate from him as we might expect of the work of the historian.
David comes to accept the story of the past he is telling for the benefit
of the Codlings as his own. In a revealing moment David's future is
linked to theirs through an object which he comes to share with them,
even though it belongs to the Codlings. This is the object which, first
drawing him into their story, keeps him there.

David's first task as detective predates his meeting with the Codlings.
He finds a canoe which has slipped its moorings and floated down
river to his house, whose garden backs onto the river. David longs for a
canoe, but as much as he wants to keep it, he sets about finding its
owner. His clue is the remnant of a rotting block of wood to which the
canoe had been moored. He is, of course, successful. The canoe belongs
to the Codlings, but, like much else of theirs, it is in disrepair. David
and Adam take on the task of repairing the canoe together.

Mr Moss, David's father, drives a bus for a living, a bus which goes
between the nearest big town, Castleford, and the villages in which the
boys live. One day, following a clue, David is on the side of the road,
having lost a shoe, and hoping for a ride. His father, who has recently
adapted to a new company code which does not allow picking people up
except at bus stops, is furious. People who cling to the old (and recent)
ways, in which they hailed buses wherever they liked, and expected to be
dropped near their destination, wherever that was, are '"no better than
pirates"' (179). There appears to be no point to this story within a story,
nothing hangs on it; if anything it serves to confuse Mr Moss's characterization. Yet as an alternative account of memory and history to that
which David is uncovering and creating, it is vital.

The detection David undertakes on behalf of the Codlings requires him to piece together a story which no one remembers. At the end of the novel David finally sees how all the pieces fit together. Were he Sherlock Holmes or even Inspector Dalgleish this would be the moment in which, revealing all, he would show himself to have mastered the past, understood the plot. But just as he is about to tell his story he is stopped, silenced by Adam's aunt, Miss Codling, who tells him to listen instead to a nightingale singing by the river.

The story of the buses from Castleford is a parabasis, an aside. It suspends the main narrative and addresses the reader directly as 'you' (177). It reflects upon the story told in the rest of the novel, and indirectly comments upon it. Like that story, the parabasis is about the past, but rather than providing an account of history's recovery, this is a story about memory's failure. Before the introduction of the new buses passengers could be picked up and put down at will; the new management requires that people alight and get picked up only at bus stops. To begin with, this was ignored, but slowly, even those who grumbled about it got used to waiting at the newfangled stops. What the people of the villages remembered about their bus service – that it would pick you up and drop you off at your door – is repudiated. Indeed, after initial complaints, the villagers begin to act in a way that amounts to forgetting as they comply with the new requirements.

The memory which is in the process of failure here (soon, no one will remember, and those who do will be 'no better than pirates' as Mr Moss says) is a version of the past, a collective story about village life. And this story is in the process of loss, overridden by a differently authorized concept of how things should be.

The parabasis is a *mise en abîme* which seems at first to tell an alternative story about history and memory to that told in the main body of the text. In this short account the failure of memory is the result of coercion. Unlike Judith Codling's memory failure, which is that of a child who cannot form the kinds of connections between signifier and signified – rhyme and the world – which would support her memory, the villagers have been pressured to forget: a new version of something they already knew had been imposed upon them in the name of progress. The parabasis makes it clear that the skirmish between memory and an authority which wished to deny it has been won by a faceless and unfeeling bureaucracy.

When Miss Codling silences David she puts a stop to a similar story, in which other village memories are drawn into an account of the past. The story of the treasure and its finding, of David's filiation with the

Codlings and of the boys' adventure, is one in which memory and history seem to have worked together to the advantage of both. A forgotten rhyme has been restored, a treasure found, the complete story of its hiding and finding understood. When the detective steps forward to speak his narrative, all that went before will be subsumed by it, made to play its part in the history which detection has produced. The detective's story brings closure: he has gone over old ground, replotted it and completed it.

Yet were it to be narrated this too would be a story told at the expense of memory, in this case David's and his family's. As the Mosses have been drawn into the Codlings' plot they have surrendered their right to remember a distinctive account of their own past. When Adam and David have finished repairing the canoe (which always remains moored at the Codlings'), in spite of Adam's '"[s]he's as much yours as mine"' (41), David slaps the boat in an excess of pleasure. The craft would 'forever' bear the 'five fingerprints of David Moss' (42). David's fingerprints are his trace, a residue of his presence which will last 'forever' just as the rhyme which was forgotten was also a trace: a relic of the man who wrote and the child who did not remember. David's trace 'forever' appears in a story which has been shaped to the Codlings', and has been subsumed by it.

The story the parabasis tells interrogates the period's consensual politics, and the main story, interpreted in the light of David's silencing, makes a similarly troubling point. David has restored the referent in producing a history of the Codling family. The 'treasure' is found, but now it is more than family jewels; it has become part of David's heritage, too. The rewards are clear but so, too, as the parabasis indicates, are the costs. The 'treasure' is restored as a heritage object at the expense of other possible narratives of the past. The Festival of Britain 'forgot' stories of the war, which was tantamount to casting aside most of its visitors' pasts. Pearce's novel indicates the ways in which the newly developing stories of 'heritage' perform similar forgettings.

Kate Tranter's task in the later *The Way to Sattin Shore* differs from David's in that the story she hopes to uncover is without doubt her own. But it is obscure and frightening to the child she is. Her father is dead, and Kate has found his tombstone in the churchyard. She traces his name with her finger: he died, it seems, on the day she was born. But one day the tombstone disappears, and from that day on Kate takes upon herself the task of detection, a work she undertakes for her own sake. She discovers the paternal grandmother she never knew who lives near Sattin Shore and, eventually, meets her (living) father.

Kate's plotting is undertaken in the face of a distorted history; she has no memories of her father, nor have her family supplied them for her. Instead she has the past's representation in writing, a writing which she misreads. The novel returns to the problem of the relation of signifier to signified that concerned *Minnow on the Say*. In assuming that the name on the tombstone is her father's Kate in fact creates what she takes for granted: she thinks that the link between signifier and signified is guaranteed whereas, as her later experience proves, it is arbitrary. The name on the tombstone is not that of her father at all, but his dead brother, whom her father was thought to have left to die. Kate's mistake leads to redemption; her father proves his innocence, and the family is reunited. But unlike David's, Kate's narration of what she has discovered and particularly of her mistake about what appeared to be written in stone, absolute in its referent, is essential to the novel's outcome.

Kate's paternal grandmother, so recently found, has long known that a childhood friend of her son's was in fact the person who left him to die. And yet she has come to love and depend upon her dead son's friend. This Kate learns too, and accepts as another history, another 'true' story. In her search for origins, for a firm place from which to begin the story of her own life, Kate finds solidity, but it is not, as she learns, a grounding which will serve for everyone, not even for the woman who is literally the beginning of it all. While Kate unravels mysteries to find a truth for herself within the stories she can tell, it is clear that others can find their truths in quite different accounts. In this novel, Pearce indicates her willingness to be optimistic as she imagines a present whose relation to its past, and thus to its future, is based on a stability which must be constantly created, and which will in any case seldom speak similarly to all.

The shift in attitude from *Minnow on the Say*'s history-making is considerable. Both Kate and David are concerned with history and the past; both replot the past for their own ends, make it over into a story of value to the present. But Kate's is a story in which the valency of the individual and her or his memory forms the focus of the history she writes, while the narratives of *Minnow on the Say* break down precisely at the point at which it seems that the individual's account of the past is likely to contradict that of consensus and collective memory. David must 'never tell', and Kate must keep a secret. The difference is that Kate's secret operates within her history as redemptive and enabling. The path from David's silencing to Kate's redemptive story passes through a midnight garden and memory.

Memories, both collective and individual, are created and sustained by groups and their stability. In Britain from the late eighteenth century the stability of groups, from the family itself to the greater communities of village, town and workplace, was threatened as it had not been since the Black Death of the fourteenth century. People were mobile in unprecedented ways and numbers, and urbanization produced new spheres of sociality tending, as many critics in the nineteenth century argued, to fragmentation and alienation. Shorn of traditional forms and interactive situations, removed from the stability of long-established communities and cut off from history, memory itself, developed in terms of shared experiences and expectations, declined.

Personal memory, Maurice Halbwachs argues, depends upon collective memory. We know what it is important to remember in terms of our membership of groups. Whether, for example, we remember birthdays tends to depend upon the expectations learned within the family group: some families remember, others do not. Other memories are similarly created within group expectations; in terms of nationhood, these are frequently marked by ceremonies and traditions. The breakup of groups, then, not only fragments physical communities but erases collective memories and the versions of the past constructed within them. When collective memory declines – memories which attached us to certain world-views, places, events and ensured that we shared a sense of their centrality – we are left with an affective void, Nora argues. Nora has written extensively about the failure of collective memory in the late twentieth century. Distinguishing memory from history, he argues that memory has been overtaken by history, with a concomitant dilution of a sense of connectedness to the past, since history is about a past which is over, done with. Memory, by contrast, makes links with the past. The need for memory continues, however; but in the absence of what he calls *milieux* of memory it has become individualized and psychologized rather than collective. An example of this is the declining collective memory of the old system of bus stops in David Moss's village. Where once the whole community would remember, the individual is now forced to remember for her or himself. And it is to such a form of remembrance that *Tom's Midnight Garden* is an outrider, a taste of things to come.

Tom Long is to spend the summer holidays with a childless uncle and aunt who live in a large house, now converted into flats. His boredom and indolence are broken into one night when the clock, in an otherwise empty downstairs hall, strikes thirteen. Going down to investigate, he finds the house surrounded by a glorious and mysterious garden. The opening of Pearce's novel takes up themes familiar from other children's fantasies: a child alone discovers the entry point to a place which will provide him with a friendship and adventure. The element of wish-fulfilment that such books provide is evident; they mirror the child's capacity to imagine her or himself in another world, where she or he is recognized as special and remarkable. A reflection of narcissistic yearning, the fantasy that such books offer also provides a space in which the child can safely project a selfhood which remains as yet incompletely formed in the actual world. The movement between the two worlds of the book, real and fantastic, repeats the child's own experience; the absorption of the child in the fantastic other world of the book is matched by the actual child's experience of daydream and play and his or her relation to the quotidian.

Tom's Midnight Garden is distinguished by its attention to memory and its relation to time, and particularly by the fact that the memory in question is not the child protagonist's, but an old woman's. Tom's visits to the garden take place day after day in his real time, but do not repeat that chronological progression. He never knows whether the garden will show itself in winter or summer guise; nor does he know whether Hatty will be a very little girl, or a slightly bigger one, or even a young woman. As the story unfolds, little is made of this aspect of the garden's surprises; indeed, from Tom's perspective it is Hatty and the garden and house which are odd, so anything might be expected of them. Told from Tom's perspective, then, the events in the garden are part of a magic world which, like others of its kind, works from within its own unknowable logic. But in this case logic is revealed: Hatty has been dreaming of her past, and of the precious but few and far between days she spent in the company of a little boy wearing only pyjamas.

It seems that Tom has been a figment of Hatty's dreams, and that her dreams have had the power of transporting him back into the past. Pearce is adamant about this power: on one of Tom's later visits to the garden he and Hatty skate on the frozen river towards Ely. Tom asks Hatty to leave the skates for him in a room which he has by now recognized as the one he inhabits in the 'real' world, where it is part of his aunt's flat. She does so: they are there when he looks in the morning. They are accompanied by a note, written years ago and yesterday.

Novels have no need to match their imaginative world exactly to the real world; the writer's art lies in tactful departure from the expected and paradigmatic. But the points of departure are always a source of critical interest, and are often a creative response to an otherwise insoluble problem. Pearce's account of memory metaphorizes its power in an interesting and profound way. Memory is the key to identity in the obvious sense that without it one simply cannot know who one is – cannot, indeed, undertake the most simple cognitive task. And it is within memory that the individual grapples with experiences, relegating some to the ephemeral and laying down others within associative chains which will form the basis of a life. Which experiences will pass into such foundational form and which will float free is not, as Freud teaches us, within the individual's power to decide. This is not to deny the art of memory, the ability to train oneself to remember things, but rather to point to a topography of memory in which the most basic and the most foundational memories are held in the unconscious. Such memories often come back in ways which surprise us, when, as it were, we were least expecting them. Equally, what is at issue in memory is not so much the veridical quality of what is remembered as the effect that memories, some of which we do not even know we possess, have on the structuring of our lives.

Pearce invests the power of personal memory with the potential to forge links between people in the absence of collective memory. Hatty 'remembering' Tom, a child who happens to be in her house, has an effect in the real world: she leaves, and he finds, a pair of skates. How this can be so remains a mystery, and the fact of this mystery is as important and materially effective as the detection practised by David Moss and Kate Tranter.

The mystery of the skates lies between the two detective stories. David's is undertaken in the spirit of the earliest detectives; he is out to find the truth of the matter, to understand it completely, and interpret it fully. He does so. That he cannot speak what he knows is evidence that the kind of history he has told is already breaking down. In David's careful plotting, the creation of that kind of history, and its tactics of suppression, have been revealed. By contrast Kate Tranter's history has no aspirations to a single truth. Her story of the past is many-faceted, created from memories, bits of (misread) history, narratives half-heard and half understood. Yet it is enough: it is, indeed, redemptive.

Memory's place in the story of the past, repudiated by one narrative of detection, is re-established by another. When Mrs Codling silences David she does so in order to sustain mystery, to obscure the past's contradictory stories among which memory is included. Kate's detection unravels a different plot in which memory and history are reunited to present a story in which a hidden detail, the key to the whole, is revealed, only to be kept secret in Kate's memory. Kate's grandmother knows who left her son to die and tells her grandchild. This shared secret, which Kate's detection did not reveal, enables Kate to understand that the present is an effect and outcome of the past and as such defies easy logic or inductive reasoning. The story of the past Kate writes in the end, her history, is an amalgam of others' narratives, fitted to and constitutive of her own.

The classic detective of whom Terdiman and Knight write was concerned to unravel the mysteries which had become newly attached to human behaviour. The imponderable gave up its secrets as the detective employed his period's methodologies: science, reason, method. Pearce's response to her period's mysteries indicates that it is the relation of the present to the past, and in particular the role of memory in that relation, which has become a key concern, as alternative accounts of the past jostle for place. The demands of the immediate postwar realignment of old stories with new which are examined in *Minnow on the Say* give way to the familiar inclusiveness which was a feature of the 1980s, part of that period's own economic, political, and ideological revolutions. Pearce's inclusion of memory as the essential emulsifier for the mix of the 1980s is evidence of the changes that have taken place in the three decades which separate her first child detective from her latest. *Minnow on the Say* is concerned with memory as a possession of the culture as a whole, with the stories of the past which the Festival of Britain embodied. By the time Kate Tranter wanders onto Sattin Shore that issue has given way to a focus on the individual: Kate is forced to produce her own history, and finds it unique, a story which only she knows, whose relevance will remain hidden from others. Kate's secret is kept for her own sake, not history's.

In this development the psychologization of which Pierre Nora writes can be detected, but to it Pearce adds her own twist. Memory, that essential but still mysterious function, in spite of our best efforts to unravel its secrets, is returned to the centre of the story of the past. This is an outcome which Nora locates in the 1990s, when he concludes his monumental 12-volume work on the French past. Pearce proves once again that the children's novel of mystery, at its perceptive best, sees clearly in ways that mark books such as hers with a particular, almost prophetic, power.

Works cited

Barham, M. and Hillier, B. *A Tonic to the Nation: the Festival of Britain 1951.* London: Thames & Hudson, 1976.

Halbwachs, Maurice. *The Collective Memory*, trans. Francis J. Diter and Vida Yazdi Diter. New York: Harper & Row, 1980.

Hobsbawm, Eric. *The Age of Extremes: The Short Twentieth Century 1914–1991.* London: Abacus, 1995.

Knight, Stephen. *Form and Ideology in Crime Fiction.* London: Macmillan, 1980.

Nora, Pierre. *Les Lieux du mémoire.* 12 vols. 1984–97. Abridged and translated as *Realms of Memory: Rethinking the French Past.* 3 vols. Ed. Lawrence D. Kritzman. Trans. Arthur Goldhammer. New York: Columbia University Press, 1996–98.

Pearce, Philippa. *Minnow on the Say* [1955]. London: Puffin, 1981.

——. *Tom's Midnight Garden.* Oxford: Oxford University Press, 1958.

——. *The Way to Sattin Shore* [1983]. London: Puffin, 1985.

Samuel, Raphael. *Theatres of Memory*, Vol 1: *Past and Present in Contemporary Culture.* London: Verso, 1994.

Terdiman, Richard. *Present Past: Modernity and the Memory Crisis.* Ithaca, NY and London: Cornell University Press, 1993.

Townsend, John Rowe. *Written for Children: An Outline of English-language Children's Literature.* Harmondsworth: Penguin, 1983.

8

The Secret Development of a Girl Writer: Louise Fitzhugh's *Harriet the Spy*

Robin Amelia Morris

Two genres, the female *Künstlerroman* and the detective novel, intersect in Louise Fitzhugh's 1964 *Harriet the Spy*, recasting the development of a girl writer as a tale of unfolding mystery. The mystery that Harriet encounters in the course of her spying activities is one of personal identity: how does one make sense of the complex interaction between individual existence and community? While the *Bildungsroman* traditionally traces a young person's development, and the even more specifically focused *Künstlerroman* traces the development of an artist, as exemplified in the female tradition by Louisa May Alcott's *Little Women* (1868), detective stories for girls have stood at the opposite pole. These novels, such as the famous Nancy Drew series, rarely allow their protagonists to change or mature. The mysteries their sleuths face are outside of themselves: their own identities are never in question. However, because of the generic conventions involving crime and discovery, they can offer a vision of an independent, active female that the more mundane *Künstlerroman* cannot.

Set to work upon each other, the *Künstlerroman* and the mystery story produce a hybrid text in *Harriet the Spy* that allows its protagonist to achieve her goals successfully. Earlier protagonists of female *Künstlerromane* tended to become entangled in the dominant romance plot, as Rachel Blau DuPlessis observes in her study *Writing Beyond the Ending*. For eleven-year-old Harriet M. Welsch, the process of discovering her gendered subjectivity at the particular historical moment when women were beginning to question the 'feminine mystique' (Betty Friedan's book of that name, critiquing the ideology which pushed middle-class women back into the homemaking role after their temporary liberation during the Second World War, had just been published a year before *Harriet the Spy*), provides the novel with the subtextual mystery it investigates beneath its witty surface. The forging of one's identity – in particular, one's sexual identity – is the great project of childhood, and Fitzhugh's exploration of this in terms of a spy's information-gathering is an apt metaphor which goes beyond the two genres on which it draws. Julia Kristeva describes the emergence of a speaking subject in her *Revolution in Poetic Language* (1984), basing her psychoanalytic conjectures on poststructuralist linguistic explorations. These theories prove highly illuminating in tracing Harriet's development from pursuer of unspecified mysteries into a writer.

In her 1989 article, 'The Feminist Writer as Heroine in *Harriet the Spy*', Lissa Paul observes that *Harriet the Spy* breaks with the female *Künstlerroman* tradition, which is usually 'about failure', because Harriet achieves journalistic success (70). In this tradition, females have to struggle against the idea that expressing oneself in writing is an act of self-absorption, antithetical to the ideal of the selfless, nurturing woman. Many of these novels, written, evidently, by writers who had gone through that struggle and found a way to justify writing, conclude that women's writing fosters family and community ties and is therefore not a selfish activity. Implicit in numerous novels, this view achieves theoretical consolidation by DuPlessis when she notes that 'the figure of the female artist counters the modernist tradition of exile, alienation, and refusal of social roles – the *non serviam* of the class artist hero, Stephen Dedalus' (101). Deconstructing the myth of the remote male genius was a necessary stage in constructing a place from which women could value their own literary contributions. By refiguring literature to make it a means of participating in the family and the larger community, writing characters are able to resolve the hard choice between life and art which the *Künstlerroman* plot demands of its protagonists. Characters who are good examples of this are: Jo in *Little Women*, Emily of New Moon and Anne of Green Gables in the L. M. Montgomery series named for them, Francie in Betty Smith's *A Tree Grows in Brooklyn* (1943) and Esperanza in Sandra Cisneros's *The House on Mango Street* (1984).

However liberating this alternative may have been for earlier ambitious protagonists and their authors who had to fight hard just for publication, by Fitzhugh's time it was reifying into ideology. Simple rejection of the model of male individual success grew confining. If Harriet's female *Künstlerroman* predecessors deposed the myth of the isolated male artist hero, and yet that was the ideal she desired, she would have to look elsewhere for a model which valorized that independence. Lissa Paul's insight regarding the centrality of failure in the female *Künstlerroman* begins to suggest why this novel cannot remain within the *Künstlerroman* narrative but must play with the more popular detective genre. By utilizing the mystery plot, where previous *Künstlerromane* by women writers were drawn into either the romance plot, or 'a triangular plot of nurturance' as DuPlessis explains, Fitzhugh is able to effect a significant shift in the narrative of female artistic development (84, 91). Harriet's model would come, not in the form of earlier fictional girls who wrote, like Jo March, but in spies who operate in secrecy.

Spies are the ultimate outsiders, usually operating during times of war, either in their own occupied country or in enemy territory. Like Harriet they collect data that do not always have an apparent use, storing up information as the most valuable commodity. It is telling that Harriet considers herself a spy, rather than the more socially acceptable detective, who operates on the side of order and who is, indeed, often a police officer. Harriet, a girl with ambition, sees the social order as an obstacle, rather than something to be defended or restored as it is to Nancy Drew. Unlike the typical detective, Harriet has no particular mystery to solve. She is an operative, facing a deeper mystery than the novel makes explicit but which we can here begin to understand.

To Harriet, as to many young children, most of life is a mystery: why others live their lives in ways different from one's own is particularly perplexing. By sneaking into people's homes and peeking in through their windows, Harriet is able to consider how other people's various circumstances affect their lives, and she comes to learn that not all families are as privileged as her own. We see this process taking place in her investigation of the Italian family who run the local grocery. The narrator sets the scene of writing: 'Harriet squatted under the window and wrote out everything she had seen' (57). Then Harriet follows up on this detailed description by drawing a conclusion: '"[t]hat Fabio may be bad but I don't blame him"' (57). It is as if detailed observation allows her to probe the mystery of people's inner selves: this knowledge sometimes makes her more sympathetic to those who are different from herself.

Harriet is a bit harsher on those of her own class, like Mrs Plumber who takes to her bed in order to select a profession, prompting Harriet, hidden in the dumbwaiter, to scribble: '"[i]t's just what Ole Golly says. Rich people are boring"' (45). Many of the people she observes make strange choices. About an older man who creates elaborate bird cages, she notes, '"I wouldn't mind living like Harrison Withers because he looks happy except I wouldn't like *all* those cats. I might even like a dog"' (72–3). In contemplating and writing about these different lifestyles, she is not only understanding their individuality, but she is solving the mystery of who she is and where she fits into this complex social system.

Further, the primordial mystery, which all children confront, is the question of where they come from: their own birth. Indeed, as Bobbie Ann Mason notes, in her discussion of Harriet's predecessor in sleuthing, Nancy Drew, '[m]ysteries are a substitute for sex, since sex is the greatest mystery of all for adolescents. The Nancy Drew books cleverly (and no doubt unintentionally) conceal sexual fascination' (63). In *Harriet the Spy* this quest for knowledge continues to function at an unacknowledged, subliminal level, filtering through the intersecting genre plots. For example, the novel opens with omniscient narration, showing Harriet teaching her friend Sport how to play her favourite game, Town, in which she creates a fictional world and imagines events occurring within it. Reproducing the social order she sees around her in this fabricated world, Harriet concocts an adventure plot that revolves around men while the women are busy giving birth.

The physical reality of childbearing appears in the novel only here, as a projection of Harriet's imagination. Harriet conjures up a mother, Mrs Harrison, whose name she has apparently borrowed from one of the people on her spy route, the bird cage artisan Harrison Withers. Both Virginia L. Wolf and Hamida Bosmajian convincingly argue that he represents one of Harriet's potential selves: Withers is a model of the isolated artist that she ought not emulate because, as Bosmajian points out, 'Harriet would "wither" if she were to imitate him' (78). Although he seems happy, the fact that his art involves creating cages, a symbol frequently used throughout female *Künstlerromane* to indicate the sense of entrapment experienced by many girls who wish to be artists, as both Barbara White and Linda Huf document, affirms Wolf and Bosmajian's sense of him as more of a warning than a model. Thus Harriet's bestowing the name of one of her shadow selves on a woman in labour suggests that Harriet is envisioning a version of herself, giving birth to what must also be herself.

Harriet seems to enter a trance to conjure this birth: Fitzhugh describes her looking 'down at the town as though hypnotized' (6). Harriet proceeds to describe a robbery at a gas station in vivid detail while Sport listens in awe. '"Then what?"' he encourages her.

'At this same minute Mrs. Harrison's baby is born and Dr. Jones says, "you have a fine baby girl, Mrs. Harrison, a fine baby girl, ho, ho, ho."'

'Make it a boy.'

'No, it's a girl. She already has a boy.'

'What does the baby look like?'

'She's ugly. Now, also at this very minute, on the other side of town, over here past the gas station, almost to the mountain, the robbers have stopped at a farmhouse which belongs to Ole Farmer Dodge.' (7)

Clearly she is much more comfortable with the adventure plot, yet she has felt compelled to include the birth narrative, and then dismiss it by commenting on the baby's ugliness. The connection between herself and the baby becomes clearer when we see how, a few pages later, she herself 'feels ugly'.

The reality of life begins, in the first scene of the novel, to intrude on comforting fantasy. Ole Golly, Harriet's nurse, interrupts the game of Town with the announcement that she is going to take Harriet to see something. This glimpse of the world comes in the form of Ole Golly's mother, a woman who is grotesquely obese and not 'very bright' (16). Her mentality is such that, in Mrs Golly's hearing and without eliciting any reaction, Ole Golly can tell Harriet to behold '"a woman who never had any interest in anyone else, nor in any book, nor in any school, nor in any way of life, but has lived her whole life in this room, eating and sleeping and waiting to die"' (18). Such a description would seem to belie the woman's ability to have raised a daughter such as Ole Golly but that is one mystery that remains unsolved. Certainly, the description conveys a character opposite to Harriet, who treats everyone and everything as a mystery to be solved. Mrs Golly is also the antithesis of her daughter, the erudite nurse, Harriet's substitute mother. Like Harriet, Ole Golly loves routine and dislikes physical affection; her corporeal presence – a thin rigidity enveloped in tweed – renders her asexual. Unable to contain her shock at this unlikely maternal relationship between Ole Golly and her grotesque mother, Harriet acts childishly. She makes fun of Sport's real name and feels 'very ugly all of a sudden' (15). She feels, it appears, like the female baby she had so very recently declared to be ugly. In the presence of this massive, barely verbal lump of female flesh, Harriet becomes an ugly baby.

The whole experience frightens her. For the first time, Harriet can read sadness in her nurse's face. Ole Golly must struggle to evoke her familiar firmness to free them from her hysterical, engulfing mother. This opening scene of the novel sets out in graphic terms the urgency of Harriet's project. She must separate from her mother substitute and dwell in the realm of language – the symbolic realm in Julia Kristeva's terms – in order to be the strong and independent individual she aspires to be.

According to Kristevan psychoanalytic theory, enunciation begins to arise when the Self acknowledges its separateness from the Other; this occurs at the stage called the thetic break and gives rise to the Symbolic. 'The symbolic – and therefore syntax and all linguistic categories – is a social effect of the relation to the other' (Kristeva 29). Harriet frequently compares the lives of those she investigates and her own life in her spy book entries such as: 'I'll tell you one thing, I don't want to live like Miss Whitehead' (33). These are traces of the process by which she is discovering her own separate self. Kristeva argues that from this splitting of the subject (the Self) from the object (the Other) arises enunciation, which produces narrative and myth. In other words, you have to know that you are a separate individual before you can begin to tell stories. Symbolic discourse supports the social order and suppresses the semiotic – that non-linguistic process expressing pre-Oedipal fusion with the maternal body.

Kristeva differs from other French feminists, such as Hélène Cixous, who construe the semiotic as the aspect of the signifying process most conducive to recovering feminine power. Such an emphasis has produced an ideal referred to as *l'écriture féminine*. However, Rita Felski notes that the attribution of the characteristics of the semiotic, such as irrationality and non-linearity, to 'the feminine' simply reinforces traditional notions about women that have contributed to their oppression. Indeed, it seems that Harriet senses something oppressive about the non-verbal condition and has no desire to swim in the semiotic. If anything, the pre-Oedipal state horrifies her. She does not want to merge with her mother, or with Ole Golly.

Written in 1964, before such notions as *l'écriture féminine* had been articulated, Fitzhugh's protagonist struggles to leave the semiotic behind in order to engage in the symbolic: the realm of public discourse, the place where her father has a 'high-pressure job' and battles it out with 'finks'. Of course, one can argue that Harriet merely identifies with the oppressor and adopts his language (she imitates his use of the word 'fink' and echoes his opinions about how boring her real mother's pastime of bridge-playing is). If the choices available to a female child in 1964 were not so starkly drawn between vocation and idleness (upper-class wives like her mother appear idle to her, prompt-ing an entry wondering '"[d]oes my mother mooch off my father? I'll never do that"' (46)) Harriet might have been able to find her own way to producing that mysterious feminine writing. As it is, she falters in using her father's language: after trying to avoid using the forbidden word 'damned' by replacing it with 'finked', she is told that fink cannot be used as a verb (83–4).

If orality is tricky, there is greater stability in the written word, to which both Harriet and Ole Golly cling. Harriet writes compulsively in her notebook and Ole Golly explains life by quoting texts even if she cannot always explicate them. During the unsettling encounter with her mother, Ole Golly takes time out to quote Henry James's observa-tion about the agreeableness of '"the hour dedicated to the ceremony known as afternoon tea"' (18). One of her many literary references, it is noteworthy in this context because it evokes ritual, another one of Harriet and Ole Golly's cherished means of containing the uncontain-able. Meanwhile, 'Harriet fairly itched to take notes on' Mrs Golly (14), to contain this maternal mountain and defend herself with words that reinforce her separate identity.

A sizeable number of fictional girls who write are orphans. They live with aunts similar to Ole Golly or other women who are not biologi-cally maternal. The 'mother' of all these heroines is the eponymous Aurora of Elizabeth Barrett Browning's *Aurora Leigh* (1864). She is fol-lowed by Susan Coolidge's Katy, of *What Katy Did* (1872), as well as Montgomery's Anne of Green Gables and Emily of New Moon. DuPlessis explains that this phenomenon

> covertly announces that the mother might be less than inspiring ... The death or generational displacement of the mother in plots involving a daughter artist may be the writer's way of solving one form of the conflict between role and vocation, between the mutual costs ... of maternal nurturance and filial autonomy. (99)

Perhaps the one trait that Nancy Drew has in common with protagon-ists of female *Künstlerromane*, like Aurora Leigh and Anne Shirley, is that she too is motherless. Carolyn Heilbrun, asserting Nancy Drew's significance to feminist history, writes that:

> Even more important than the roadster [which provided mobility], Nancy Drew has no mother, no female mentor from the patriarchy to tell her to cool it, be nice, let the boys win, don't say what you

mean. Mothers have long been and were, in Nancy Drew's day and before, those who prepare their daughters to take their proper place in the patriarchy, which is why in so many novels with interesting women heroes, whether by Charlotte Brontë or Mildred Benson, the female heroes are motherless. (18)

More recent novels dare to critique motherhood overtly and consider that the woman who has herself been forced to submit to limitation may not be willing or able to provide the kind of encouragement an ambitious daughter needs. *Harriet the Spy* stands in a state of tension between the tradition of dead mothers and the newer appearance of ineffective mothers by providing Harriet with both a distant birth mother and a nanny, neither of whom are completely satisfactory role models.

Nonetheless, Harriet's discovery that her seemingly asexual nurse has a boyfriend precipitates a major crisis. Mr Waldenstein appears, disrupting the symbiotic union between Harriet and Ole Golly and reconfiguring them as a nuclear family – or at least a looking-glass version of one. Although Harriet is at first hostile to him as a threat to her world, he wins her over and she accepts his invitation to go to a movie. However, instead of using the standard station wagon to make this imitation of a family trip to the movies, they must travel there on Mr Waldenstein's delivery bicycle, with Harriet riding in its cart. While highlighting the fact that this manufactured family is not of the same economic class as her own, this unusual means of conveyance also allows Harriet to experience a new kind of security. Riding in the cart, she feels 'so delicious that she almost fell asleep on the ride back' (120). It is as if she is re-entering the womb.

However, her birth is a rude awakening, as most births are. She emerges from the womb-like security of the bicycle cart to a scene of anger and confusion. Her real parents, having arrived home early, are frantic and angry to find no one home and her mother fires Ole Golly. Although this dismissal is later withdrawn, Ole Golly still plans to depart because she has accepted an offer to marry Mr Waldenstein and because '"the time has come"' (128). This enigmatic explanation, alluding to Lewis Carroll, hints at the mystery of sexual desire and childbirth from which the child is excluded. The inevitable mother/daughter separation, symbolically enacted by the ride in the cart and Harriet's expulsion from the cart/womb, provokes a sense of terrible loss for Harriet. Despite this, her quest to understand all the mysteries life holds will not be quelled: the next day she is full of questions for Ole Golly regarding her engagement.

Continuing to pursue her spying activities, her solitude no longer part of the game but a reality, Harriet witnesses yet another symbolic birth. The Robinsons, a rich, self-satisfied couple on Harriet's spy route, have purchased something in a large crate, so large that Harriet is forced to consider how this object could be squeezed through the small space of the door, much as children who know the basic facts of life wonder how a baby could emerge from such a tiny hole as the vagina. Fitzhugh provides a detailed description of the unpacking of this object, complete with the assistance of a 'Railway Express' man who helps the delivery along while the couple hold hands and look on in 'speechless joy' (158). Finally a large wooden sculpture of a baby emerges. Harriet at last witnesses the ultimate mystery of birth: just like the baby Harriet's imagination saw fit to give birth to, this one is unattractive. It is also enormous, dwarfing the tiny mother figure it holds in its hands.

This is more than just a humorous reversal of the usual mother and child iconography. It is an accurate representation of the enormous ego of the infant who, totally dependent upon the mother, wishes to be able to control her as easily as this baby can. But, while the tiny hand-held mother may fulfil the infant's craving for control, it also threatens with the implication of the mother's powerlessness. She cannot possibly protect or nurture this baby. Here again, the sense that mothers are inadequate, unable to provide satisfactory role models for their ambitious daughters, confronts us. Now we can see why, when Harriet walks away from their window remembering that Ole Golly is no longer around to hear about this, she feels 'something akin to rage' (159).

The delivery man gapes in astonishment when he finds out the sculptor is a woman, saying '"[a] dame made that?"' (158). The fact that the baby's creator is female reminds us of the difficult choice facing both Harriet and her creator, Louise Fitzhugh, who was a painter as well as a writer and illustrator. They must choose between flesh and blood connections or artistic creation. This sterile birth, in which sawdust replaces blood and fluid, takes place shortly after Ole Golly has left Harriet and seems to be mocking her own sense of having been connected to her nanny. The comfort of being in the cart has been negated by subsequent abandonment. Her expulsion from the womb hardly seems to have any rewards. Indeed, it seems that the birth of the artist always produces monstrous creatures. Grace Stewart, in her book *A New Mythos: The Novel of the Artist as Heroine*, observes how frequently the theme of women giving birth to freaks or monsters recurs, and attributes this to the idea that unlike the male genius, the woman is not supposed to give birth to herself or to a work of art: she's supposed to give birth to a baby. Stewart asserts that creating a new mythos involves 'a recognition of this offspring, no matter how ugly or weak' (178).

The artist may be seen as, or may even be, an enormous, engulfing ego, and as a result, be isolated from others. Harriet's loneliness after Ole Golly's departure is compounded by isolation from her classmates who reject her after having read her notebook with all its uncompromising reflections on them. This is in keeping with the typical *Künstlerroman* which usually presents its protagonist with a stark choice between life and art. By letter, Ole Golly suggests a way to reconcile the artistic self with the community. For one thing, she tells Harriet that she must lie. Then she offers the instruction that '"writing is to put love in the world"' (276).

This edict is, in a nutshell, the justification that most aspiring female writers in novels from *Little Women* to *The House on Mango Street* have used to vindicate their literary ambitions. Indeed, the most significant factor these female *Künstlerromane* have in common, which differs from the 'universal' pattern based on male protagonists, is that their heroes do not wish to set themselves against family and community. Although they often end up rejected by the community, they struggle to reintegrate, to have themselves and their works accepted.

When DuPlessis examined this tendency to view artistic production as something that both emerges from and enhances community as opposed to the autonomous individual, she found it an effective technique for resolving the 'binary alternatives' that the nineteenth-century text presents between domesticity and artistic life (104). Susan Stanford Friedman provides us with an explanation of why writing from and for a communal self became a useful strategy with her observation that only the privileged (unmarked) can view themselves as individuals: a woman cannot

> experience herself as an entirely unique entity because she is always aware of how she is being defined *as woman*, that is, as a member of a group whose identity has been defined by the dominant male culture. (38)

In rejecting the hegemony of the singular identity as the only literary voice that matters, new possibilities for female writing can be encouraged.

On one level, it may appear that *Harriet the Spy* also takes advantage of these opportunities, and presents the female writer as the voice of a larger community. Harriet does seem to be a part of an extended but intimate neighbourhood, which provides her with subject matter. A hardly recognizable New York City where an eleven-year-old girl can slink about unescorted, peeping into people's windows and even sneaking into their abandoned dumbwaiters, certainly appears to be a world of close connection. But in fact, Harriet's role as an unseen observer, her note-taking and the very emphatic class differences between herself and her subjects of scrutiny indicate a lack of true community. Even her own parents are mysterious, alien beings to Harriet, every bit as much as the people from different social realms that she observes. Indeed, it is only because she is a spy that Harriet is aware of these other inhabitants of a rather fragmented urban environment. As I noted earlier, a spy is alone in enemy territory. This is another way of depicting what W. E. B. Du Bois called 'double consciousness', that sense 'of always looking at one's self through the eyes of others' (16–17). This dual consciousness permits Harriet to see and write of the discordances in the social structures she inhabits. The entries in Harriet's spy book function to help her understand her unique place in this complex social order and establish her own independent identity.

Harriet's writing is a continual act of separation; she writes to define other people's identities and in so doing begins to define her own. For example, her spy journal contains the following entries: '"I don't think I'd like to live where any of these people live or do the things they do"' (12); '"Once I thought I wanted to be Franca and live in that family. But she's so dull if I was her I couldn't stand myself"' (57). This investigation into the nature of identity is very private, not meant to be read by anyone but herself, and when it is it produces more alienation than Harriet can handle. The act of becoming public brings the nature of notebook writing into focus: it is primarily critical, and in defining a self, it detaches that self from others. Spies work alone.

The connection between writing and forging a separate identity is illustrated even more clearly by the pleasure Harriet takes in writing her name at the top of a fresh piece of paper. She includes a middle initial that she has selected herself, her parents having neglected to give her a middle name. This letter, M, seems no accident but an additional assertion of her I 'am'-ness. As her classmates desert her, she struggles to maintain her identity and to take her usual pleasure in writing her name. Then a deliberate act of malice causes ink to spill, 'and a stain of spreading, running blue ink went over the Harriet M. Welsch, making it disappear, and continued toward Harriet, as she watched in horror' (216). Moving from signifier to signified, it seems as if the ink blot will cause Harriet herself to disappear and be blotted out. Not only does formlessness overcome her hard-wrought identity, but it happens with the very tool that allows her to inscribe herself: ink. Writing can create a separate identity; it also makes that identity vulnerable to erasure by allowing it autonomous existence. This symbolic dissolution of her inscribed identity is devastating for Harriet – her betrayal by the tools of her writing trade is analogous to the fact that her own words have resulted in her exile. This illustrates that a writer lives at least as dangerous an existence as a spy.

Furthermore, all these instances show how crucial the written word is to Harriet's identity formation. To apply Kristeva's terms, Harriet struggles to situate herself firmly within the symbolic order. As cute or cruel as some readers may see her notebook entries, they are, in fact, highly analytical, representing the act of transforming raw experience into language. By her frequent comparisons of other people's lives to her own, culminating in her highly moving entry, '"I love myself"' (210) – a phrase that shows acceptance of her own, isolate identity – Harriet demonstrates that she is going through the thetic break in which the Self acknowledges its separation from the Other and moves into the symbolic realm. She writes this entry, among her briefest, while sitting upon the toilet. Since the act of defecation is part of the anal, pre-Oedipal stage, the difficulty of achieving a successful thetic break which the phrase 'I love myself' represents is highlighted all the more poignantly. She is right in the midst of it.

Harriet defines herself as both writer and spy (both professions, at first, in ungendered terms), and her notebook, in which she writes down her extensive observations, is the only one of her many spy tools she uses. It is the place where life's mysteries become text and thus closer to intelligibility. When her classmates find her notebook and turn against her, Ole Golly intervenes to push Harriet towards an understanding of her vocation as primarily a writer rather than a spy. Although both careers involve unravelling mysteries, the writer has a somewhat more respectable place in the social order. Ole Golly instigates behind-the-scene machinations that install Harriet as editor of her school paper's Sixth Grade Page. More importantly, Ole Golly transmits to Harriet the aforementioned advice to girls who would be writers, that writing is to 'put love into the world' (276) – with the unusual qualification that this may necessitate telling white lies.

The publication of Harriet's private, starkly candid observations about those she spies on hardly appears to fulfil Ole Golly's dictum about putting love into the world; rather it holds up the less fortunate to her classmates' ridicule. However, Harriet is fulfilling a function that society recognizes a need for: she becomes, in effect, a gossip columnist. She wins her friends back because she orally lies about her notes on them, not because she has changed the way she writes. Her penultimate notebook entry states that '"Ole Golly is right. Sometimes you have to lie"' (297). She never affirms the other pieces of advice. It is not Harriet's writing that has reunited her with her friends but her lying. Love and friendship need not be relinquished, but the female artist must employ social skills and perform her gender role even more adroitly if she is to maintain relationships as well as a vocation. She must behave like a spy. This deviation from the tradition, in which writing may be marginally acceptable because it can prevent girls from that most heinous trait in a female – lying – underscores the clandestine quality of Harriet's work. Both of Montgomery's characters, Anne of Green Gables and Emily of New Moon, must contend with guardians firmly opposed to their fictional creativity because they view imaginative expression as the equivalent of lying. The Calvinist morality out of which this view emerges, in an attitude that seems to be a vestige of a more orally based society, considers a spoken lie even more immoral than a written one. Thus fiction may be useful if it prevents lying. As recently as 1943, the belief that fiction is just a slightly more acceptable form of lying appears in Betty Smith's *A Tree Grows in Brooklyn*. Smith writes: '[i]t was at a Thanksgiving time that Francie told her first organized lie, was found out and determined to become a writer' (148). Francie's teacher encourages her to '*tell* the truth, and *write* the story' (150). As Lissa Paul states, 'lying is a survival tactic for the feminist writer' (70). Observing people, reporting honestly in writing and dissembling to their faces is even more akin to espionage than it is to our conceptions of what a writer does, particularly a female writer.

Just as Harriet learns to become, not simply a writer, but a female writer, in order not to be ostracized by society, she learns to become, not just a spy, but a female spy. The revelation comes to her in the midst of a crisis precipitated by her mother's demand that she take dance lessons. Labouring under the impression that real spies do not dance, Harriet tries to answer Ole Golly's question about how spies are trained:

'They learn languages and guerrilla fighting and everything about a country so if they're captured they'll know all the old football scores and things like that.'

'That's *boy* spies, Harriet. You're not thinking.' (86)

Naturally, in a patriarchy, which defines the unmarked as male, the model to which Harriet had adhered, before becoming conscious of gender, was the male one. Now she learns that girl spies must learn the same things as the boys '"and a few more"' (87). Ole Golly refers to a movie they had seen and reminds Harriet that Mata Hari had had to dance with a general (87). Women must have very different ways of gathering information than men. Harriet's 'ungendered' models will have to be replaced by female ones like Mata Hari.

Ole Golly's example also hints at the connection between female espionage and prostitution. While the cleaned-up movie version, suitable for children's consumption, only pictures Mata Hari dancing with generals, the common knowledge about her behaviour, and the behaviour of other women engaged in espionage during the world wars, was that they seduced and betrayed men from occupying countries. According to Patricia Craig and Mary Cadogan who trace the literary history of female detectives and spies, the public image of women spies changed during the First World War, when they began to be perceived as women who were serving their country and as 'vivid symbols of independence' (52) but the taint of moral impurity about them remained paramount. Women may have had powerful weapons for espionage: one, the fact that they were considered too fragile for such dangerous work, and two, their sexuality, but these were weapons that could hardly be honoured the way men's more forthright ones could be. They were also weapons that could readily be used against them.

This sexualized reality is one Harriet cannot ignore but will have to come to terms with in order to be successful in her chosen vocation. She must begin playing the role society has assigned her in order to reach her goals. What is unique about *Harriet the Spy*'s approach to the pubescent assumption of gender identity is that Ole Golly and Harriet conspire together in their understanding that it is a role, a disguise, a tactic. Becoming a woman for Harriet is comparable to being a spy in enemy territory.

While her fictional female predecessors in the *Künstlerroman*, for the most part, gave themselves up to the master's language, Harriet is aware that she is acting, that she is a spy in disguise, like Mata Hari, performing her gender role to achieve her own aims. Ole Golly's advice on how to be a woman and a writer is of the same cloth. Harriet will always be a spy in alien territory. But that territory, the realm of symbolic discourse, is where she must go in order to individuate.

For Harriet, the fall from the state of pre-Oedipal semiotic bliss (as it would appear to be from Kristeva's characterization of it) into the symbolic realm of language is ultimately a happy fall. Though plunging into a state of total isolation, Harriet finally succeeds in communicating her vision. As she discovers, self-definition, and its corollary, isolation, can be more dangerous than any of her spy adventures. Rather than reinforcing the idea that writing for girls is morally justifiable because it enhances communal bonds, as the female *Künstlerroman* usually did, Fitzhugh uses the gains made by female protagonists of detective fiction to allow Harriet to achieve the kind of success in a public genre experienced by protagonists of the male novel of artistic development. Harriet's life of espionage, of unravelling the endless mysteries of what goes on in other people's private moments, becomes the source of her real career – writing. Writing has helped her create a self.

Works cited

Bosmajian, Hamida. 'Louise Fitzhugh's *Harriet the Spy*: Nonsense and Sense', in Perry Nodelman (ed.) *Touchstones: Reflections on the Best of Children's Literature*, Vol. 1. West Lafayette, IN: Children's Literature Association, 1985, pp. 71–83.

Craig, Patricia and Mary Cadogan. *The Lady Investigates: Women Detectives and Spies in Fiction.* New York: St. Martin's Press, 1981.

Du Bois, W. E. Burghardt. *The Souls of Black Folks.* New York: Fawcett, 1961.

DuPlessis, Rachel Blau. *Writing Beyond the Ending: Narrative Strategies of Twentieth-Century Women Writers.* Bloomington, IN: Indiana University Press, 1985.

Felski, Rita. *Beyond Feminist Aesthetics: Feminist Literature and Social Change.* Cambridge, MA: Harvard University Press, 1989.

Fitzhugh, Louise. *Harriet the Spy.* New York: Dell, 1964.

Friedman, Susan Stanford. 'Women's Autobiographical Selves: Theory and Practice', in Shari Benstock (ed.) *The Private Self: Theory and Practice of Women's Autobiographical Writings.* Chapel Hill: University of North Carolina Press, 1988, pp. 34–62.

Heilbrun, Carolyn G. 'Nancy Drew: A Moment in Feminist History', in Carolyn Steward Dyer and Nancy Tillman Romalov (eds), *Rediscovering Nancy Drew.* Iowa City: University of Iowa Press, 1995, pp. 11–21.

Huf, Linda. *A Portrait of the Artist as a Young Woman: The Writer as Heroine in American Literature.* New York: Ungar, 1983.

Kristeva, Julia. *Revolution in Poetic Language* [1974], trans. Margaret Walker. New York: Columbia University Press, 1984.

Mason, Bobbie Ann. *The Girl Sleuth: A Feminist Guide*. New York: Feminist Press, 1975.

Paul, Lissa. 'The Feminist Writer as Heroine in *Harriet the Spy*', *The Lion and the Unicorn*, 13 (1989): 67–73.

Smith, Betty. *A Tree Grows in Brooklyn*. Philadelphia: Blakiston, 1943.

Stewart, Grace. *A New Mythos: The Novel of the Artist as Heroine*. St. Alban's, VT: Eden Press, 1979.

White, Barbara. *Growing Up Female: Adolescent Girlhood in American Fiction*. Westport, CT: Greenwood Press, 1985.

Wolf, Virginia L. *Louise Fitzhugh*. New York: Twayne, 1991.

9

Apparition and Apprehension: Supernatural Mystery and Emergent Womanhood in *Jane Eyre, Wuthering Heights*, and Novels by Margaret Mahy

Adrienne E. Gavin

> *Women fly while men are not watching.*
>
> (Author unknown)

'Women fly while men are not watching' is a phrase which connects mysterious powers with womanhood and draws on popular and historical associations between women and magic. Its claim that women exhibit their powers when men are not watching emphasizes that these mysterious powers are the province of women rather than men and that these powers are secret, unknown to or unobserved by men. This connection between mysterious abilities and womanhood is often used by women writers of supernatural mysteries for children. In their novels, characters who are emerging from girlhood into womanhood commonly follow a pattern in which they are initially frightened by the supernatural and then take on supernatural powers themselves, establishing powerful and magical self-identities as women.

Critics have pointed to the fluid nature of the boundary between the natural and the supernatural in women's ghost stories, a fluidity which lends to the supernatural a familiar quality, enabling it to be claimed by women (Carpenter and Kolmar 12). In women's supernatural fictions for children, familiarity with, and the acquisition of, supernatural powers distinguishes womanhood from both girlhood and maleness. This is particularly true in novels of supernatural realism in which the supernatural infuses otherwise realist narratives. In these works there is little of the scepticism about the supernatural often found in classic ghost stories, nor is the supernatural comic, consistently terrifying, or ultimately disproved as it frequently is in works by male authors or by women writers about boy characters.

The argument of this essay is in part presaged on the multiple yet particular meanings of two words: apparition and apprehension. Apparition means a ghost or ghost-like figure but it also relates to the act of appearing or being visible. Apprehension means alternatively: fear or anxiety, the act of capturing or arresting, or belief or comprehension. Each of these meanings is significant in examining the pattern by which womanhood emerges in children's supernatural mysteries by women.

In the first stage of this pattern girl characters who are on the cusp of womanhood see or experience supernatural apparitions which cause them apprehension in the sense of fear, discomfort, or anxiety. First, a ghostly apparition appears in a mirror or mirror-like surface, reflecting the girl's own incipient supernatural womanhood. Non-recognition of herself in the mirror creates fear in the girl, both of the supernatural and of her future. Soon afterwards she becomes percipient to other apparitions, usually one or more male supernatural characters who escalate her fear further. That these characters are male is connected with the girl's apprehensions about men, sex, and romance, but also serves as a premonition of the patriarchal power she will encounter more directly as a woman. Both types of apparition – mirror-visions and male 'ghosts' – provoke the emergent woman's apprehensions about the unknown and about change; change in the way she appears to herself, and in the way the world sees her.

Fear of apparitions is followed by a second stage in which the emergent woman character apprehends the supernatural in the sense of arresting or containing it. This occurs through her acquisition of supernatural powers which she then uses to control or destroy the powers of male supernatural characters.

The third stage, like the first, is marked by both apparition and apprehension. Now, however, it is apprehension in the sense of belief in and understanding of the supernatural, and apparition in the sense of appearing or making visible her new self as a woman. Significant in her apparition is vocalization of the self; both her appearance and her speech demand recognition from other characters: recognition that she is a woman, that she has special powers, and that she is a mystery in her own right.

This literary pattern by which fear of the supernatural is followed by the acquisition of supernatural qualities on the part of female characters is widespread in children's novels by women writers such as Gillian Cross, Helen Cresswell, Penelope Farmer, Penelope Lively, Philippa Pearce, and Catherine Storr. Discussion here concentrates on the two novels which have most influenced this pattern in female writing: Charlotte Brontë's *Jane Eyre* (1847) and Emily Brontë's *Wuthering Heights* (1847), and on the two contemporary novels which best exemplify it: *The Changeover* (1984) and *The Tricksters* (1986) both by Margaret Mahy.

Typically first read in adolescence by the many women writers whose work they have influenced, the Brontës' novels remain key texts in the canon of children's fiction. Mahy, for her part, has been rightly termed the 'most powerful and popular exponent of witches, magicians, and ghosts flourishing in the clear light of day' (Egoff and Sutton 385). Discussing female protagonists in children's literature, Lissa Paul suggests that 'there has been a shift in children's literature: from Golden Age entrapment to the transcendence in the young adult fiction of the 1980s' (196). This claim holds partially true when we compare the Brontës' Victorian accounts of emerging womanhood with Mahy's late twentieth-century envisionings of this same female movement towards supernaturalism.

Jane Eyre's fears of the supernatural are provoked at the onset of her adolescence when, aged ten, she expresses passionate rage at her treatment in the Reed household. Of her resistance to being borne captive to the red-room into which she is to be locked in punishment she says: 'I was a trifle beside myself; or rather *out* of myself, as the French would say' (12). This sense of not being herself is exacerbated in the red-room where she is terrified by a vision she sees in the mirror: 'the strange little figure there gazing at me, with a white face and arms specking in the gloom, and glittering eyes of fear moving where all else was still, had the effect of a real spirit' (14). Her mood of hot-blooded rebellion chills to fear as, provoked by her mirror image, she imagines her Uncle's ghost suddenly appearing in the red-room in which he died. '[T]urning a fascinated eye towards the dimly gleaming mirror' (16–17), she feels her fear escalating into terror. Finally she collapses, overwrought, in 'a species of fit: unconsciousness closed the scene' (18).

This red-room scene has fascinated feminist critics who have read it as symbolic of emergence into womanhood in various ways: the red of the room symbolizing menstruation, for example, or its enclosed nature representing a womb from which Jane is born into a sense of herself. Vanessa D. Dickerson argues that in 'the mirror scene, Jane does not prove so much a stranger to herself as one who acknowledges her strangeness and recognizes her own ghostliness' (59 n. 13). Yet this recognition is not immediate; Jane's fear is provoked by a vision of herself as other than what she has known.

Scenes in which a girl character is frightened by a ghostly reflected image of herself recur in women's writing. Jenijoy La Belle in her study of the looking-glass in literature comments:

> At those times in the lives of female characters when they are most concerned with their self-identities, or when crises in their lives throw them back on their sole selves, they turn with remarkable frequency to the contemplation of their images in the glass. (2)

Jane faces both crisis and questions of self-identity in the red-room.

Initially frightening to her, Jane's supernatural qualities soon become the core of her womanhood and are revealed most clearly through the romance plot. Rochester is attracted to, but cannot understand, Jane's mysterious, supernatural qualities: '"[s]he comes from the other world,"' he says, '"from the abode of people who are dead ... If I dared, I'd touch you, to see if you are substance or shadow, you elf!"' (247). '"You are altogether a human being, Jane? You are certain of that?"' (442) he asks her.

In contrast, Rochester's attempted usurpation of 'female' powers in his guise as a fortune-telling gipsy woman reveals his lack of strong supernatural powers. Although Jane knows that Rochester does hold power over her, she becomes aware that it is not fully supernatural: 'he is not a ghost,' she thinks, 'yet every nerve I have is unstrung: for a moment I am beyond my own mastery' (246). She regains mastery by gradually claiming her powers and demanding that he recognize her self, which, through love, he does.

Jane must also conquer St John Rivers's powers; sensing his eye upon her she feels 'as if [she] were sitting in the room with something uncanny' (402). On the verge of accepting his proposal of marriage she feels momentarily powerless: 'motionless under [her] hierophant's touch' (423). Yet Rivers is an ineffective hierophant; he cannot explain all mysteries. Supernaturally attuned, Jane is resurgent a few moments later as she psychically hears Rochester's call to her and St John's powers are thereafter lost: '[i]t was *my* turn to assume ascendancy,' she states. '*My* powers were in play, and in force' (425). By the end of the novel Jane has become an apparition to both Rivers and Rochester in the sense of becoming visible to them; both men are forced to recognize her for herself as she overcomes the power each has exerted over her. After her marriage to Rochester, Jane becomes '(what [Rochester] often called me) the apple of his eye' (456). Being blind, Rochester is literally forced to see things from her perspective. Jane ends in full womanhood as an apparition who has accepted her own mysterious qualities.

Although her fear of and entry into the supernatural occur towards the end rather than the beginning of her adolescence, Catherine Linton née Earnshaw's progress into womanhood in *Wuthering Heights* follows a similar pattern to Jane Eyre's. Having rejected Heathcliff in favour of marrying Edgar Linton, Catherine, aged nineteen, dies soon after giving birth to her daughter. During her pregnancy she goes through an illness and period of self-starvation in which she experiences fear of the supernatural provoked by non-recognition of herself in the mirror. She imagines she sees a face in the black press that was in the room of her Wuthering Heights childhood, but in fact she is staring at herself in the mirror of her current room at Thrushcross Grange, as Nelly Dean recounts:

> 'Don't *you* see that face?' she enquired, gazing earnestly at the mirror.
> And say what I could, I was incapable of making her comprehend it to be her own ...
> 'Oh! Nelly, the room is haunted! I'm afraid of being alone!' ...
> 'There's nobody here!' I insisted. 'It was *yourself*, Mrs Linton.' (123–4)

Patricia Meyer Spacks reads Catherine's terror as a fear of loneliness:

> The ghost that haunts the mirror is her solitary self ... which contains the seeds of terror. Freud reports his own unnerving experience of seeing himself, for a moment unrecognizable, in a mirrored train-compartment door. 'Uncanniness,' he argues is the essence of such experience, the product of its unexpectedness, its reversal of underlying certitudes. (143)

Sandra M. Gilbert and Susan Gubar suggest that what Catherine sees in the mirror is 'neither gothic nor alien ... but hideously familiar'; she sees who she has 'really become in the world's terms: Mrs. Linton, the lady of Thrushcross Grange' (283). In its ghostly, terrifying nature, however, the mirror image can most significantly be read as reflecting the supernatural nature of what Catherine must become and her fear of her own future – her fear, in other words, of what La Belle, using a phrase from Elizabeth Taylor's *A Game of Hide and Seek*, calls a 'forward-going ghost' (La Belle 81). In order to find and reveal her real self and achieve true womanhood – as opposed to the pseudo-womanhood she experiences in her marriage to Linton – Catherine must literally become a ghost. Unlike Jane Eyre who has entered into womanhood and her supernatural powers before marriage, Catherine, not yet fully cognizant of her own magical qualities, has married under the combined impetus of adolescent fickleness and social inducements (Linton being the culturally-sanctioned 'better catch'). The only way out of this marriage is through the death of one of the spouses. In seeing the ghost in the mirror, Catherine sees her own ghosthood; she must die in order to find her self as a woman.

Catherine appears in Lockwood's nightmare as a child ghost because it is in her childhood relationship with Heathcliff that she has last felt her true self. Lockwood, 'who wants to be free of this eerie exposure of the female's self, brutally saws the ghost's arm across the broken pane of glass' (Dickerson 76). 'For the rational Lockwood,' as Dickerson suggests, 'the supernatural is tantamount to a loss of control, while for Catherine the supernatural ultimately translates into force, power, and control' (78). Soon after the mirror scene in which she confronts her supernatural future, Catherine has said to Nelly '"I wish I were a girl again ... I'm sure I should be myself were I once among the heather on those hills"' (126). Yet it is impossible to return to childhood. In becoming a ghost Catherine has entered into and accepted the supernatural, has become an apparition in both senses, and has reduced Heathcliff's power over her through haunting him: '"she has disturbed me, night and day, through eighteen years – incessantly – remorselessly,"' he tells Nelly (289). Catherine has, however, also earlier claimed '"I *am* Heathcliff"' (82), and it is only when, on adult terms, she is reunited with Heathcliff, who is so much a part of herself, that she can fully experience true womanhood. That she achieves this is evidenced by the words of the little boy who reveals to Lockwood at the close of the novel: '"[t]hey's Heathcliff and a *woman*, yonder, under t' Nab ... un' Aw darnut pass 'em"' (336, emphasis added). Catherine has become a woman, a woman whose supernatural and mysterious power is made manifest.

Despite having overcome fears of apparitions, controlled male power, and successfully entered into the mysteries of womanhood and supernatural powers, Jane Eyre and Catherine Linton end in situations which, in Paul's terms, 'entrap' those powers. Both Jane and Catherine end up in desolate places, joined to a male partner rather than completely independent and, more significantly, with Rochester blind (later partially sighted) and Catherine a scarcely sighted ghost, recognition of their powers by other characters becomes limited because those powers effectively become unseen. Their supernatural qualities have been revealed to readers, to other characters, and to their lovers, but by the novels' ends there is a form of retrenchment. This retrenchment insists that, after a womanhood-signalling manifestation, Jane's and Catherine's powers become largely invisible. In other words, Jane and Catherine can 'fly' but only 'when men – or those subject to Victorian patriarchy – are not watching.'

Mahy's *The Changeover: A Supernatural Romance* signals the concerns of this essay in its title. Laura Chant's ceremonial and quest-like experience of changing over marks clearly the point at which she accepts the supernatural by taking on powers as a witch and signals her entry into womanhood. Typically of Mahy's novels, as critics such as Elliott Gose and Adam Berkin note, *The Changeover* is palimpsestically and intertextually thick with allusions to myths, fairy tales, and other literature. Mahy both uses and subverts – without simplistically inverting – the texts to which she alludes, particularly, as Josephine Raburn and Lissa Paul each discuss, in her depiction of gender roles and female characters. As in *The Tricksters*, and other Mahy novels which reveal a supernatural progress into womanhood such as *The Haunting* (1982) and *The Other Side of Silence* (1995), *The Changeover* sets mystery against a background of changing family dynamics, but strong familial love. Mahy is, as Joan Gibbons suggests, 'a leader in the field of writers on family relationships' (11) and Laura's entry into the supernatural and womanhood intertwines with familial situations as well as with the romantic and sexual tensions in her developing relationship with Sorry Carlisle.

Like Jane Eyre and Catherine Linton, Laura Chant experiences fear of the supernatural which is initially signalled by a mirror scene. Aged fourteen, Laura looks at herself in the mirror after taking a shower: '[t]he mirror ... showed her a blurred ghost ... its vagueness suited her, for she was uncertain about her reflection and often preferred it misty rather than distinct' (2). Moments later she is frightened by a supernatural 'warning', and a distinct vision of herself in her bedroom mirror fills her with fear:

> her reflection was treacherous. Looking at it, she became more than uneasy; she became frightened ... the face was not her face for it knew something that she did not. It looked back at her from some

mysterious place alive with fears and pleasures she could not entirely recognize. (3–4)

Laura's fear is caused by the non-recognition of self; she fears her own future womanhood and her own mysteriousness. As Nicholas Tucker suggests, '[l]ooking in the mirror and seeing someone else is not just a feature of ghost stories; it also relates to adolescents' occasional surprise about the rapidity of the changes in their physical appearance' (8). For girls and women, as La Belle points out, there is often, too, a 'close congruity between what is revealed by the mirror and what a male sees' (116), and Laura's fear of the supernatural is soon exacerbated by her experiences with two male supernatural figures, Carmody Braque and Sorry Carlisle.

Carmody Braque, '"an old and careful demon"' (88) who smells of stale peppermint, puts a stamp on Laura's three-year-old brother Jacko's hand causing in him a life-threatening illness. Laura shows Jacko's stamped hand to her mother 'as if it were a vital clue in a mystery' (27), and Jacko himself becomes a 'medical mystery … a puzzling case that would have to be solved' (77). Laura's sensitivity to the supernatural tells her that Braque is regaining youth through his supernatural draining of Jacko's life force: '[s]he could not sing in tune but she could resonate with mystery, and some part of her brain could understand and interpret the resonance' (53). She solves the mystery of Jacko's illness by going through the changeover in order to save his life.

Sorensen Carlisle, 'seventh form prefect and secret witch' (54), who indulges in rings, black caftans, and reading 'women's romances, such as [Laura] and Kate despised' (61) is also, Laura knows, a danger to her as well as an attraction. His 'tricky, looking-glass eyes' provoke in her fears similar to those induced by her own mirror (13). His mother Miryam and his grandmother Winter, also witches – '"daughters of the moon"' (88) – tell Laura about Sorry's '"ambiguous nature"' (70):

'It's very much a feminine magic – or so we think … And Sorensen sometimes resents it. He doesn't like being called a witch, although of course that is really what he is. Sometimes he feels that he's not completely a man or a witch but some hybrid, and he struggles too hard to be either one thing or the other.' (70)

They tell Laura they are glad that she has recognized Sorry but warn her that 'Sorry might be dangerous to her' (94).

Walking through the subdivision towards Sorry's house for the first time, Laura has already experienced fear as she thinks of the tangible dangers evidenced by the rape of a student in the trees bordering the Gardendale Reserve ten days before. The attraction between herself and Sorry enhances her fears about her emerging womanhood:

> She was not altogether easy with the new, and in some ways blatantly female, body that had recently opened out of her earlier childish one, but was obliged to accept its advantages and drawbacks, as well as all the obligations of caution that came with it. (57)

Seeing Sorry in his study, she is afraid: 'her hair stood quite simply on end, for in this room he was somehow expanded, less simple, less mild, less *good* – overflowing with blackness' (61). Yet she notices that she causes fear in him too: 'he stared at her incredulously as if she had had a precisely similar effect on him. Appearing in his doorway, a visitation hoped for and feared' (61). She is made uncomfortable by his poster of a naked woman which she later sees has a grainy photo of herself pinned to it, and by his looking at, then touching, her breasts without being 'invited'. As their relationship develops, however, she becomes aware of her own powers and comes to realize that his power over her is not as strong as she might have thought. '"Now you're in my power!"' Sorry says to her pleasantly on one occasion. '"Think of that and tremble."' '"Big deal"' Laura replies (87).

Already a 'sensitive' and able to apprehend (see) witches, Laura gains her real powers in going through the changeover ritual guided by the Carlisle witches. Before the changeover begins Miryam tells her to look in the mirror, saying, '"look – it's a wonderful, mysterious thing to be a girl"' (138). The magical womanhood Laura is about to emerge into, however, is even more mysterious. '"Sometimes I think all women are imaginary creatures, as Sorry chooses to put it,"' Miryam tells her.

> 'He doesn't mean that we're simply imagined, you know, but that our power flows out of the imagination, and that's the faculty that makes magicians of all of us. Witches just act upon it with such conviction that their dreams turn into reality.' (134)

Going through the changeover 'the true path [is] always marked by [Laura's] own drop of blood and she follow[s] it faithfully' (145–6), suggesting, as Anna Lawrence-Pietroni points out, 'the ongoing rhythms of menstruation' indicative of womanhood (36). Looking in a mirror after having emerged as a witch, Laura sees 'plainly that she [is] remade, ha[s] brought to life some sleeping part of herself' (152). When Sorry tells her that the '"Sleeping Beauty always loves the prince who wakes her,"' she responds '"I woke myself"' (151), claiming her own powers as a woman and an isolate self-identity. Sorry recognizes her new, mysterious self. '"You're just as scary as [Braque] is,"' he tells her, '"something shifted in you ... you remade yourself"' (159).

As a witch, Laura has the power to put a mark on the unsuspecting Carmody Braque, thus saving her brother. Although terrified, by offering herself to Braque in exchange for her brother and thus getting him to 'invite' her in, she is able to mark him with her own magic stamp. Watching Braque collapse to his knees and feeling her new powers she notices

> the world suddenly alt[er], growing lighter and more luminous. An energy as strong and sweet as honey flowed into her ... with shock and triumph she discerned her own ghost, looking back at her out of her victim's desperate eyes. (166–7)

Seeing Braque again at the school gates she feels 'enormously strong as she suddenly bec[omes] aware of the full extent of her power over him' (183), but she learns to use her magic wisely not cruelly. She is alone in her final confrontation with Braque, which takes place on the Gardendale Reserve near where Jacynth Close was raped. She knows that an open space, like womanhood, offers both visibility and danger. In destroying Braque through her own magic, Laura exerts control not only over supernatural threats but over the fear of attack that her womanhood evokes in her. In doing so she reveals not only her own powers but her achieved womanhood.

The difference in supernatural quality between Braque and Sorry is that Sorry is a human witch who, because of his difficult childhood, has repressed his own feelings, whereas Braque is a non-human, evil spirit who steals other people's feelings. Laura, in entering into her own mysterious womanhood, conquers both their powers, by provoking love in Sorry and causing death in Braque. She exercises her new found power over Sorry by telling him: '"[y]ou can take down that poster in your room. Keep my photograph, I don't mind, but not pinned to the poster"' (170). Her magical strength makes her realize that she will not be objectified and made unindividual, and that Sorry must seek individual subjective knowledge of her. As Lucy Norton suggests, looking and seeing are a very important part of adolescent experience in this novel, and Sorry must see Laura as herself.

Sorry claims male mystery for himself when he says '"one thing Winter and Miryam forget when they talk about feminine mystery is that being a man is very mysterious too"' (199), but his example of this mystery – '"I suppose shaving's part of it"' – (199), does not ultimately convince. What is most mysterious within him are his 'feminine' magic powers which, through his love for Laura, he is coming to accept in himself. At the conclusion of the novel Laura has made herself and her mysteriousness visible not only to those who initially frighten her, but to her family. Both her mother and her father notice changes in her just as she sees changes in herself. Looking in the mirror she sees 'the very face she had been promised weeks earlier on the day of the warnings' (208).

Sarah Ellis argues that like 'Jane Eyre, Laura will find that her destiny lies with the romantic hero' (312), yet there is no certainty that Laura and Sorry will remain together after Sorry's four years of training and Laura's completing high school. They end being able to read each other's minds telepathically, in a manner reminiscent of the supernatural link between Catherine and Heathcliff, but they are also physically separated. As Raburn notes, '[t]he sexual union at the end of [Northrop] Frye's romance is not present in this story. Mahy's heroine does not need a sexual union to complete her identity. She achieves it on her own' (34). 'In the end Laura is clearly the hero,' Berkin states; 'Mahy underscores feminine mystery and strength' (250). Laura has entered into womanhood and into her supernatural powers, powers which are both mysterious and evident.

For Harry Hamilton, the seventeen-year-old protagonist of Mahy's complex and mystery-riddled novel *The Tricksters*, entry into the supernatural and womanhood is also spliced with familial, sexual, and self-identity concerns. The middle of the five Hamilton siblings, Harry is quiet and hidden, 'a family listener and watcher' (29) who is the holder of secrets. One of her secrets is that she is 'a writer' (13); another is her knowledge of the skeleton in the family closet which she never intends to reveal. Overshadowed and mocked by her dynamic and beautiful elder sister Christobel, in emergent womanhood Harry seeks recognition of her own mysteriousness and wants to be seen as 'wonderful Ariadne' which is her real name (22).

Like Jane, Catherine, and Laura, Harry has a mirror experience which initially reveals her supernatural qualities to her. Looking into the mirror in her little attic room she catches 'the trace of a vanishing expression that surprised her, as if, only a moment earlier, she had not been a fugitive, but an enchantress' (15). Later the same day, through a complex combination of the fiction she is writing, her own reflection, and belief in a 'possible ghost', Harry operates as a conduit for the apparition of a male supernatural figure. Sliding into the sea through her own reflection in the water, she explores an underwater cave with her hand, but is terrified when she feels as if her hand has been severed, then feels a 'chilly hand' holding hers (25). Surfacing frightens her further when she sees a man sitting on her rock: 'he was not con-tinuous, only an intermittent presence trying to make a place for himself in the world' (27). Her fear escalates when she recognizes him as the dead Teddy Carnival, the 'possible ghost' of Carnival's Hide, the house where the Hamiltons and their guests stay at Christmastime. The following morning she is frightened again when she is sole witness to the materialization of three men on the beach who she senses have 'crawled out of a wrong gap in the world ... they had struggled through holding on to the silken clew of her own story' (53). They are a triple, aberrant manifestation of the ghost of Teddy Carnival.

The mysterious nature and conjuring tricks of these ghostly brothers, the tricksters of the novel's title, together with their claims to be descendants of the Carnivals lead to their acceptance by the family. Harry knows, however, that they are dangerous – as men and as ghosts: 'everything about [the] fair-headed man suggested menace to Harry' (54) and 'the dark brothers ... ma[ke] [her] skin creep with fear' (64). Representing respectively rationality, love, and lust, the triplets Ovid, Felix, and Hadfield, struggle among themselves for dominance. That they physically resemble characters in the story she has been writing heightens Harry's fear of them.

In becoming a woman, Harry has to overcome her fear of the Carnival brothers and grow beyond reliance on familial protection. Initially she oscillates between the adult desires revealed in both her writing and her attraction to Felix and her desire to remain a child: '[s]omewhere, waiting to be found again ... was an old, innocent self, sexless as a tennis racquet ... [But it] was gone forever, and something else was trying to replace it' (88–9). That Felix-love and Hadfield-lust are '"mirror-image identicals"' (70) is dangerous for Harry and reflects her confusion over what is trying to replace her 'sexless' childhood, a confusion also revealed by her creation of the brothers' fictional coun-terpart, the seducer-by-force and 'enemy-lover' Belen (95). As she enters into her own supernatural powers, however, Harry vanquishes each of the brothers in turn.

She conquers Hadfield's predatory powers physically. Accosted at night on the beach by a trickster who says he is Felix and who touches her breast and will not let her go, Harry is terrified. 'She did not like the feeling she was accessible, whereas, holding her from behind, he remained secret and powerful ... His touch was not an accident, but an assault' (98). She fights him off, giving him the 'notable black eye' (108) which the following day reveals to her that Hadfield, whose '"heart is not in the right place"' (70), rather than Felix was her attacker. Now realizing that it would not be 'exciting to have choice taken away from her' (106), she crosses out the words in her book describing Belen sexually overpowering her heroine Jessica. Hadfield is unrepentant about his attack, but Harry's own strength has destroyed his supernatural power over her and he does not tangle so directly with her again.

Harry overcomes her fear of Felix in the same way in which Jane Eyre conquers her apprehensions of Rochester and Laura Chant conquers her apprehensions about Sorry: through the power of love and through the realization that she also frightens and has supernatural powers over her lover. She is attracted to, but initially wary of, Felix who she senses is 'like a wolf playing at being a pet' (87), but soon tells him: '"I'm not scared of you ... I wrote you and I can probably rewrite you, or even cross you out if I have to"' (125). He challenges her invention of him, however, claiming his own existence: '"I mightn't be completely real, but I'm real enough"' (126). Like Harry, he wants to gain power over dominant siblings.

As their relationship blossoms both Harry and Felix do gain power. Felix, through his love for Harry, gains dominance within the brotherhood and Harry develops a sense of herself as a woman. Looking in her mirror she suddenly feels 'certain she [is] beautiful ... like an enchantress' (172). At the moment she notices this new magical self, however, the third male supernatural threat, Ovid, appears ominously behind her. Ovid is dangerous to Harry because he goes for the 'weak place in her life' (175), tempting her with ideas of gaining power over Christobel. Yet she is entering increasingly assuredly into her own magical powers. She resists Ovid's attempts to persuade her to give up Felix and rebuffs all his threats. When he tells her that she is '"not so very pretty"' (173), she confidently responds: '"I can *seem* beautiful"' ... and [sees] his expression change as if he suddenly recognized something unexpectedly formidable in her' (174). When he threatens to use her to destroy her family, she tells him firmly '"[w]e're not yours to destroy"' (177). After her encounter with Ovid she feels 'an excitement she had never felt before. It was to do with becoming powerful for the first time in her life' (178).

Harry's final defeat of Ovid coincides with her becoming an apparition to her family and revealing her mysterious self to them. 'It was no
longer enough to be Ariadne alone up in her room. Revealed to Felix,
recognized by Ovid, she now wanted everyone in her family to know
her, too' (188). Her Christmas Eve fancy dress costume is to be her
'true, astonishing self, inventor of beautiful winged demons, conqueror
of the ravishing Hadfield, adversary of Ovid – the very girl who had
tempted Felix under the furious blade of the lightning' (188). After the
party she and Felix make love, but Harry cannot 'recognize ordinary
happiness in her feelings, unless an achieved mystery at the heart of
her life should turn out to be happiness after all. A profound secret had
begun to yield to her' (221). It is the secret of her womanhood and of
her own mysteriousness.

'Secrecy', as John Daniel Stahl suggests, 'is often the child's method
of declaring and developing his or her individuality and independence'
(39). Discussing Louise Fitzhugh's *Harriet the Spy* (1964), he suggests
that '[s]ecrecy, especially the privacy of her notebooks, is important to
[Harriet] because she needs the opportunity of judging without
shaping her responses to the expectations of others, adults, and peers'
(40). In a similar way, Harry, the writer of a secret romance in which
she experiments with love and passion in ways she soon sees do not
match up with reality, has not only kept her imaginative work secret,
but has also kept the secret at the heart of her family. She is now forced
into revelation of her first secret by Ovid's subterfuge and provoked
into revelation of the family secret in retaliation for Christobel's
mockery of her writing and as a statement of her own identity.

Walking in upon Christobel entertaining the family and their
guests by reading aloud from '"a remarkably dreadful book, written
by someone who's devoted their life to good works and square-
dancing at the YMCA and is secretly longing to be raped by a winged
stallion"' (227), Harry is mortified to realize that the book is hers. As
she hears their taunting jibes, she knows that Ovid and Hadfield
have set this situation up. She is forced into revealing that she
wrote the book. '"Harry the Silent"' (71) speaks out, becoming an
apparition before her family and demanding that they recognize her
own special powers:

> Even without a mirror before her, she knew she was wearing her
> enchantress face. She could see it, as if she had caught fire and was
> reflecting a hot light on all the other family faces turned towards
> her ...

'You don't know anything about me!' she cried, speaking through Christobel to all of them. (230)

Harry is driven to reveal her second secret, devastating Christobel who learns for the first time that their own father, Jack, is the father of her friend Emma's two-year old daughter. Although as Harry speaks 'she s[ees] Ovid, beaming and nodding at her, and kn[owing] she had done what he had intended all along' (230), she also knows 'that she had always wanted to be the one to tell Christobel this secret, and now it was told' (230). She has conquered Christobel's power over her and at the same time finally overcomes the Carnival ghosts. Her powerful and mysterious womanhood allows Felix to achieve final dominance among the brothers through the love it inspires in him, which means that Ovid can threaten no longer. Felix dissolves, 'white as death, but *triumphant* death' and with his brothers he vanishes (234).

Harry has earlier imagined a '"book [that] would make something happen in the outside world by the power of its stories"' (63–4). Her own book has done this in two ways: it has enabled the apparition of the Carnival triplets, the conquering of whom has revealed her own powers, and it has provoked the declaration of both her secrets to her family, forcing a recognition from them of her own mysterious nature. After the emotional storm that erupts dies down slightly as family members go off to deal with the night's revelations in their own ways, Harry walks down to the beach where she burns her book. Through the bonfire she sees the now integrated and non-threatening ghost of Teddy Carnival who then disappears. She wonders 'if she herself was replacing Teddy as the ghost of the house and half hoped she was' (242).

Her new mysteriousness entrenches itself within her when, on New Year's Day, Harry finds a shell ring on the sand which she puts on, repeating the invocation she has used at the beginning of the novel: '"I've married the sea. I'm Mrs Oceanus. Everything comes out of me"' (263). As she does so 'something indescribable happen[s] … The world shift[s] mysteriously'; she feels filled with light and fire, unified with the elements and complete in herself (263). Her new sense of her self as a woman also enables her to begin writing again. As Roberta Seelinger Trites points out, '[a]lthough for a time she rejects her own writing because she is so scared of this power, by the end of the narrative she reclaims her subject position as a writer' (45). Harry knows that, like her womanhood, her new book has '"the possibility of everything in it"' (*Tricksters*, 265) and she embraces its mysterious potential positively and without fear.

The four female characters discussed here follow a pattern which is prevalent in women's supernatural fictions for children and young adults. Jane Eyre, Catherine Linton, Laura Chant, and Harry Hamilton all enter into the mysteries of womanhood as they simultaneously become aware of their own supernatural powers. They each move from a girlhood in which the supernatural causes them apprehension, in the sense of fear and anxiety, to a womanhood in which the supernatural is apprehended, in the sense of being understood. They each move from seeing apparitions to being apparitions. In doing so they move beyond their fears of the unrecognized future selves they see in 'mirror visions' and succeed in controlling or destroying the powers of male supernatural figures. They each enter into a self-identity in womanhood that is powerful, mysterious, and recognized by others.

The pattern followed is the same in all of the novels examined here, but the parameters of 'recognition by others' differ when we compare the Brontës' Victorian novels with Mahy's late twentieth-century texts. Jane Eyre's and Catherine Linton's supernatural powers, having been revealed, become invisible, or nearly so, in the concluding pages of the novels in which they appear. Although their supernatural powers clearly exist, they are at least partially 'entrapped' by becoming invisible, secret, and unseen rather than evident. Mahy's novels, on the other hand, reflect Paul's claims about 'transcendence in the young adult fiction of the 1980s' (196).

For Laura and Harry 'transcendence' is achieved. Although Laura ends in a romantic relationship with Sorry, their impending separation indicates her independence and freedom to change. Riding to Carmody Braque's house on the back of Sorry's Vespa she has held her arms out wide claiming '"[s]omeday I'll fly"' (157). In conquering Braque she has metaphorically flown and the novel leaves no doubt that by its end she is capable of literally flying if she chooses to. In *The Tricksters* Harry ends alone and powerful; naked in the sea she feels herself delicately 'possessed by the brute blood of the air' (263) and mysteriously 'filled with light' (263). The light that fills her is radiant light but also implies the lightness necessary for flight. While Laura and Harry preserve to themselves some special private moments in which they experience and use their supernatural powers, Mahy's texts insist, too, that their magic must be made visible. At the conclusions to the novels in which they appear their powerful new identities are made manifest to those around them as well as to readers. They will neither be objectified nor made invisible in their new form as women. Their powers are not entrapped but transcendent. In other words, contemporary emergent women characters like Laura and Harry have gained the power to fly while men – or any other beings – *are* watching.

Works cited

Berkin, Adam. '"I Woke Myself": *The Changeover* as a Modern Adaptation of "Sleeping Beauty"' *Children's Literature in Education*, 21 (4) [79] (1990): 245–51.

Brontë, Charlotte. *Jane Eyre* [1847], ed. Margaret Smith, The World's Classics. Oxford: Oxford University Press, 1988.

Brontë, Emily. *Wuthering Heights* [1847], ed. Ian Jack, intro. Patsy Stoneman, The World's Classics. Oxford: Oxford University Press, 1995.

Carpenter, Lynette and Wendy K. Kolmar. 'Introduction', in Lynette Carpenter and Wendy K. Kolmar (eds), *Haunting the House of Fiction: Feminist Perspectives on Ghost Stories by American Women*. Knoxville, TN: University of Tennessee Press, 1991, pp. 1–25.

Dickerson, Vanessa D. *Victorian Ghosts in the Noontide: Women Writers and the Supernatural*. Columbia, MO: University of Missouri Press, 1996.

Egoff, Sheila and Wendy Sutton. 'Epilogue: Some Thoughts on Connecting' in Sheila Egoff et al. (eds), *Only Connect: Readings on Children's Literature*, 3rd edn. Toronto: Oxford University, Press, 1996, pp. 377–94.

Egoff, Sheila, Gordon Stubbs, Ralph Ashley and Wendy Sutton (eds), *Only Connect: Readings on Children's Literature*, 3rd edn. Toronto: Oxford University Press, 1996.

Ellis, Sarah. 'Innocence and Experience in the Young Adult Romance', in Sheila Egoff et al. (eds), *Only Connect: Readings on Children's Literature*, 3rd edn. Toronto: Oxford University Press, 1996, pp. 304–14.

Gibbons, Joan. 'Family Relationships in the Stories of Margaret Mahy', *Papers*, 5 (1) (1994): 11–27.

Gilbert, Sandra M. and Susan Gubar. *The Madwoman in the Attic: The Woman Writer and the Nineteenth-Century Literary Imagination* [1979]. New Haven, CT: Yale University Press, 1984.

Gose, Elliott. 'Fairy Tale and Myth in Mahy's *The Changeover* and *The Tricksters*', *Children's Literature Association Quarterly*, 16 (1) (1991): 6–11.

La Belle, Jenijoy. *Herself Beheld: The Literature of the Looking Glass*. Ithaca, NY: Cornell University Press, 1988.

Lawrence-Pietroni, Anna. '*The Tricksters, The Changeover*, and the Fluidity of Adolescent Literature', *Children's Literature Association Quarterly*, 21 (1) (1996): 34–9.

Mahy, Margaret. *The Changeover [: A Supernatural Romance]* [1984]. London: Puffin, 1995.

——. *The Tricksters* [1986]. London: Puffin, 1995.

Norton, Lucy. 'Seeing is Believing: Magical Realism and Visual Narrative in Margaret Mahy's *The Changeover*', *Bookbird*, 36 (2) (1998): 29–32.

Paul, Lissa. 'Enigma Variations: What Feminist Theory Knows About Children's Literature', *Signal*, 54 (1987): 186–202.

Raburn, Josephine. '*The Changeover*, a Fantasy of Opposites', *Children's Literature in Education*, 23 (1) [84] (1992): 27–38.

Spacks, Patricia Meyer. *The Female Imagination: A Literary and Psychological Investigation of Women's Writing* [1972]. London: George Allen & Unwin, 1976.

Stahl, John Daniel. 'The Imaginative Uses of Secrecy in Children's Literature', in Sheila Egoff et al. (eds), *Only Connect: Readings on Children's Literature*, 3rd edn. Toronto: Oxford University Press, 1996, pp. 39–47.

Trites, Roberta Seelinger. *Waking Sleeping Beauty: Feminist Voices in Children's Novels*. Iowa City: University of Iowa Press, 1997.

Tucker, Nicholas. 'Margaret Mahy's Fairy Tale Universe', *Books for Keeps*, 96 (1996): 8.

10
Possessed by the Beast: Subjectivity and Agency in *Pictures in the Dark* and *Foxspell*

Clare Bradford

Narratives which focus on human subjectivity frequently invoke metaphors of margins and of hybridity, which encode the mysterious processes whereby humans become active subjects, or are prevented from doing so. The margins between self and not-self, or between self and Other, are disclosed in a particularly dramatic way in narratives of bodily metamorphosis. Such narratives, whether comic or tragic, always hinge upon notions of subjectivity, since they feature humans who assume (or have imposed upon them) identities which depart from their habitual ways of being and of knowing. Such a shift of identity may be from one human to another, as occurs in the transition from Dr Jekyll to Mr Hyde, or from human to animal, as in Apuleius's *The Golden Ass*. Or it may involve a transformation from human to magical or monstrous creature, as Franz Kafka's Gregor Samsa, in *Metamorphosis*, changes into a monstrous cockroach, or from human to machine, as in Italo Calvino's *Cosmicomics*, or from human to inanimate object, as Lot's wife becomes a pillar of salt in the Book of Genesis. Fundamental to these narratives is the sense that human subjectivity is imbricated within various *schemata* involving the mysterious and especially the supernatural. For stories of transformation often carry mythical resonances; they draw upon ideas of the unconscious, and in contemporary texts they frequently intersect with features of poststructuralism and postmodernism, both of which resist the idea of fixed and stable meanings. In the novels I discuss, mystery is located in the shifting meanings which surround transformations from human to animal and from animal to human; in both, the mystery of metamorphosis discloses the mysteriousness of psychological and psychic processes in humans.

149

Two characteristics mark narratives of metamorphosis: first, their effects are profoundly intertextual, since they cannot help but evoke other such narratives. Children's texts which involve metamorphoses are written to and for relatively inexperienced readers, whose prior experience of such narratives is generally haphazard and partial. Nevertheless, stories involving shape-changing are common in texts for children, ranging from folktales to literary narratives of transformation, from Diana Wynne Jones's fantasy novels to film and television reworkings of metamorphic narratives (including those involving werewolves). Jones's novels display a range of metamorphic narratives: for example, a boy becomes a wolf, and a girl and her mother become cats in *Black Maria* (1991); in *Dogsbody* (1975) the Dog Star Sirius, banished from his constellation, is born on earth as a dog; and in *Castle in the Air* (1990) bandits are turned into toads, a cat which periodically changes into a panther is transformed back into her original shape as a young woman; a djinn becomes a dog; and a demon is changed into a flying carpet, among other metamorphic moves. Children's stories involving bodily transformation produce meanings which inevitably relate to the intexts – a large and diverse set of narratives – which they recall.

Secondly, narratives of metamorphosis are always metaphorical, always located within the realm of the fantastic, so that the trope of bodily transformation stands for a range of meanings typically centred around identity, gender, and sociality. I draw here on the distinction, argued by John Stephens in *Language and Ideology in Children's Fiction*, between fantasy as a metaphoric mode and realism as a metonymic mode, which may employ metaphor but which works metonymically through representing aspects of story and discourse as part of larger signifying patterns (246–51).

My focus in this discussion is on the metamorphosis of human bodies into animals, and to illustrate how this trope encodes contemporary concerns about subjectivity and agency I examine two recent texts: Gillian Cross's *Pictures in the Dark* (1996) and Gillian Rubinstein's *Foxspell* (1994). In both novels, adolescent boys (Peter Luttrell in *Pictures in the Dark*, and Tod Crofton in *Foxspell*), are involved in metamorphic episodes; in both cases, the animals into which they are transformed (respectively otter and fox) belong to threatened and hunted species. Representations of animals in contemporary texts are inevitably shaped by twentieth-century ecological politics, and in both texts binary oppositions such as civilized–savage, human–animal, and good–evil are problematized by questions concerning human responsibility for environmental degradation and the extinction of animal species. While *Pictures in the Dark* is set in an English town, the events in *Foxspell* take place in the suburbs of an Australian city, and the settings for the novels' metamorphic episodes are inscribed with quite different ideologies: *Pictures in the Dark* draws on ideas of a dehumanizing and paranoid modernity, while the Australian setting of *Foxspell*, in which the fox is an introduced and now unwelcome species, evokes colonial and postcolonial meanings. The two authors are a contrasting pair: while Cross's work is located within British cultural contexts, Rubinstein, born in England but now living in Australia, thematizes the displacement of those who live in a country not theirs by birth.

The human bodies involved in literary metamorphoses enter a phase of dispossession or vacancy, and are no longer capable of encoding stable identities; more than this, a metamorphosis always involves the possibility that once transformed, the anterior body will fail to rematerialize, so that it may be permanently trapped in an identity other than its original or 'normal' form. The texts which I discuss feature adolescent characters and imply adolescent readers, for whom metamorphic changes are apt to symbolize both the physical changes of adolescence, and the cognitive and psychological processes involved in the development of individual identity and autonomy.

The mythic resonances of metamorphoses, and their capacity to produce significances by erupting into 'real' landscapes and social formations, mean that narratives of transformation have much in common with allegory. Specifically, they share with allegory what Walter Benjamin describes as 'the movement from history to nature' (182), since time is transformed at the moment of metamorphosis into timelessness, and history is converted into a *schema* within which events and individuals are attributed archetypal meanings. Just as allegory 'at one stroke ... transforms things and works into stirring writing' (Benjamin 176), so metamorphosis and textuality are interdependent; as Bruce Clarke notes:

> metamorphosis in literature may be read as an allegory of writing and its effects – reading, (mis)interpretation, figuration, intertextual transmission, and so forth. The metamorphic changes represented within texts are allegories of the metamorphic changes *of* texts. (2)

In *Pictures in the Dark* and *Foxspell*, textuality is both the ground within which transformation occurs and the marker of shifting subjectivities. In *Pictures in the Dark*, Peter finds a place of refuge in the school library, where he hides in the Encyclopaedia section, behind a 'wall of books' (43) which encodes both his alienation and his desire to order his experience. When he prepares a map of the river system, his intimacy (as otter) with the smallest details of currents and riverbanks is dangerously exposed, translated into signs which can be construed in the everyday human world. In *Foxspell*, Tod's incapacity to read books is contrasted with his ability, as fox, to read the signs of animals and humans, and it is when he adopts the language of animals (by making the sound of a young, hurt animal) that he takes the first step towards metamorphosis.

Children's books commonly thematize ideas about personal growth and development, frequently within a *schema* in which focalized characters move along a continuum in which they are depicted as manifesting progress – for example, from a state of self-centredness to one which recognizes the emotional and psychological needs of others; or from relative ignorance about cultural and social factors to a more informed position; or, in a more general sense, from childhood towards adulthood. The catalyst for such movement is generally an event or series of events in which a character is tested by the necessity of making choices or decisions. *Pictures in the Dark* and *Foxspell* enact similar kinds of psychological and emotional change, but they do so in a particularly dramatic way, in that when characters such as Peter and Tod undergo metamorphic episodes, they assume subjectivities previously perceived as Other. These moments of transformation may hover between the uncanny and the marvellous (to use Tzvetan Todorov's terminology), but they are always mysterious, because they encode unstable subjectivities and resist commonsense explanations, evading any final solution or closure which might undercut the mystery at the heart of their narratives. Notions of agency are likewise shifting and ambiguous in both novels, since neither Peter nor Tod is entirely capable of controlling his transformation from or to a human form. Familiar Western epistemologies such as those concerning human development and the separation of human from animal are thus destabilized and made strange.

Gillian Cross's novel *Wolf* (1990) deconstructs those ancient stories in which wolves are cast as villains, predators of women and girls, threatening shapes lurking at the edges of human settlement, and maps the Red Riding Hood narrative onto a web of political and social formations. No 'real' transformation occurs, but the *idea* of the metamorphosis of man into wolf, present in the landscapes of Cassie's dreams, is used metaphorically to display the unsettling gaps between appearance and 'reality', between the various and different

subject-positions which individuals adopt, and Cassie's desire for stability. *Pictures in the Dark* shifts the trope of metamorphosis into the
mode of fantasy, but Peter's transformation from boy to otter is mediated for readers through the focalizing view of Charlie Willcox, an
observer-interpreter whose progress from disbelief to horrified belief
serves to disclose the meanings of Peter's metamorphosis.

Charlie's interest in photography invests him with a specular function, in a novel shot through with visual images; the story of Peter's
transformation begins when Charlie takes a photograph which turns
out to be 'the strangest ... of his life' (1), for its view of the river from
the Old Bridge includes a pattern of ripples caused by a swimming
animal which Charlie identifies as an otter, an animal long extinct in
the area, and rarely seen in other parts of the country. Charlie's role as
observer extends to the school setting within which much of the
action occurs: he is present, for example, during an early episode in the
school grounds, when Peter Luttrell is accused of looking at a girl in a
way which causes her to fall from a high wall. While Charlie resists the
impulse to accept the view of Peter held by his school-friends and by
his cousin Zoë, he also notes the otherness of Peter's behaviour and
appearance: his pale eyes, 'like water over pebbles', and the 'strange,
obstinate look' (7) on his face. These contradictory responses construct
a reading position aligned with Charlie's view of the events of the narrative – one both sceptical of majority opinion, and open to the possibility of events outside the 'normal'. As Charlie realizes that his reading
of events cannot be accommodated simply through recourse to rationality, the reader is positioned to acquiesce with those moments in
the text which modulate into the mysterious and the supernatural.
This strategy promotes a reading position similarly open to the possibility of mystery.

Two family groupings are opposed in *Pictures in the Dark*: Charlie's
parents, his aunt and uncle, and cousins Zoë and Rachel, constitute a
cohesive, energetic, jokey group, set against the Luttrell household,
where Peter's paranoid father enforces a regime characterized by an
obsessive regard for neatness and order. But Cross does not deal in
facile oppositions; Charlie's cousin Zoë is a leader in the victimization
of Peter Luttrell, whom she believes to be a witch, so that Charlie is
torn between family loyalties and his disgust at the intolerance of difference which lies beneath Zoë's behaviour. On Charlie's first visit to
the Luttrells, his view of the family's back garden displays a contrast
which works as a metaphor for the conflict between Peter and his
father: '[t]he whole careful, ultra-tidy view was completely ruined by

the river that sprawled behind the wall, making a joke of the Luttrells' garden' (21). For Peter's alignment with the wildness of the river and its surrounds evades the rules and prohibitions by which his father seeks to impose order upon aspects of his life which are disordered. These include the strange animal which invades the Luttrell garden, Peter's failure to observe his father's rules and the dementia suffered by Mr Luttrell's mother. When Peter is punished by being locked at night in the garden shed, his metamorphosis into an otter offers him the freedom of the river and the mobility of a wild animal.

Jacques Lacan's work on the unconscious and subjectivity is particularly useful as a way of understanding how *Pictures in the Dark* construes metamorphosis. For Lacan, the unconscious constitutes the realm lying between the two domains of the subject and the Other, and is always present as an 'active break' (839) at the point where subjectivity is constructed through the symbolic (that is, through language). Further, the subject employs the pronoun 'I' in order, as Paul Smith explains, to create 'its own pretence or its own illusion that it has no effective unconscious – a disavowal which subvents the ability to act and speak at all' (76). But Peter Luttrell is unable to 'act and speak' through signs which are capable of being recognized and understood within the signifying system of school or family. The process which Lacan calls 'suture' (the subject's strategy of constructing an 'I' which fills the gap between the subject and the endless chain of signifiers which constitutes discourse) is thus disrupted, so that Peter's unconscious materializes in the form of a wild animal. The symbolic register of language is, as I have noted, the ground within which metamorphosis occurs; Peter's lack of words and his desire to be freed from his father's prohibitions find their expression through a bodily transformation in which the otter signifies a compensatory freedom and plenitude. On the other side of the divide, Zoë and her friends have recourse to discourses of superstition and intolerance, accusing Peter of possessing 'the evil eye'. Their mobilization of these discourses represents their confusion in the face of Peter's rejection of the 'normal' and everyday terms in which they construe their world.

The paranoia suffered by Peter's father is also explicable within a psychoanalytical framework, since he projects onto external phenomena those features which he most fears in himself. Thus, his anger and fear are projected onto the disorderly animal which enters his pristine, ordered garden; when his paranoia reaches its peak, he uproots shrubs, digs up the grass in his garden and replaces plants with concrete, nailing boards across the gate to prevent the otter from entering his property and placing a net where he knows the animal enters the river.

The climax of the narrative occurs when Zoë and her friend carry out a test which, they believe, will demonstrate that Peter is a witch: they gag and bind him, and throw him into the river to see if he will float. When Peter 'escapes' into his otter form, he is caught in the trap which his father has set, and is saved from drowning only by the efforts of Charlie, who at the cost of being bitten by the otter frees it, sustaining the savage blow which Mr Luttrell aims at the animal. Meanwhile, Peter's body has been dragged from the water by Zoë, who redeems herself by attempting to resuscitate him. The moment at which Peter 'comes back' is when his father looks at him and does not turn away, 'even when the tears started rolling down his face, streaking his smooth-shaved cheeks and seeping into his immaculate, snow-white collar' (194). This recuperation of father–son communication symbolizes the possibility of suture, as Peter enters the symbolic system, stretching out his hand to his father, and his 'recovery' is encoded through Charlie's recognition that Peter's metamorphic episodes are over:

> [Charlie's hand] was swelling, and beginning to bleed again. 'I got bitten by an otter.'
> 'Don't be silly,' Zoë said. 'There aren't any otters in this river.'
> Charlie didn't bother to argue. It didn't matter now. He didn't think he would ever see the otter again. (195)

Such dual reintegration (of Peter's subjectivity and of the intersubjective relationship of father and son) seems to resolve too suddenly in *Pictures in the Dark*, as though the mystery of the narrative's metamorphic episodes, which subvert rationality and the laws of the physical world, evades the novel's closure. This sense of disjunction derives from tensions particular to narratives of metamorphosis: they hover between two timescales (that of the 'real world' in which characters and events occur, and of the mysterious moment outside time when metamorphosis occurs), and between two models of spatiality – the realistic settings in which characters and events are located, and the mythic significances with which these settings are inscribed.

A set of contradictory signifiers is deployed to depict the physical and social worlds of the novel. Thus, the gradual disappearance of otters from the river clearly relates to the degradation of the animal's habitat over generations of human activity, and details such as the 'mess of cans and carrier bags' (21) snagged on the willows make their own environmental comments. On the other hand, Charlie's photographic sequence displays the robust ecological world of the river, 'rich with all kinds of life, from the tiny water-boatmen skimming over the surface to the tall, stooped heron in the reeds' (197). Charlie's capacity to 'see' through his camera is, ironically, informed by Peter Luttrell's knowledge of the river, so that Peter's metamorphosis (itself a signifier of inarticulacy) enlarges Charlie's vision. While the figure of the endangered otter seems to encode a muted nostalgia for a pre-industrial England in which otters used to swim in rivers, the contemporary river of Charlie's photographs is by no means a wasteland. The obvious intertext here is Philippa Pearce's *Tom's Midnight Garden* (1958), in which the river is a central signifier, evoking the passage of time; Hatty's progress from child to woman; the mysterious connection between Tom and Hatty. Pearce's river, unlike that in *Pictures in the Dark*, encodes nostalgia for a pre-industrial English landscape, through the comparison between the polluted and unhealthy waterway of Tom's time, and the river of Hatty's period, which 'flowed beside meadows' and abounded in fish, geese and waterfowl (162).

The river of *Pictures in the Dark*, in contrast, encodes a tempered optimism concerning the survival of the otter and of the river itself as a viable ecological system. And Charlie's enlarged view of the river discloses his ability to see what others do not, and to care about the survival of otters: 'maybe, some day, [Charlie] would see another otter, swimming free and strange in the bright river' (197). A similar kind of complex representation is present in the construction of family relationships in the novel. Peter's transformation into the otter has its roots in the dysfunctionality of his family, and specifically in his father's paranoia, both of which relate to contemporary concerns about the depersonalization and isolation of individuals and groups lacking the support of familial and social networks. At the same time the example of Zoë, who belongs to a cohesive, tolerant, and supportive family, suggests that individuals' ideologies cannot be explained simply in relation to familial values.

Cross's construction of shifting and uncertain ideological and epistemological frameworks extends to questions of agency in *Pictures in the Dark*. Peter is, in one sense, the victim of his father's obsessions (especially when he is barred from his home and forced to sleep, like an animal, in the shed), but his transformation to otter represents his resistance to his father and to the children who victimize him. Moreover, his possession of knowledge of the secrets of the river is deeply pleasurable; when he shows Charlie the tracery of snow on tree roots, he does so with the pride of ownership:

'Hey!' Charlie said. 'That's brilliant!'
Peter laughed suddenly. A high, surprising sound in the cold air.
'I knew you'd like it.' (102)

When he finally 'returns' to his human body, he does so through an act of will, responding to his father's mute appeal. Agency in Peter is thus not a simple or coherent expression of his subjectivity, but shifts between resistance and submission to external demands.

Like Peter Luttrell, Tod Crofton, in *Foxspell*, is caught within a family setting marked by conflict and uncertainty, but many of the tensions which simmer in his family relate to those effects of displacement and homelessness which surround migrant experience. Gillian Rubinstein, who migrated to Australia from England over twenty years ago, has written about her own sense of having 'lost a sense of place' ('Unlucky', 171), of being located as a writer somewhere between the English landscapes of her childhood memories and the Australian landscape in which she writes; in this respect, Tod's transformation into a fox constitutes a highly ambivalent metaphor, since foxes, a species introduced to Australia from England, are now regarded as pests because of their destruction of native Australian animals.

At the beginning of *Foxspell* Tod is himself displaced, having travelled from Sydney to Adelaide with his mother and two sisters to live with his maternal grandmother following his father's decision to return to his home in England. The departure of his father has plunged Tod into a female world in which he is as powerless as his grandmother's drake, 'the only other male around', who 'let himself be bossed about by an old chook called May' (8). This metaphorical representation of Tod as 'henpecked' relates to a broader set of ideologies within the novel, in which female characters (especially Tod's mother and grandmother) are depicted as tough and resilient, male characters as inept and insecure. Like Peter Luttrell, Tod is unable to access a symbolic system through which to construct his subjectivity; he cannot read and can barely write, and his metamorphosis, like Peter's, can be read in psychoanalytical terms, as a metaphor for the inarticulate 'I' of his everyday life. Thus, both texts dramatize contemporary anxieties about boys whose language development lags behind that of girls, as well as about boys and men who are unable to express their feelings: Mr Luttrell 'can't share things. He keeps it all shut inside' (*Pictures*,

144), and Tod's father sends (literally) mixed messages about returning to his family. But Rubinstein's treatment of metamorphosis also carries an anti-feminist edge, for Tod's mother Leonie, a stand-up comic, exploits his obsession with foxes to obtain material for her comedy routine: 'She had stood up in front of dozens of strangers and made jokes about foxes and sex and puberty, and hearing him howl at the moon like a werewolf, and having to feed him raw meat' (*Foxspell*, 161). When Tod, transformed into a fox, kills and devours his grandmother's hens, his motivation is, in part, anger at Leonie's act of appropriating his fantasy, so that the gender politics of this text come perilously close to a representation of the feminine (and specifically the maternal) as a devouring and emasculating force.

While Peter Luttrell's metamorphosis represents a rejection of his father's prohibitions, Tod's transformation into a fox involves his search for a father to replace his own, who has returned to England because of his homesickness for the landscape of his childhood. After Tod discovers a young, dead fox which has been shot and strung up on a wire fence, his act of burying the animal brings him to the attention of the old fox, Dan Russell, which lives in the quarry near his grandmother's house. Dan Russell is, in fact, an uncanny mixture of fox, spirit, and man, and in his fox form he initiates Tod into the moment of metamorphosis:

> The wild feeling leaped again, leaped right through with nothing blocking it. It flowed through Tod ... and he felt his body turn and change, but not strangely. His new body was familiar to him from his dreams, and he felt as much at home in it as in his old one. He ran his pointy red tongue round his sharp teeth, and swished his white-tipped brush, licked his neat paws a few times and grinned at the big fox standing next to him. (*Foxspell*, 118)

Dan Russell's name derives from the following line in Geoffrey Chaucer's 'The Nun's Priest's Tale': 'And daun Russell the fox stirte up atones.' A similar reference to Old World names deployed in a New World setting is suggested by Tod's name. Having discovered Beatrix Potter's *The Tale of Mr Tod* in the school library, Tod asks whether he has been named 'after a book' (*Foxspell*, 50), whereupon his mother tells him that he was in fact named after the Todd River in Alice Springs, where he was conceived, but that his father spelled the name of the river incorrectly on the registration form. The name Tod is, as his mother tells him, 'an old word for fox' (51), but it also carries associations with *death*, its meaning in German. Through this mingling of Old World and New World names, Rubinstein encodes Tod's indeterminate identity, between fox and boy and between English and Australian cultures, as well as his father's incapacity to *know* Australia (signified through his misspelling of 'Tod'). As well, the link of 'Tod' with 'death' confers weight on the name and prefigures the book's ending.

Whereas Peter's metamorphoses in *Pictures in the Dark* are displayed through the focalizing view of Charlie (who never observes the moment of transformation), Tod is the focalizer for his own metamorphosis, and through this textual strategy Rubinstein constructs for him a subjectivity split between fox and boy. This strategy provides for a comparison, as it were, from within – between opposing epistemologies. Thus, as a boy, Tod views foxes in relation to the distinction between native and introduced species, and values native animals more highly; as fox, however, he knows only that small marsupials constitute a source of food. In Michel Foucault's terms, subjectivity is produced through the discursive systems which shape an individual's experience and knowledge of the world; Tod's metamorphic state thus represents a clash of discourses, articulated in Tod's awareness of the chasm between his two selves:

> [Tod] realised he knew absolutely nothing about anything. He wanted to learn, but he was beginning to feel frightened. Dan Russell didn't think like a person at all. Tod remembered that when he had been a fox everything Dan Russell had communicated had been true, and he'd obeyed him immediately. It was only being human again that made him doubtful and scared. (*Foxspell*, 123)

Tod's sense of a subjectivity split between opposing frameworks of knowledge and conflicting ideologies, and his experience of displacement, enact a dilemma explicable in postcolonial terms. Tod's father has been unable to sustain his sense of self within an Australian landscape which is alien to him: '[s]ometimes [Tod's father] hit himself on the chest and said he had a huge hollow space inside him which was homesickness for the landscape he grew up in' (19). When he is transformed into a young fox, Tod finds a surrogate father in Dan Russell, who recalls for Tod the experience of the foxes transported in cages on ships sailing from England to Australia to provide hunting for English settlers. These two father-figures exemplify contrasting reactions to the experience of displacement: Tod's father retreats to the landscape of his childhood, so rejecting his Australian family and the otherness of Australia itself. Dan Russell, on the other hand, represents what is described, in *The Empire Writes Back*, as *'cultural denigration*, the conscious and unconscious oppression of the indigenous personality and culture by a supposedly superior racial or cultural model' (Ashcroft, Griffiths, and Tiffin 9); the foxes' destruction of the small marsupials native to the area is construed by Dan Russell as the inevitable consequence of their superior strength and cunning. This contrast between Tod's two father-figures evokes the mystery of psychological and psychic connections between humans and the lands where they are 'at home', a mystery undercut by the pragmatism of Dan Russell's colonial solution.

Rubinstein's own awareness of the complexities of colonial and post-colonial displacement is evident in her reference to European plants, animals, and people now naturalized in Australia: '[i]t is impossible to deplore the existence of the fox or the cat, the olive or the ash, without deploring my own existence as a migrant' ('Unlucky', 170). But this very anxiety about legitimacy – about who has 'the right to be here' ('Unlucky', 170) – and its projection, in *Foxspell*, onto Tod's metamorphosis into a fox serves to erase the fundamental fact of colonization in Australia: that it involved the dispossession and death of indigenous people, widespread environmental degradation, and the extinction of many species of native animals. More than this, the metamorphic episodes in *Foxspell* deploy strategies common in colonial discourse, in that they seek to legitimize colonization by claiming for the newcomer a deep connection with the land which is equivalent to, and as powerful as, that which indigenous animals and people have with the places where they have lived for many thousands of years.

The most obvious expression of this claim for legitimacy is Rubinstein's mobilization of European mythologies, which she locates within the Australian landscape. Dan Russell's spirit self was summoned from his English home by the foxes transported to Australia: '"[m]y children call out to me from this strange land ... So I come ... Teach them to live here in this new land, look after them"' (121). Tod, troubled by the memory of the native animals threatened or rendered extinct, asks about the spirits native to the land: '"[d]on't the gum trees have a guardian? And the native animals? Didn't their guardians try and stop you moving in?"' (122). These questions, which appear to encode an evenhanded regard for animals and their spirit guardians, effect a slippage which proposes a universal system of spiritual beings in place of the highly specialized and local traditions of spirituality which characterize Australian indigenous traditions. In this global system, the struggle between native and introduced animals (and, by inference, between indigenous people and white settlers) enacts the survival of the fittest, since, as Dan Russell tells Tod, '"[t]heir guardians weak ... Guardian spirits faded and little animals disappeared"' (122). The mobilization of references to a 'new' spirit world thus constitutes a powerful claim for authenticity by producing a homogenized system in which Yggdrasil and Athene (respectively, Scandinavian and Greek mythological figures) exist on the same plane as the spirits of the (introduced) rabbit and the (native) magpie.

The setting in which Tod's metamorphoses occur is a quarry, a site scarred by the activities of European settlers who have sought to extract bounty from the land and which has subsequently been claimed by the ash and oak, the fox and the feral cat. It is a landscape effectively colonized by newcomers to the land; it is also a space inscribed as masculine, for those who roam in it are Dan Russell, Tod, and the youths who shoot foxes and vandalize the council depot located in the rubbish dump which adjoins the quarry. In contrast, Tod's home (or, rather, his grandmother's home) is a feminine space, a location at once comforting and engulfing. Tod's movement from home to quarry signals the tensions between his desire for a masculine identity and the call of home and safety, but the version of masculinity proposed by the text is posited on a system in which the masculine is the normative, positive term, and the feminine its negative.

The fox and the quarry are so clearly marked with the signs of colonizing power that the novel's episodes of metamorphosis, and Tod's adoption of Dan Russell as his surrogate father, construct a subjectivity which colludes with the colonizers and affirms their right to transform the land. In this way, Tod's metamorphosing body symbolizes the landscape, whose features are erased, 'written over', and transformed into a space where its original inhabitants are disempowered and displaced. Throughout the novel, the principal narrative (that of Tod's metamorphic episodes) is interwoven with a subplot concerning Tod's relations with the gang of boys who frequent the quarry. At the end, Adrian, the young brother of one of the gang members, falls beneath a train and is killed, and in this moment the two narratives meet, for Dan Russell, witnessing Tod's anguish at the death, barks to Tod and 'wait[s] for his cub to look up and meet his gaze' (190). The indeterminacy of the novel's ending hinges upon a moment of choice outside the narrative, when Tod will either meet Dan Russell's gaze (and transform finally and forever into a fox) or return to the human world.

Peter Luttrell's decision to 'return to himself' is enacted when the boy reaches out to touch his father's hand, a gesture which constitutes Peter as a subject through his entry to the symbolic system. In *Foxspell*, Tod is offered the bleakest of choices: between human life without a father and within a smothering matriarchy, and existence as a fugitive and hunted animal. The 'strange sounds' made by Tod as he '[pants] in a heavy anguished way' are ambiguous, as though he is arrested in a state of hybridity, without recourse to the language of human or animal (190). In part, this hybridity reflects the ambivalence – 'neither here nor there' – of postcolonial experience; in part, it arises from the uneasy conflation, in *Foxspell*, of human with animal. Dan Russell, for example, is a fox-spirit who assumes the shape of a man but whose instincts and beliefs are all fox; Tod, in his metamorphic episodes, is aware of the ideological conflicts between fox and human, but is compelled to act as an animal. Questions of agency in *Foxspell* are thus subject to a greater degree of slippage than is the case in *Pictures in the Dark*, and to some degree this slippage derives from the postcolonial significances of the narrative.

Rubinstein's sympathy for the fox (like her, a newcomer to an ancient land) is palpable in *Foxspell*, and manifests itself in a set of implicit ideologies which contest the very idea of human agency. The conflation of human with animal suggests, for example, that just as the fox will always displace indigenous animals, so the displacement of colonized peoples is inevitable and lasting; the representation of indigenous animals as weak and powerless, with no strategies for their own survival, is strikingly similar to colonial representations of Aborigines. Human agency is subsumed within a deterministic *schema* in which the subject is construed as docile and pliant in the face of political and social structures – thus, the reader is positioned to view Tod as (almost literally) torn apart by the competing demands of his family and of Dan Russell.

The very fluidity of the metamorphic moment is itself a metaphor for the shifting and uncertain subjectivities which it encodes. For this reason, Rosemary Jackson's formulation of a contrast between metamorphic narratives which arise from 'strangeness within the self', the 'Frankenstein type of myth' (58), and those which arise from a source external to the self, the 'Dracula type of myth' (59), seems overly programmatic; certainly it does not ring true of the metamorphic narratives of the two novels I have considered. In *Pictures in the Dark*, the subjectivity of Peter Luttrell is both collusive and resistant, impelled by both external and interior forces; in *Foxspell*, Tod Crofton's metamorphosis from boy to fox more closely approximates Jackson's second model, but the indeterminacy of the book's closure leaves open questions about the balance between external and internal forces.

While the trope of metamorphosis is loaded with the echoes and memories of its manifestations in other texts, it is always susceptible to the particular inflections of the cultural contexts within which it is reworked, and in both *Pictures in the Dark* and *Foxspell* it constitutes a locus for treatments of subjectivity, agency, sociality, and masculinity. The principal significances of Peter's and Tod's metamorphic experiences (which of course evoke the bodily changes of adolescent boys) relate to the insertion of the self into social, cultural, and political structures. Both novels implicate paternal figures and cultural constructions of masculinity in conflicts which find their expression in metamorphic episodes, but these conflicts are played out within quite different ideological frameworks which can readily be seen in their respective deployments of the symbolism of the gaze, in episodes which occur at key moments of choice in both novels. Peter Luttrell, 'absent' from his body following the trauma of his father's attack, 'returns' when he responds to Mr Luttrell's gaze: 'Peter's eyes changed, and he blinked. With a great effort, as if he were coming out of some distant place, he focused on his father's face' (*Pictures*, 194–5). This reciprocal gaze encodes Mr Luttrell's acknowledgement of his son's identity, and Peter's preparedness to forgive his father; at the level of narrative closure, it symbolizes a difficult and uncertain project, that of a new form of interaction between father and son. In *Foxspell*, Dan Russell's gaze calls Tod to make a choice between human and animal, and between rationality and the mysterious. This choice implies two others, for Tod must also choose between the feminine world of home and the masculine environment of Dan Russell, and between the claims of colonized and colonizers. The closure of *Pictures in the Dark* promotes a view of the human subject which allows for what Paul Smith calls 'the *simultaneous* non-unity or non-consistency of subject-positions' (118), whereas in *Foxspell* the choice of one subject position is assumed to eliminate the possibility of all others. Thus, the trope of metamorphosis, true to the slippery and fluctuating significations which it encodes, carries out quite different kinds of ideological work in the two texts, and signifies contrasting models of subjectivity.

Works cited

Ashcroft, Bill, Gareth Griffiths, and Helen Tiffin. *The Empire Writes Back: Theory and Practice in Post-Colonial Literatures*. London and New York: Routledge, 1989.

Benjamin, Walter. *The Origin of German Tragic Drama*, trans. John Osborne. London: NLB, 1977.

Clarke, Bruce. *Allegories of Writing: The Subject of Metamorphosis*. Albany, NY: State University of New York Press, 1995.

Cross, Gillian. *Pictures in the Dark*. Oxford: Oxford University Press, 1996.

——. *Wolf*. Harmondsworth: Penguin, 1990.

Foucault, Michel. *The Archaeology of Knowledge*. London: Tavistock, 1972.

——. *Power/Knowledge: Selected Interviews*, ed. C. Gordon. Brighton: Harvester, 1980.

Jackson, Rosemary. *Fantasy: The Literature of Subversion*. London and New York: Methuen, 1981.

Lacan, Jacques. *Écrits*. Paris: Editions du Seuil, 1966.

Pearce, Philippa. *Tom's Midnight Garden*. Oxford: Oxford University Press, 1958.

Rubinstein, Gillian. *Foxspell*. Melbourne: Hyland House, 1994.

——. 'Unlucky the Writer who Belongs to Two Cultures', in Wendy Parsons and Robert Goodwin (eds), *Landscape and Identity: Perspectives from Australia*. Adelaide: Auslib Press, 1994, pp. 168–71.

Smith, Paul. *Discerning the Subject*. Minneapolis: University of Minnesota Press, 1988.

Stephens, John. *Language and Ideology in Children's Fiction*. London and New York: Longman, 1992.

Todorov, Tzvetan. *The Fantastic: A Structural Approach to a Literary Genre*, trans. Richard Howard. Ithaca, NY: Cornell University Press, 1975.

11

'There Are Worse Things Than Ghosts': Reworking Horror Chronotopes in Australian Children's Fiction

John Stephens and Robyn McCallum

The paranormal, mystery, the uncanny, magic, beings from other places or other dimensions (sometimes benevolent, but more often demonic), all have a powerful appeal to contemporary audiences for fiction and film. In adolescent fiction, the genres which feature the paranormal have been the ghost story, fantasy, and horror, although in the later twentieth century boundaries between these genres and between these and realist fiction became more fluid and narratives more hybridic. Perhaps this genric fluidity is consonant with the more fluid conceptions of subjectivity in the postmodern world, and becomes a vehicle for introducing versions of subjectivation uncharacteristic of adolescent fiction in general (see McCallum.)

A central concern in genres dealing with the paranormal is the irruption of the uncanny, a moment of apprehension which brings a frisson of fear, whether to represented characters or to readers, and is not susceptible to logical explication. The uncanny thus points to a mystery deeper than the transitory mystery of, say, a detective story, where we expect that eventually all or most puzzles will find resolution. Instead of celebrating the rationality of a primary puzzle solver, the uncanny confronts us with human limitation. Hence the intensity of the 'mystery' encountered is enhanced by our awareness that although a plot may resolve, the uncanny element which had driven it is resolved only temporarily; a reader's imagination assumes some subsequent irruption, perhaps in another form or another place. The immediate function of the uncanny is thus to disrupt our senses of everydayness and of what we think of as 'real' by implicating us in mental states posited on 'primitive' superstitions and irrational fears. A further

165

function, now of central importance in adolescent fictions, is to inter-rogate the meanings we make of our everyday lives – of who we are, and of how we signify in relation to the world we inhabit. Robyn Ferrell makes the important point that '[t]he uncanny must be fleeting, peripheral, threatened. It is a type of moment rather than a class of objects; an effect of a process of perceiving rather than of an image per-ceived' (132). Hence a mystery narrative which pivots on the uncanny prompts us to rethink the materiality of the world and the solidity of its customs. It invites us to look at familiar places and objects and to see them not as different but as signifying differently. Relationships between self and place become redefined.

The transformative effect of uncanny moments in adolescent litera-ture of the paranormal is a global phenomenon, just as the literature itself is radically intertextual because of the range and diversity of its origins and affiliations. It bears traces from the great English fantasists of the 1970s – Susan Cooper, Alan Garner, Penelope Lively, for example – and is shaped under the aegis of horror films from Hammer to Hollywood and of Gothic horror fiction from Mary Shelley to Stephen King and Christopher Pike. But, as Ferrell suggests, the uncanny is centrally concerned with signification despite its marginal-ity to our everyday experiencing of the world, and it functions, like margins more generally, to 'keep the central in its place' (132), so it becomes possible for the global, hybridized genre to express specific and localized relationships between self and place and thence to func-tion as a critique of culture. Such critique is not the most obvious thing about this kind of writing and is often present only as an implicit ideological effect. Nevertheless, we think it can be shown that whereas in general Australian children's fiction depicts selves as being given shape and significance by their embeddedness in place, recent hybridic genres involving the paranormal depict how, in postmodern culture, identity is apt to become fragmented by that very embeddedness. The irruption of the uncanny thus brings into the open the fissures within everyday lives.

The works discussed in this essay share an apprehension about the brittleness of social formations, disclosing this through the impact of the actual and presumed uncanny on members of a community. Narrative closure is characterized by tensions between the satisfac-tory resolution of story elements – explanations, rewards, and pun-ishments duly apportioned – and thematic irresolution that suggests outcomes are fleeting and temporary and explanations are makeshift and partial. In any case, readers are left with the image of a fragile society stretched across an abyss of uncertainty and fear, threatened by collapse.

A convenient introduction to contemporary mystery writing aimed at an Australian adolescent readership is Gary Crew's anthology *Dark House* (1995), a collection of original stories by twelve authors who were given the motif of the 'Dark House' as their subject. The dark house is a cliché in Gothic and horror fiction and film, but as a setting it always has a strong association with the paranormal and uncanny – Freud's *Unheimlich* – inasmuch as the dark house inexorably becomes 'unhomelike', defamiliarized even as it expresses its own clichéd motifs and structures. A catalyst for radical change emerges with some shift in the configuration of the setting, such as the protagonist arriving at the house for the first time, or a stranger entering the domestic circle, so that the elements of ordinariness, domesticity, sociality, and (often) inexplicit sexuality are displaced into macabre or perverted variants. Most of the stories in this collection incorporate a paranormal or uncanny component, though only a minority pivot on a character's *hesitation* between natural and supernatural explanations for an apparently uncanny event or experience, which, according to Tzvetan Todorov, generally marks the uncanny. For most of these stories we follow the argument of more recent commentators on the uncanny who have questioned Todorov's formulation and identify uncanny effects of other kinds. In particular, Mladen Dolar has proposed three kinds of uncanny effect which, in our view, are very pertinent to the *Dark House* stories (Dolar 21–3).

First, Dolar states that it is often assumed that supernatural postulates are intrinsically uncanny. Victor Kelleher's 'Aunt Maud's Bequest' turns on two supernatural, uncanny assumptions: that an invisible, vampiric spirit could inhabit a house and, draining the life from young men, transform them into paintings of themselves; and that the process is rendered inescapable because it is textually realized as, simultaneously, the reader reads the story and the victim reads the very same words mysteriously, inexplicably, inscribed in the book of his death. Second, Kelleher's metafictive turn here also points to Dolar's next construction of the uncanny, as a tension in audience response between knowledge and belief ('I know such things do not normally happen, but they terrify me'). By repeating earlier narrative segments in the embedded book, and bringing them closer together until they coincide at the moment of the character's death, Kelleher flaunts how readers may recognize that the uncanny is a product of representation and yet be implicated in an accession to its actuality. James Moloney's *doppelgänger* story, 'The Cat and the Crow', in which a child is haunted by the spirit of his separated and deceased Siamese twin, is a simpler example of this second type of the uncanny because it incorporates a possible explanation: the child is projecting his feelings of loss, grief and guilt about his dead brother, though readers are finally denied this as a realistic resolution of the supernatural uncanny.

Finally, Dolar proposes that the uncanny effect may lie in a tension between the certainty that something horrific will happen and the unconscious hope that it will be avoided. This effect may be experienced both by characters within the narrative and by readers of the narrative. An example is Peter Lawrance's 'All the King's Men', in which readers may hope for but not expect an outcome other than that presaged by the inexorable illogic of a psychopathic narrator. In contrast, Jenny Pausacker's 'The Princess in the Tower' illustrates how this third form of the uncanny is embodied within the psyche of a character. Here, a young girl imagines that her dead father comes to her room at night to tell her a fantasy story about a magic-working princess's encounters with evil. The information that the father is dead, and hence Ginny is conjuring the story from imagination and memory, is withheld until the final paragraphs. Each instalment of the princess-story is a negotiation, as Ginny strives to produce a story which combines exciting events, an empowered role for the princess, and a positive outcome, but her father maintains control by means of a narration which is variously melodramatic, patronizing and manipulative. As the story unfolds and the 'father's' version pushes the plot further towards the macabre and horrific, Pausacker engineers a complex psychological tension. The struggle within the embedded story marks a child's resistance to a horror narrative in which 'the vampires ... the ghosts ... the living dead' (39) triumph over the human protagonists. Implicitly, J. R. R. Tolkien's *The Lord of the Rings* is being rewritten, envisaging a final victory for Sauron, evoked here in a crowned shadow who leads the monsters and the undead and is the princess's father. What this further discloses is a classic example of Freud's definition of the uncanny – something familiar which has been estranged by a process of repression, the *unheimlich* secret shut up within the *heimlich* personal space of a room 'full of all the things I'd ever owned' (21). In short, it discloses a memory of incest which the child keeps repressed by substituting a different story outcome, and hence expresses the tension between the certainty that something horrific will happen (has happened and will be recalled) and the unconscious hope that it will be avoided:

'She recognised her father the king, who had taught her everything she knew. So how could the princess possibly hope to stand against him?'

My father leans even closer. His shadow looms up and falls across the bed and falls across me. His shadow is smothering me. I start to choke. (40)

Ginny dispels the shadows with a torch and her mother comes to comfort her:

My mother heard me choking and sobbing. She came straightaway. I was shivering and scared in the darkness, so I told her every detail of what had happened.

'Oh, Ginny,' she said, sounding as frightened as I was. 'Oh, Ginny, how long is this going to go on for. It's been two and a half years since your father died.' (40–1)

This is a moment of significant disclosure for readers, but not for the character herself, who as the story ends snuggles back down in the dark waiting for her father to arrive to tell her 'another story', vowing that she will not be 'scared and stupid' this time. The narrative is thus open-ended at the level both of story and of theme. Readers may be able to allay the uncanny moment by means of a realistic explanation, but this entails the conclusion that the character suffers from an unresolved psychotic delusion stemming from her previous subjection to abuse. For Ginny, who has a literal belief in her father's appearances, the experience remains uncanny because she sustains a misinterpretation. The agency she seeks but rarely gains in her dialogic storytellings is even less available in her life experience, where her repression of the past leaves her literally and figuratively subjected to the perverse, manipulative word of the father.

'The Princess in the Tower' is an excellent depiction of how the unconscious is inscribed on conscious life and how mystery fiction implies deeper significances by opposing the experiences of characters in the fiction to the effects perceived by readers. The story also makes strategic use of a third element in the signifying process, what Allan Lloyd Smith has defined as 'the conscious (that is, the explicit) and the unconscious (that is the concealed or silenced) knowledge of the larger historical/political culture' (287–8). Pausacker grounds the story in the everyday Melbourne life of shopping trips, weekend excursions, and relationships with siblings and peers, and Ginny's bedtime narration is woven from an international intertextual domain – 'fairy tales, Tolkien, Isobelle Carmody, Virginia Andrews' (23), unspecified horror films, and Dungeons-and-Dragons role-play games. This particular list seems to be a clue to the covert story of patriarchal control of power, child abuse, and incest. Instead of depicting the supernatural irrupting into the everyday, as is a common strategy in both horror and fantasy, and hence in hybrid forms such as Isobelle Carmody's *The Gathering*, 'The Princess in the Tower' textualizes the supernatural and suggests that the real horrors and monsters do not lie in some dimension behind or beyond the everyday, but inhere within 'homeliness'. The facade of the family home may conceal worse things than vampires, ghosts, or the living dead.

Having argued that the uncanny moment is prompted by a return of something repressed, Freud collapsed his argument back into the Oedipal story. Ferrell makes the important point that the Oedipal story is not a disclosure of how things are but an instrument of cultural imposition whereby women become alienated from subjectivity:

> The Oedipal story is one that a woman might look at, first in incredulous amusement and next in terror, when she sees that, despite this being some man's delusion, he has the power to impose it. That this shall become meaning. (142)

In capturing a narrative version of this insight in 'The Princess in the Tower', Pausacker has produced a story which resists any naive Freudian interpretation. As such, it is also a key point of resistance within the *Dark House* anthology in that the stories as a group demonstrate how pervasive as an unconscious cultural assumption is the conjunction of the uncanny and the 'castrating' female, perhaps mediated here by an implicit associational chain equating the house with the female. Be that as it may, eight of the twelve stories in *Dark House* (those by Garry Disher, Victor Kelleher, Gillian Rubinstein, Arnold Zable, Peter Lawrance, Marion Halligan, Isobelle Carmody, and Gary Crew) hinge on a (monstrous) female who seeks to destroy, devour, or otherwise symbolically castrate one or more of the male characters.

Lawrance's 'All the King's Men', in particular, reproduces the assumptions articulated in Freud's essay on the uncanny, blending these into horror fiction in a way rather reminiscent of Hitchcock's *Psycho*. The first person narrator, a professional detective, is involved in two apparently unrelated concerns: his girlfriend, Perri, has moved in with him, and he wishes to get her out of the house again; and he has been assigned to the investigation of a particularly nasty sex-related murder. The second story strand thus suggests that part of the mystery here will or could be addressed in detective story mode, and so move towards an outcome by the processes of sifting clues, establishing chronologies and cause-and-effect relationships, and identifying. This does not happen, however, and Lawrance attempts to generate indeterminacy and tension through unreliable narration, the indeterminability of the relationships among signs, clues and meaning, and open-endedness. He does not employ the supernatural uncanny, however, but instead the return of the repressed, overtly specified as the narrator's obsessive Oedipal attachment to the memory of his dead mother, produces a prowler story as he terrorizes his girlfriend and younger brother, Chester.

The story is often awkward and overstated, as in the rather heavy-handed invocation of the Oedipal story in the opening paragraph – 'I adjusted my tie; caressed the knot at my throat, the final touch to the seriousness of dressing. I occasionally thought of Mother at this point. Sometimes I caught a glimpse of her face, staring back at me through that mirror' (161) – but is nevertheless an interesting example of how genres become hybridized. The familiar story of the couple in the dark house stalked by a psychopathic prowler is reshaped by conventions pertinent to the detective story: the secondary strand involves a gruesome murder, a detective, and clues which suggest the murderer is a psychopath – the dead woman has been mutilated and dismembered and her limbs scattered, and she has been stabbed in the eyes. The narrator self-consciously draws attention to his detective-work in solving the story, and 'problem', of the girlfriend he no longer wants and who, in reaction to his hostility, has occupied his deceased mother's bedroom. However, his confidence in his own interpretation of events and motives and his self-assurance that '[a]fter all, [he] was a policeman, trained to see how actions and events were conceived' (165), signals a confusion of subjective experience with objective description and foregrounds the narrator's irrationality. The mystery is sustained beyond the close of the story because readers can never determine whether the threats and betrayals the narrator responds to are produced in the phenomenal world or are really inventions of his increasingly deranged mind.

The detail of the stabbed eyes takes the story back into the realm of the uncanny in that it recalls E. T. A. Hoffmann's famous story, 'The Sandman', which Freud took as his paradigmatic example of the uncanny. For Freud, the uncanny effect depends on castration, which he saw symbolized in the motif of blinding in Hoffmann's story, and hence it prevents the fulfilment of subjectivity. Lawrance emphasizes the same connection when his narrator contemplates the possibility of stabbing the eyes of his brother, whom he suspects of a liaison with Perri. It is also present in Perri's occupation as a dancer in a striptease club, although unlike the automaton Olympia of Hoffmann's story she does not merely perform femininity as an object of the male gaze but also articulates her own thoughts and desires.

The various genres drawn upon merge when the narrator/detective discloses that he too is a psychopath with a history of mental instability, who is fixated on his dead mother and appalled by female sexuality. The dismembered body he investigates becomes a projection of his own feeling of castration: the dead woman's hair has been 'removed from the head and arranged at the neck, at the point where the flesh had been severed' (169), reminding the narrator of his tie/penis, which he caresses as he looks at the severed head. Tony Magistrale and Michael A. Morrison point out that from the 1980s onwards the monster in American horror has become the sociopath, a killer 'seething on the inside, but one of us on the outside' (6). They go on to argue that the criminal sociopath establishes a closer affinity between audience and monster than happens when monsters are unlike human beings and indubitably Other. 'Even as he preys upon us, he externalizes our awareness of imminent societal collapse, the demise of values, the illusoriness of security, and our rage at being unable to change any of this' (Magistrale and Morrison 7). Lawrance takes this societal collapse a further step by conflating sociopath and detective, and so when he closes 'All the King's Men' with a confrontation of victims and monster reminiscent of a filmic freeze-frame he points to that sense of helplessness in a world of crumbling values:

> They heard the tap I made on the window. They looked at me, standing outside, staring in. They clutched each other. They cried out. (180)

In their responses to the Freudian notion of the uncanny, the stories by Pausacker and Lawrance offer a substantial contrast, but as a component of their common terms of reference the uncanny is part of a bundle of international genric features that both draw on. In asking whether hybridic horror stories can have a local Australian nuance, we seek to come to terms with the relationship between setting and forms of social critique. To pose this more precisely, we can ask whether hybridic fictional forms grounded in mystery or horror genres are characterized by recognizable chronotopes, and then whether those chronotopes include examples not explicable solely in terms of pretexts to be found in American or British fiction and film. As Mikhail Bakhtin defines it, a chronotope denotes 'the intrinsic interconnectedness of temporal and spatial relationships that are artistically expressed in literature' (84). Particular narrative genres are characterized by specific formal combinations of time and place (that is, by chronotopes) which structure a novel. The concept of the chronotope is forceful here, in that it goes beyond being a conceptual substitute for the idea of plot to encompass how narratives take on particular culturally and ideologically inscribed forms (McCallum 185). Maria Nikolajeva extends this by the observation that novelistic chronotopes are gendered. Thus she argues that 'male' texts tend to structure time as linear and space as open, whereas 'female' texts structure time as circular and space as closed and confined (125). The particular formation of this in the literature of the uncanny is that the space in which decisive action occurs is not just closed and confined but often in some way isolated as well – for example, stories in *Dark House* have overgrown gardens (Kelleher, Rubinstein) or are rendered remote in other ways (Disher, Neilsen, Moloney). Female space is thus constituted as threatening space, an effect accentuated by circular narrative structures in, for example, 'Aunt Maud's Bequest' and 'All the King's Men'.

At the most general level, the base chronotope of contemporary mystery hybrids is the 'present everyday', that is a setting in present time and everyday locations, presumably so as to bring readers into a close cultural alignment with the chronotope. Chronotopes thus invariably have an ideological effect as well as a function as a unit of narrative analysis: their cultural specificity imbues them with a capacity to be in 'dialogue with extraliterary historical contexts' (Holquist 112). Roderick McGillis has observed that a kind of intertextuality, in the form of obtrusive but narrowly based allusions to 'obvious aspects of popular culture', has a similar function in R. L. Stine's books: '[t]he attempt is to remain familiar and yet to fill the familiar with uncanny happenings. The message is: The familiar world we live in is dangerous, and you'd best get used to it' (103). This allusiveness is, in fact, a common component of the horror chronotope. McGillis points to the misogyny pervading the texts he discusses, so it is perhaps not surprising to find that women perform a negative role in the majority of stories in *Dark House*. Mystery chronotopes in adolescent fiction thus seem to be characterized by particular forms of gendered behaviour.

Female characters with a more agential and positive subjectivity have appeared in contemporary Gothic narratives, as Carol Clover has observed (60), and a female hero paradigm is emerging in contemporary children's fantasy (Stephens and McCallum 117–24), but mystery and horror chronotopes still appear to exclude such subjectivities. Finally, the social world of the setting is one in which family members are alienated one from another, self-interest rules and violence is endemic. Magistrale and Morrison argue that a distinction needs to be made between the *art* of horror and its mere exploitation, because the best horror art is 'visionary' and 'tests and shakes our complacency as individuals and as members of a larger culture' (7). How far can it do this, however, if a chronotope depends on reader recognition and alignment, but that chronotope is, for example, specifically North American?

There is no tradition of mystery or horror writing in Australian children's literature, so there is still a tendency to carry over chronotopes from (mainly) American sources. The domination of the Australian market by American series such as Goosebumps and Fear Street naturalizes their chronotopes, but arguably a corollary is that there will be greater distance between texts and readers. An example of a detail of physical setting so obvious as to be virtually invisible is the propensity for the houses in *Dark House* to have upper floors and hence staircases (in nine of the twelve stories), even where this has no particular function, whereas it would not be a reflex assumption among young Australian readers that a house would have more than one floor. The domestic architecture thus unobtrusively signifies that the chronotope probably refers to another culture. For most of the stories in *Dark House* the authors have accepted that the genre does not have local chronotopes, and either locate the action in England (Kelleher), or in North America (Crew and Carmody), or else leave the location unspecified, with the present everyday now defined by linguistic usage and idiom.

Four stories in *Dark House* have an explicitly Australian setting. One of these, Carmel Bird's 'The Conservatory', does not concern us here, as it is genrically out of place in the collection. In the other three setting is part of signification. Pausacker fashions her own chronotope to make the point that child abuse is a very present local phenomenon. Arnold Zable, in 'Beyond Night', tells a quasi ghost story which is rather a fable about Australian multiculturalism. After his mother's death, the narrator spends the night in darkness in his mother's house in inner-city Melbourne in order 'to come to terms with the darker presences that had hovered about her, and which seemed still to permeate the house [he] had been raised in' (133). These 'darker presences' are not paranormal in the usual sense, however, but are a complex of memories, griefs, and guilt stemming from the fact that she left Lithuania in 1937 and the family, friends, and culture left behind were swept away by successive Soviet and German invasions. Finally, Gary Disher exploits the discrepancy between a Sydney location and a genric chronotope in 'Dead Set', where the narrator, Ben, alienated by his hateful job selling encyclopedias and his bullying supervisor, conjures up a dark house and a beautiful female occupant out of his need, desire, and imagination. Simultaneously non-existent and materially present to Ben, house and woman exist in intertextual space and are not a part of common intersubjective space. Moreover, their conjunction disrupts the 'present everyday' chronotope. The house is a stereotypical Gothic mansion, from lion's head door knocker to the paintings on the walls and the candle-lit rooms. Caterina, its inhabitant, is Ben's imagined other half, his ideal object of desire, modern in dress and manner, and his height and age. She is also a vampire, however, both Eros and Thanatos, filling the narrator's needs by inducting him into sexuality and acting as 'the death dealer' (66) for his abusive boss, Curtis. Within the materiality of Ben's imaginings the Eros/Thanatos conjunction thus reconstitutes the present everyday as a desirable intersubjective space.

Paranormal phenomena are commonly exploited in fiction and film for the frisson of fear they produce, and because in order to do that they depict a world in which morality and justice no longer prevail it is tempting to see such texts – as McGillis, for example, sees them – as a kind of postmodernist acceptance, even celebration, of cynicism, conceptual and moral relativism, self-destruction and chaos (McGillis 104; Magistrale and Morrison 7). The paranormal can also function as a displaced representation of elements of culture, as the stories by Disher, Pausacker and Zable illustrate, and is also evident in two recent Australian novels, Isobelle Carmody's *The Gathering* (1993) and Judith Clarke's *The Lost Day* (1997). These novels are genrically identifiable as, respectively, fantasy and contemporary realism, but show a pervasive influence from horror chronotopes.

Through elements of plot, narrative technique, and theme, *The Gathering* brings together three main genres: high fantasy, horror, and historical mystery. Crucially, the novel has a first-person narrator, still a rare narrative strategy in fantasy texts, though long a key source of the uncanny in horror texts. Thus in this novel the uncanny is an effect of perception rather than of the plot, which rather conforms to the 'good versus evil' metanarrative of traditional fantasies. The attempt to hybridize the various genres results in a thematic ambivalence but also an implicit conservatism. Of the texts we are considering, *The Gathering* best exemplifies how the uncanny functions to reaffirm the dominant ideology of the culture.

The novel deals with the central young adult novel themes of individuality and conformity, the operation of power in society, the importance of understanding past and present generations in order to evolve one's own subjectivity, and the importance of imaginative engagement with the world. When the narrator, Nathanial, and his mother move to the town of Cheshunt, they enter a totalitarian community organized in conformity with what Michel Foucault identified as the 'panopticon.'

> The exercise of discipline presupposes a mechanism that coerces by means of observation; an apparatus in which the techniques that make it possible to see induce effects of power, and in which, conversely, the means of coercion make those on whom they are applied clearly visible. (Foucault 170–1)

Thus the organization of the town's teenagers into 'the gathering', with a vigilante offshoot, the imposition of a curfew, constant surveillance of individuals and domination of this system by people in powerful community positions constitutes a tyranny against which Nathanial and 'the Chain', the small group of like-minded individualists he teams up with, struggle and prevail.

The basis of the novel in fantasy links the paranormal with the cosmic struggle between good and evil. The narrator's awareness of this struggle emerges as an aspect of his perception of the uncanny. This is signalled in the opening sentence: '[s]ometimes you get a feeling about a thing that you can't explain; a premonition of wrongness' (xi). The return of what has been repressed has both a social and an individual aspect. On the one hand, Cheshunt is the site of some unspecified evil action in the distant past, which returns recurrently, channelled via the possession of chosen vessels such as the school principal, Karle; on the other, Nathanial has lived in Cheshunt before, and his present experiences bring back to him repressed memories of the violent and abusive father from whom his mother had protected him by fleeing. All five members of 'the Chain' are outsiders because of comparable emotional or psychological scarring in earlier life. Fantasy presupposes a continuity between the social and the personal, and for each member of the Chain the defeat of the forces of evil coincides with confronting and expelling his or her own personal demons. The ending insists that the defeat of evil is only temporary, but that it is defeated at all, and that the members of the Chain experience personal healing, aligns the text with fantasy rather than horror.

Despite the dominance of fantasy among its genres, *The Gathering* deploys the present everyday chronotope. That this conforms with a familiar North American chronotope, rather than any local Australian version, is indicated by nuances of setting, linguistic choices (such as 'hurricane' rather than 'cyclone'), and the central thematic use of the myth of the lone dissenting hero (see Macleod 191). Female roles also conform to that chronotope. They are few and restricted, and apart from Nathanial's mother who is a classic victim figure, the only significant female characters are Lallie and Nissa. As a seer and supernatural guide, Lallie fulfils a fantasy role; Nissa is a strong and assertive female, but narratively that is constituted as her weakness, and the narrator's frequent references to her sexual desirability align her with the female as object of gaze typical of horror (see Dolar, McGillis).

Because of its basis in fantasy, *The Gathering* has access to the convention that the paranormal expresses a transcendent contest between Good and Evil, and that this contest periodically erupts in material form within human social organizations and throws up charismatic figures such as Lallie and Karle as guides or leaders on either side of the good/evil polarity. Because for almost two millennia concepts of the supernatural in Western societies have been shaped by Christian thought, there is an underlying assumption that good and evil exist in a hierarchical relation in which good denotes the base condition from which evil is always a falling away or deviation. This is implicit in the conversation between Nathanial and his mother when he asks her if she believes in good and evil. The crux of her reply is, '[e]vil and good are potentials in all of us. You have a choice whether or not to be evil because you can choose not to do evil things' (149), and she expands this with the comment that the simple binary opposition is too clear-cut to define actual lived experience. Nathaniel rejects this conception of evil as too 'mundane' (it is in fact too relativist both for him and the novel more generally), but mother and son still share an assumption about the priority of good. It is no doubt the vestiges of that assumption which prompt the recoil from the postmodernist ethic (or ethical lack) informing horror genres.

Realist fiction has long been more disposed towards relativist perspectives on morality and social organization (Stephens 242–3), so when a realist novel incorporates allusions to horror narrative forms of the paranormal and uncanny, as in Clarke's *The Lost Day*, the function of the uncanny is not to produce an affirmation of the underlying stability of the good/evil hierarchy, but to bring its characters to confront the abyss, or what Allan Lloyd Smith formulates as 'a realm of nothingness, of an unbearable absence of meaning' (289). What *The Lost Day* does affirm in the face of meaninglessness is human warmth and companionship and the capacity for *caring*. The focus on sociality here offers a significant contrast with *The Gathering*. Although by the climax of *The Gathering* the idea of 'The Chain' as a bulwark against evil has been clarified so that it is understood to consist not of its physical symbols but of people, an intense social bond has become a conduit by which individual virtue is infused with transcendent power. Uncanny moments in *The Lost Day* may hint at the possibility of a larger pattern, but the concern felt by members of a community for the focal character affirms the qualities of intersubjective human warmth and affection in the context of a larger society where individuals become random victims and the outcomes of events do not point to transcendent meanings.

The mystery about which Clarke's novel pivots involves the temporary disappearance of the main character, Vinny, and the impact this has on his relatives and friends as they seek to explain and contextualize it. Thus for sixty per cent of the novel (pages 23–113) Vinny is an absent subject, textually constructed in the thoughts of his friends, mother, and uncle and by the shifts in the tenor of their lives. For example, Josh experiences this shift as a transformation in the significance of the everyday, but especially of place. He had earlier encapsulated the discontent with everydayness which impelled himself and his friends towards the glitter of the club strip: 'Jacaranda Street, Deepdene! The place of the Living Dead! It was boring, boring, boring. Stupid and – small' (13). (George A. Romero's cult horror film *Night of the Living Dead* (1968) is a *de rigueur* inclusion in the corpus of popular culture texts alluded to in contemporary adolescent horror narratives.) However, Vinny's disappearance prompts a nascent awareness of the subtle nuances of place:

> The houses and gardens of Jacaranda Street were just the same as ever, but to Josh every single thing seemed to burn with secret difference, because now they were part of a world from which Vinny might have gone, where he simply wouldn't be any more. (86)

The impact of this secret difference is dual: it testifies to the forcefulness of the intersubjective relationship shared by the group, and how it is this which imbues place with meaning, and it points to the radically unsettling effect of an unsolved mystery. Further, until Vinny's reappearance readers have no more knowledge of what has happened than the characters, and so will generate their own hypotheses. The scene in which Vinny disappears in the street outside a nightclub is focalized by his friend Jasper, and because Jasper sees nothing readers are given no information. The moment itself is not intrinsically uncanny, although inexplicable to Jasper, but Clarke has laid a sufficiently visible false trail in the opening twenty pages of the novel to invite an uncanny interpretation. On the one hand is an apparent premonition experienced by Vinny as he leaves home: '[a]n eerie feeling had fallen over him, like a net flung from the sky. A feeling that there was something wrong about tonight, something strange and dangerous and just – wrong' (10). The slight frisson of the uncanny and the hint of powerful, outside forces in the language of the simile are almost immediately resolved in Vinny's mind as products of one of Melbourne's sudden atmospheric shifts, but the naturalistic explanation is then called into question a few pages later with his disappearance.

A still more radical suggestion of the uncanny, or at least the paranormal, is offered when, in setting the scene for the Saturday night activities of the young adult characters, the opening lines of the novel hint at some existential ambiguity. Once again a recourse to figurative language reinforces the sense of difference from ordinary everydayness:

> Saturday night!
> The city shines. Its towers blaze up against the darkness and gleam down on the surface of the river, as if there's another city hidden under there. (1)

This doubleness suggested by the other, hidden city mirrors and critiques the everyday world, and both threatens and affirms it. It enters into the consciousness of all the major characters as the mystery deepens: Sam, Josh, Jasper, Vinny's girlfriend Frances, his Uncle Barry, and Vinny himself. The solution of the mystery – that Vinny had been lured away by an apparently ordinary, middle-aged man who had pretended he wanted help to find his missing daughter and who had given him a drugged drink – is only ever a partial solution because Vinny cannot remember most of what happened while he was drugged. The incident is marked as irregular, aberrant, deviant, and leaves Vinny feeling tainted, but is also significant for what did not happen. He was not raped, not maimed, not murdered, and he did not disappear forever, but these are not just possibilities alluded to – they happen to other characters on the margin of the novel and are the sphere of the other, hidden city. As in Pausacker's 'The Princess in the Tower', the discourse of the paranormal, especially in relation to the present everyday chronotope, gives way to a discourse of the real, only to disclose that everyday, aberrant human behaviour is much more frightening. On the one hand, this is marked by characters' responses still oriented towards the paranormal. Thinking about what might have happened to Vinny, Josh concludes that '[t]here were worse things in the world than ghosts. Much worse' (139). Frances experiences a deep sense of fear, which is again figured in terms of place, familiarity and otherness:

> She wasn't afraid of Vinny, but of where Vinny had been, like someone who'd come from a country you wanted to keep on believing was a long way away, not here, close by, just across a border you mightn't even notice was there. (135)

The muted allusion to the irruption of the paranormal into the present everyday restates Josh's observation: the actual and present demons of our culture inhabit its everydayness.

On the other hand, the domain of the real is firmly asserted through the narrative frame as it brings the novel to a close. In an extended move towards closure, several characters appear in brief vignettes illustrating some reorientation of self to world, or some shifted or deepened understanding. The final section, however, a reprise of the opening pages, returns to some of the things that might have happened to Vinny and did happen to other young people. The example which concludes the novel is of a girl who had caught Vinny's attention in King Street when he first agreed to go with his eventual abductor:

> he spotted a girl who might be the one; standing by herself at a bus-stop, and crying, too. She had long fair hair and though she was wearing a black coat, there could be a blue dress hidden underneath it. (125)

The irony of Vinny's position here, himself made vulnerable because he felt compassion for his abductor's pretended plight, does not emerge until the novel's concluding lines:

Jinny Allan, 18, was last seen leaving the Field of Dreams in King Street at five o'clock on Sunday morning. She has long fair hair and she was wearing a black coat with a lilac dress beneath. She'd had a row with her boyfriend in the club and had set off home by herself.

No one's seen or heard from Jinny Allan since, and no one ever will.

She'll never come home again. (150)

The narrative frame thus discomposes the muted positive ending to Vinny's story. Clarke has got to this point by exploiting parallels between the experiences and fears played out in horror genres and the inexplicably aberrant and often brutal behaviour of people who transform the present everyday into a country 'just across a border you mightn't even notice was there.' Hence the narrative displaces elements of the everyday towards the paranormal, but then the mystery does not reside in the paranormal but in the inexplicability of human behaviour. *The Lost Day* does not deliver the triumphant answers of *The Gathering*: that Vinny was relatively unharmed is as random a chance as was his abduction, as the case of Jinny Allan reminds readers. But nor does the novel depict a cynical and disintegrating society. The shining city, the mundane suburbs, and the hidden city all contribute to a grounding chronotope which encompasses order and disorder, and good and bad happenings, but not in a cosmos which hierarchically sets good above evil, as in fantasy, or evil above good, as in horror. In a world where meaning lies only in human behaviour, declined paranormal explanations demand that represented characters and readers interrogate their sense of who they are, and of how they signify in relation to sociality.

The chronotopes of horror have an international currency and probably resist being modified to incorporate settings from outside Britain or North America. In the texts we have considered here it has been rare to see the spatial aspect of the chronotopes being treated innovatively. Only three of the stories from *Dark House* use local settings constructively. To Australian readers, *The Gathering* seems to be set in North America, principally because it has drawn upon conventional horror chronotopes. In contrast, *The Lost Day* uses the resources of its grounding realism to actualize a local setting which then transforms the horror chronotopes alluded to by the evocation of the uncanny. Significantly, those narratives which do modify the chronotopes also seek to move beyond the themes, outcomes and responses conventionally associated with horror chronotopes, now subsuming them into social comment. They suggest a way forward for genres hybridized with horror, but the lack of a tradition of horror or mystery writing in Australia means that the hard work of evolving a local discourse will still have to be done.

Works cited

Bakhtin, Mikhail. *The Dialogic Imagination*. Austin: University of Texas Press, 1981.

Carmody, Isobelle. *The Gathering*. Ringwood, Victoria: Penguin, 1993.

Clarke, Judith. *The Lost Day*. Ringwood, Victoria: Penguin, 1997.

Clover, Carol. *Men, Women, and Chain Saws: Gender in the Modern Horror Film*. Princeton, NJ: Princeton University Press, 1992.

Crew, Gary (ed.) *Dark House*. Port Melbourne: Mammoth, 1995.

Disher, Gary. 'Dead Set', in Gary Crew (ed.), *Dark House*. Port Melbourne: Mammoth, 1995, pp. 43–67.

Dolar, Mladen. '"I Shall Be with You on Your Wedding Night:" Lacan and the Uncanny', *October*, 58 (1991): 5–23.

Ferrell, Robyn. 'Life Threatening Life: Angela Carter and the Uncanny', in Alan Cholodenko (ed.), *The Illusion of Life: Essays on Animation*. Sydney: Power Publications, 1991, pp. 131–44.

Foucault, Michel. *Discipline and Punish*. London: Penguin Books, 1979.

Freud, Sigmund. 'The Uncanny', ed. James Strachey, in *The Standard Edition of the Complete Psychological Works of Sigmund Freud*, Vol. XVII. London: Hogarth Press, 1955, pp. 217–56.

Holquist, Michael. *Dialogism*. London and New York: Routledge, 1990.

Kelleher, Victor. 'Aunt Maud's Bequest', in Gary Crew (ed.), *Dark House*. Port Melbourne: Mammoth, 1995, pp. 71–86.

Lawrance, Peter. 'All the King's Men', in Gary Crew (ed.), *Dark House*. Port Melbourne: Mammoth, 1995, pp. 159–80.

McCallum, Robyn. *Ideologies of Identity in Adolescent Fiction*. New York and London: Garland, 1999.

McGillis, Roderick. '"Terror is Her Constant Companion:" The Cult of Fear in Recent Books for Teenagers', in Sandra Beckett (ed.), *Reflections of Change*. Westport, CT: Greenwood Press, 1997, pp. 99–106.

Macleod, Anne Scott. *American Childhoods*. Athens, GA: University of Georgia Press, 1994.

Magistrale, Tony and Michael A. Morrison. *A Dark Night's Dreaming: Contemporary American Horror Fiction*. Columbia, SC: University of South Carolina Press, 1996.

Moloney, James. 'The Cat and the Crow', in Gray Crew (ed.), *Dark House*. Port Melbourne Mammoth, 1995, pp. 201–17.

Nikolajeva, Maria. *Children's Literature Comes of Age*. New York and London: Garland, 1996.

Pausacker, Jenny. 'The Princess in the Tower', in Gray Crew (ed.), *Dark House*. Port Melbourne Mammoth, 1995, pp. 21–41.

Smith, Allan Lloyd. 'The Phantoms of *Drood* and *Rebecca*: The Uncanny Reencountered through Abraham and Torok's "Cryptonomy."' *Poetics Today*, 13 (2) (1992): 285–308.

Stephens, John. *Language and Ideology in Children's Fiction*. London and New York: Longman, 1992.

Stephens, John and Robyn McCallum. *Retelling Stories, Framing Culture: Traditional Story and Metanarratives in Children's Literature*. New York and London: Garland, 1998.

Todorov, Tzvetan. *The Fantastic* [1970]. Ithaca, NY: Cornell University Press, 1975.

Zable, Arnold. 'Beyond Night', in Gary Crew (ed.), *Dark House*. Port Melbourne: Mammoth, 1995, pp. 129–46.

12
The Mysteries of Postmodern Epistemology: Stratemeyer, Stine, and Contemporary Mystery for Children

Karen Coats

In the early 1930s, Edward Stratemeyer conceived of a heroine who would quickly become a cultural icon. Smart, sure-footed, and virtuous, Nancy Drew combated the evils of her time with flawless grace. With the occasional and often superfluous help of her father and friends, the young detective made River Heights and the rest of America feel confident in the competence of its youth, and reinforced a general faith in the sufficiencies of human reason to challenge and ultimately triumph over the irrational evils of war and economic crisis. But to paraphrase Dorothy from *The Wizard of Oz*, we are not in River Heights anymore. Postmodernism in many ways challenges the supremacy of the rational, opening new questions regarding the limits of our reason in the face of the irrational. That which is abject, excluded from rational inquiry and discourse, reasserts itself. Resolution, such as we find in those tidy endings in Nancy Drew mysteries, is displaced by the opening up of new networks of complexity. Hence today's mystery series fiction for youth responds to different cultural preoccupations. R. L. Stine's Goosebumps and Ghosts of Fear Street series, for instance, continually breach the borders of the world as we know it. The works of Australian writer Gary Crew elide the mysterious with the mundane making the mundane mysterious, and vice versa. Contemporary mysteries for children challenge their readers to explore new paradigms of the normal, and, concomitantly, a new paradigm of the mysterious.

Mystery is that which defines the boundaries of the known. As new knowledge comes to light, the territory of the known enlarges, and the mysterious terrain where such beasts as dragons lurk becomes smaller and smaller. Indeed, if one presumes a universe that is ultimately knowable, subject to rational laws and motivated action, then the mysterious is merely something hidden, territory not yet mapped. Knowledge is perceived as a coherent, totalizing system that is simply incomplete. Such is the modernist view of the universe, originating in the Enlightenment tendency to privilege scientific knowledge over knowledge gained through legends, myths, and other cultural narratives. Hence it is a profoundly *human* knowledge as well – not concerned with where we are in relation to our gods, as in mythological knowledge, but with where we are in relation to each other and to the natural world. In such a world, the hero is he or she who thinks rationally, keeps her head, pursues his clues until the mystery is solved. The solution is then integrated into the larger store of knowledge to enlarge the boundaries of the known, to reduce the territory taken up by the mysterious. For knowledge in modernism almost always results in action: it has effects, spurs progress, and imposes order on chaotic systems. The teleological, progressive hope in modernism is that, if we all keep our wits about us and believe in the strength of our bodies and the sufficiency of our reason, we may yet sift the mysteries of the universe around us.

It is therefore no accident that, as R. Gordon Kelly points out, the detective story genre emerged in a context of historical and ideological modernity, and, according to Michael Holquist, achieved dominance as the principal form of mystery fiction with the advent of literary modernism. According to Brian McHale, modernist fiction is dominated by questions of epistemology, of what can be known and by whom, of how we are to interpret the world in which we find ourselves. He calls the detective story 'the epistemological genre *par excellence*' (McHale 9), mirroring as it does the rational search for sure and certain knowledge of the truth. In the early decades of this century, Edward Stratemeyer made it his business to bring this genre to young readers, creating characters like Nancy Drew and the Hardy Boys who epitomize the subject on its way to knowing, competent and sure-footed in the quest to uncover truth, dauntless when faced with threats, locked doors, violent storms and equally violent miscreants, and ultimately successful in clearing up the mystery and restoring order to chaos, fortunes to the deserving, and punishment to the villains. Several critics (and most avid readers) have identified the basic plot structure of a Nancy Drew mystery: Nancy becomes acquainted with a poor soul who has in some way been swindled out of her fortune, she agrees to work on the case, she performs 'a slew of amazing feats' (Siegel 166), is threatened by the villains for meddling and is often tied up and/or locked up in a secluded spot, escapes, captures the villains, recovers the fortune, and is given some valuable token of appreciation in addition to much praise from the restored victim (Moran and Steinfirst 114). Each of these details becomes important if one considers the historical context in which these works first appeared. Mildred Wirt Benson, the first of many 'Carolyn Keenes' to author Nancy Drew books, notes:

> Dramatic changes soon came into the world, especially in communication, transportation and the attitude of people. Through it all, Nancy, as I envisioned her, stood rock-firm, untouched by war, the Depression, economic or moral problems – a trustworthy symbol for parents and children. (n. p.)

Nancy Drew becomes the prototypic rational individual standing fast against the howling winds of her time, reason triumphant against a society whose irrational undersides were beginning to show through. All around Nancy Drew, war, the Depression, and the resulting moral and ethical ambiguities, were forcing us to come to terms with two things: first, that we had in fact been 'abandoned' by any absolute moral system under which humanity could unite (Holquist 145), and secondly, the presence of what Jonathan Lear calls motivated irrationality. 'Humans regularly behave in ways they do not well understand,' he writes, 'which cause pain to themselves and others, which violate their best understanding of what they want and what they care about' (Lear 54). Against the Enlightenment hope that human reason would lead to positive progress, there emerged a growing sense that thinking might not be enough. Hence the 'untouched ... trustworthy' Nancy Drew actually functions as a defence against such recognition. Nancy Drew's faculties *are* sufficient. The villains she encounters behave in perfectly understandable ways as they act out recognizable character flaws such as greed and hubris. In designing the stories this way, Stratemeyer and his successors helped to cultivate a stance of what Lear calls 'knowingness' with respect to the world. This stance allows the reader to persist in the fantasy that the world, which includes human motivation and behaviour both good and bad, is ultimately knowable and predictable. The structure of the series contributes to the sense of knowingness as well – readers return to Nancy Drew because they know what to expect. 'Knowing already' precludes having to find out, asserts Lear, and it is for this reason that knowingness is a defensive posture. We adopt this stance to protect ourselves from something we cannot know; in this case, what we cannot know is that human reason will not save us.

Certain contemporary mysteries for children, such as those by R. L. Stine, adopt a different stance toward knowledge. They do not move from not knowing to knowing, chaos to order, tension to homeostasis. Although they do not have predictable plot structures, they do have a particular flavour in common, which consists in the fact that when the book's adventure is over, neither characters nor readers *know* anything more conclusive about the mystery or about themselves than they did before the book began. Stratemeyer and Stine have much in common with regard to marketing vision – they both write in series, they both take mystery as their primary genre, and they are both wildly popular. Their protagonists are middle- to upper-middle-class white children and young adults. Stratemeyer had a whole stable of ghostwriters producing his books; Stine has recently launched a series called Ghosts of Fear Street where the books carry his name on the cover and the name of the real author on the title page. Both the Stratemeyer series and the Goosebumps series have been dismissed as non-serious and even dangerously inferior books for children. When Nancy Drew and the Hardy Boys first came out in the early decades of the twentieth century, libraries refused to carry them; Goosebumps met (and often still meets) with a similar resistance in the 1990s. Such series books are traditionally regarded as pulp, not art. But the similarities seem to end there. The values of moral certainty, rational inquiry, and social cohesion that dominate Stratemeyer's 1930s offerings are simply no longer present in properly postmodern mysteries. While the modernist strain of mystery fiction is still alive in such works as Alfred Hitchcock's Three Investigators series, Donald J. Sobol's Encyclopedia Brown, the Hanna-Barbera cartoon series Scooby Doo, and even newer detectives like Wendelin Van Draanen's Sammy Keyes, there is definitely something different afoot in postmodern mystery fiction for children, both in the 'pulp' variety of Stine and in more 'literary' offerings. What is play for Stine becomes serious business in works by writers like Avi, Robert Cormier, Virginia A. Walter, and Gary Crew, whose award-winning *Strange Objects* (1991) I will discuss at some length.

The shift in mystery books for youth can be understood most productively by thinking about the more general shift in the status of knowledge under a postmodern paradigm. Unlike modernist thinking, postmodernism makes no presumption of an ultimately knowable or discoverable universe. Knowledge is found to be contingent and subjective; it has a perspective, if we think in ingenuous terms, or an agenda, if we lean toward the sinister. It has a narrative base, rather than a scientific or rational one. Rather than tending toward closure, as Dragan Milovanovic points out, it tends toward undecidability (14). Language and discourse create rather than describe or clarify. Bits and pieces do not come together to form a whole, rather they reveal a radical irreconcilability of world-views. Hence knowledge is no longer viewed as merely incomplete, but rather as radically inconsistent. In fact, what has come to be known as postmodernism really represents an epistemological break from forms of knowledge which privilege fantasies of total mastery, total solutions, and authorizing moral and ethical systems. Whereas Nancy Drew works in a world that is, according to Sherrie A. Inness, 'full of adventure and intrigue, but also a world that is reassuringly knowable' for the reader (3), Stine's world is one which offers 'no cohesive system of knowledge or faith or ethics that has the power to contain and control the randomness of reality' (Nodelman 123). Geographically speaking, both Nancy Drew and Stine's characters live in America's heartland, but the world of Goosebumps is cluttered with aliens, slimes, monsters, evil-inflected objects, sentient insects and lawn ornaments that wreak all sorts of havoc upon the self-identified 'normal' children of central Ohio. Modernism's defensive posture of knowingness gives way in postmodernism to a cultivated sense of indeterminacy, an often ludic, but sometimes unsettling, approach that acknowledges the impossibility or even the undesirability of knowing. Mystery becomes a feature of everyday life; rather than existing at the excluded peripheries of a human life, it structures that life as its unknowable centre. To solve the mystery would be to dissolve the self.

To illustrate how this works in terms of narrative structure, let us compare an early Nancy Drew book, *The Mystery at Lilac Inn* (1931), with *Escape of the He-Beast* (1998), one of Stine's Ghosts of Fear Street offerings. In terms of the modernist paradigm underlying *The Mystery at Lilac Inn*, the sifting of clues in an orderly, rational way is what drives the narrative. Nancy Drew follows leads to their logical conclusion, and her main job is to decide whether they are worthwhile or whether they are red herrings. She is helped along the way by coincidental encounters, but her method is generally so plausible that these implausible events transform into a sort of inevitable outcome. Nancy Drew, as it turns out, is often just plain lucky, but she is almost never read that way. While interviewing for a new housekeeper, she meets and becomes suspicious of a girl named Mary Mason who applies for the job but then flees when she realizes that Nancy's father is a criminal lawyer. While shopping with her friend, she happens to see Mary Mason, apparently no longer seeking employment, at an expensive dress shop. As it turns out, Mason interviewed at her friend's house as well. Nancy Drew follows Mason, and notes that she is having several expensive items delivered to her house just days after being out of work, and just days after a robbery. In running some errands for her new housekeeper, Nancy happens upon a stranger, who happens to drop an envelope addressed to a B. Mason. When she decides to follow first Mary and then the stranger, we know before she does that these persons are somehow connected with the crime. The act of her following them and subsequently discerning their connection to the crime obscures the implausibility of her encountering them in the first place. Her theory of the crime does not precede her gathering of evidence; rather it follows it. Thus her employment of rational methods drives the story; action leads to knowledge, which precipitates more action.

The exact opposite holds true in postmodern mystery. In *Escape of the He-Beast*, for instance, the main character must use knowledge gathered through comic book narratives in order to escape the creature he has accidentally set free from a computer program. But even knowing who the bad guys are, what their limitations are, and how the story will end is not enough. In the final battle scene, he must create an alternate ending, by drawing new weapons graphics on the computer and narrating action for a story to which the beast becomes subject. The primacy of scientific knowledge is usurped by knowledge of narrative convention; language is not merely descriptive of objective reality, but rather it has the power to actively construct reality. The final twist in this story is that the main character discovers that he himself is a computer-generated figure, created by the comic-book writer because the writer felt he needed the perfect fan. Thus knowledge of his predicament dissolves his self-identity. Note here a curious inversion: in Nancy Drew's orderly world, all depends on the chance encounter. In Stine's seemingly random world, everything is under the control of the comic-book creator who writes and draws the world into existence. Knowing, or not knowing, ultimately makes little difference. It is simply the peculiar spin of the modernist to subsume chance into a teleological structure, a myth of inevitability, whereas the postmodernist works just as hard to deny that inevitability.

In the modernist mystery's teleological structure, closure is a key element. One of the principal features of modernist interpretive strategies is that once an interpretation is made, that is once a mystery is 'solved', then the case is closed. Nancy Drew has earned her reward and she and her client can move on in their circle of parties and vacations with no residual complications. When Nancy Drew exposes the true identity of Stumpy Dowd in *The Bungalow Mystery* (1930), he is caught and incarcerated, Laura Pendleton's fortune is restored, and Laura and her true guardian, Jacob Aborn, live happily ever after. No bit of the mystery is left unresolved or unexplained. The modernist stance of knowingness in traditional mysteries gives us a sense of closure from the outset. We know that Nancy Drew is going to meet a poor unfortunate, we know that she is going to get in and out of at least one seemingly impossible situation, and we know that no money or property will be lost to its rightful heir. The repetition of a pattern does nothing to dampen our enjoyment; rather it heightens it by reinforcing a superior relation to knowledge, and by enacting a defensive structure such as Lear describes: what we already know we do not have to find out, or even think about. The reader does not have to pose questions regarding the superiority of Nancy Drew's competencies or her moral system. Moreover, because those competencies and that moral system are so firmly attached to upper-middle-class Whiteness, the reader is not called upon to reflect actively or critically on the hegemonic control these ideals exercise over the culture at large. But that is precisely what we must question every time we read a Stine book.

Stine's characters are also middle-class white kids, but they are not always on the right side of the moral questions in the text, and because the point of view is absolutely limited to the main character's perspective, the reader, by way of identification, might accidentally get it wrong along with the character. There is no superiority of knowledge with relation to the text because there is no discernible pattern to the endings. Sometimes the mystery is finished on the last page; sometimes it is not. When, in *Revenge of the Lawn Gnomes* (1995), the lawn gnomes have been successfully imprisoned and are no longer a threat to the family, the father brings home a stone gorilla who ends the story by winking at the main character. In this particular story, knowing does not help anyone, because no one will believe the children's assertion that the lawn gnomes are alive. When the evil ventriloquist's dummy is squashed flat by a bulldozer in *Night of the Living Dummy* (1993), his previously inert double awakens and the story ends. Almost every story has this little twist at the end to suggest that the evil or mischief has not been fully contained or defeated, but some do not, making it virtually impossible to know in advance what will happen. True enough, readers often take the knowing stance anyway, and this fact alone may undo the radicality of the textual gesture. Perry Nodelman makes this point in his 'Ordinary Monstrosity: The World of Goosebumps' when he says that the intrusion of the monstrous into the supposedly normal everyday world of kids has the effect of making 'that which is aberrant and monstrously self-indulgent acceptable – merely normal' (119). But his focus is on the interaction between the humans within the text. The relationship that proves more important in this analysis is the one that inheres in the child's encounter with the inhuman, the truly mysterious. It is this that calls into question the stability of the human, which produces a world that wavers rather than one that follows rational rules.

There are certainly other conventions that categorize Stine's work as postmodern, among them the obvious parody of the cliffhanger chapter ending. Benson notes that Stratemeyer told her to 'end each chapter with cliff-hanging suspense, and to include several paragraphs promoting other proposed books in the series' (n.p.). Stine is famous for his cliffhangers at the end of each chapter, but more often than not they are cheesy tricks. A dead body in a trunk turns out to be a store mannequin, a gruesome corpse turns out to be a little brother in a Hallowe'en mask. Unlike in a Nancy Drew novel, where the suspense is real – Stumpy Dowd really does lock her in the basement of an abandoned bungalow; she really is tied up in the cabin of a motorboat when it crashes into the side of a yacht – Stine's 'suspense' is more often than not simply a parodic joke.

Rod McGillis cites a paralogic universe, one that 'at one and the same time is both safe and decidedly unsafe' (18) as Stine's claim to the postmodern. Nodelman catalogues numerous other postmodern elements of Goosebumps, although he does not identify them as such. Among these he cites specifically their market-driven character, their lack of a coherent system, and the lack of any personal growth in the characters. As Holquist notes, 'the aesthetics of Post-Modernism is militantly *anti*-psychological ... and radically *anti*-mythical' (148); hence the characters in postmodern texts do not grow in knowledge about themselves, nor do they teach us anything about ourselves or the way we should live in the world. To do so would be to subscribe to the myth of progress, one of the defining and exploded myths of modernism. That is why Nancy Drew's character, although she neither ages nor learns anything new about herself, is nevertheless paradigmatic of the Modern Girl (Siegel 160), always ahead of her time. And she does progress from one era to the next, becoming less classist and racist and getting new cars with every succeeding era. A final element that distinguishes Stine's series as postmodern is his lack of a central character; postmodernism 'is about things, not people' (Holquist 148). Poststructural criticism posits that the subject has been decentred, the self no longer exists, and so on. Stratemeyer consistently organized his series around knowable characters, flat though they may be. But Stine's series are collected under a signifier, 'goosebumps', that expresses a fleeting physiological phenomenon, suggesting that these stories are more about visceral pain/pleasure rather than any enduring identity structure.

While such cataloguing of differences is important, the emphasis in this reading is on the change in what McHale, drawing on Roman Jakobson, calls a 'shift in dominant' from the epistemological concerns of modernism to the ontological concerns of postmodernism (McHale 6–11). While Nancy Drew busies herself with increasing her knowledge and perfecting her interpretations of the world, Stine's kids concern themselves with questions about the possibilities of existence in and of the world. Instead of asking 'what can I know about a world which is undeniably there for me to discover?', instead of hiding behind a posture of knowingness, the dominant questions seem to be: 'What is a world?; What kinds of worlds are there, how are they constituted, and how do they differ?; What happens when different kinds of worlds are placed in confrontation, or when boundaries between worlds are violated?' (McHale 10). With the growing presence and capabilities of technology to create new frontiers by annihilating old ones, these questions are becoming ubiquitous in our culture. Although they are exceedingly serious and often troubling, or perhaps *because* of that, Stine adopts a playful stance regarding world-making and boundary-crossing that nevertheless continually calls into question the status of the rational world. Of course, epistemological concerns are always implicated in ontological ones and vice versa – knowing is grounded in perception, but perception always proceeds from a pre-existing knowledge base – but the point McHale makes in his theory of the dominant is that certain types of literature foreground either one or the other. Stine, and his postmodern fellows, privilege the ontological, the presence of worlds rather than the knowledge of them.

Stine seems to instinctively recognize that worlds are constituted on the basis of certain exclusions. Normality is founded on the exclusion of the abnormal. But what is excluded can never be completely excluded, and this is the textual gesture that Stine continually makes. That which is excluded, being neither subject nor object, is what Julia Kristeva, in her book *Powers of Horror* calls the abject. In a world-view dominated by epistemological concerns, mystery, that which is unknown, sets the boundaries, establishes the limits. Hence we speak of the 'known universe' or the 'known world'. In a world dominated by ontological questions, however, the abject, that which is inadmissible in a clean and proper world, sets in place the boundaries, the difference between inside and outside, admissible and inadmissible, possible and impossible.

Unarguably, the abject is present in modernist detective fiction. Kristeva says: '[a]ny crime, because it draws attention to the fragility of the law, is abject, but premeditated crime, cunning murder, hypocritical revenge are even more so because they heighten the display of such fragility' (4). One may also argue that the villains in Nancy Drew come from groups of people who might be considered socially or morally abject, often because of their ethnicity or class. More than criminals, they represent, for the white middle class, something which 'disturbs identity, system, order. [Which] does not respect borders, positions, rules' (Kristeva 4). But in the case of the modernist mystery, it is not the cunning of the villain that is foregrounded, but the cunning of the knowing young detective. Premeditation merely sets the stage for discerning motive. The crime exists only to highlight the intellectual and physical prowess of the detective. The abject is used as staging for the star. In the face of human rationality, the abject has no power, poses no threat. The police, as socially sanctioned keepers of the law, may appear fragile, but the law itself never seems so because Nancy Drew bolsters it up with her own presence. The focus is on the mystery surrounding the crime and once that is solved, the power of the crime itself is dissolved and the law appears even more powerful than before.

But crime represents only one guise of the abject, and not the primary one at that. Because they are concerned with the ontological status of the world and the things in it, most postmodern mysteries do not centre around crimes at all, but address the primary locus of Kristeva's sense of the abject – the body. The reader will recall Lear's claim that the posture of knowingness is a modernist defence against motivated irrationality. But the primacy of the mind has always been, first and foremost, a defence against the presence of the body. Note that our knowing modernist heroine may get knocked down, but she rarely, if ever, *bleeds*. No matter how fast the blue roadster goes, Ms Drew never gets carsick. Her body never fails her; its substances and fluids never go awry. At worst, she gets some mud on her shoes. In postmodern literature, however, the body returns in all its abject g(l)ory. And not only the human body, but all manner of oozes and ectoplasm, shape-shifting aliens, and grisly corpses. Characters drool and vomit, they slurp down slimy, blood-sucking worms and even cannibalize each other. One girl puts earthworms in her brother's peanut butter sandwich, and he unwittingly takes a bite. In *Attack of the Vampire Worms* (1998), the children find a colony of bloodless people living in a cave. They fall into an underground stream and come up covered with leech-like white worms. The leader of the cave-people tries to get them to eat the worms so that they too will become bloodless captives of the cave. The very substantiality of their bodies is thus vulnerable in any number of ways. In other novels, a group of children become invisible by looking in a mirror and flashing a light, another gets turned into a dog, still another a bird, and two others narrowly escape becoming zombies. In one instance, a grotesquely ugly Halloween mask becomes fused to a girl's head, changing her voice and her personality. In another instance, two children realize that their father has mutated into an evil plant.

Over and over again, the children come into contact with things that do not 'respect borders, positions, rules' (Kristeva 4). Kristeva points out that certain substances stand for threats from without and others threaten from within. For our purposes, we may include sentient lawn gnomes, monsters, aliens, and so on in the former category, and the ingestion of worms and other vile things, as well as expulsions of and changes in bodily substance in the latter. Their prevalence in postmodern mystery for children suggests that, in a postmodern worldview, the abject is everywhere, and cannot be expelled, repressed, or ignored.

What is implicated in this emphasis on the abject is our belief in the sufficiency of the body. Whereas knowingness indicates an attitude toward the sufficiency of mind, our relation to the abject is directly correlated to our beliefs and desires about the body. In general, so the theory goes, we loathe the fact that we are subject to, limited by, imprisoned within our bodies. Technology is nothing other than an extension of the capabilities of the human body. And modernism's great faith in the efficacy of technology valorizes the mind's capacity to transcend the limits of the body. But the body always returns. Bacteria outsmart antibiotics, disease persists, bodies reassert themselves.

Elizabeth Grosz summarizes three responses to the abject on the plane of the social, which I would particularize for the purposes of this reading as classical, modernist, and more or less universal tendencies. Since '[c]ulture in general functions as such only by the expulsion of this social and personal horror at our own materiality and finitude' (113), we have to come up with ways to deal with abjection. Religion, she says, displaces abjection, 'replacing its "substance" with the ideal of God' (113). One might call this the classical or traditional approach to abjection. But since, according to Nietzsche, God died some time ago, modernism sought to repress the abject with 'the law-like, normative functioning of the Symbolic order' (113). Nancy Drew fits well here, upholding as she does the fiction of a society in which right always triumphs. Finally, Grosz points to the arts as 'more or less successful attempts to *sublimate* the abject' (113). But as I have pointed out, Stine's work is not often regarded as literary art. For that reason I would add a category to 'things we do with the abject' that is uniquely postmodern: Stine *commodifies* the abject. Instead of dismissing it, celebrating it, ignoring it, or denying it, he fetishizes it, using it for fun and profit. While it may be argued that this sort of commodification can be found throughout history in the context of freak shows, for example, more often than not, such display was ostensibly linked to or in the service of some other metanarrative, such as medicine, religion, or anthropology.

The postmodern gesture seems to be the abject as commodity for its own sake, that is the abject's value as a commodity is its defining feature, its reason for being. In a particularly damning article, Diana West compares Stine's work to pornography:

> in shock fiction [of which Stine's is the most prevalent], a raw catalogue of horrors and grotesqueries is used – not interpreted, not stylized, not in any way transformed by the writer for good or bad – to charge the nerve endings of young readers. (40)

In other words, she is using the terms and values of a modernism that represses and an aestheticism that sublimates the abject – those unstylized, uninterpreted 'horrors and grotesqueries' of which she speaks – to pass judgement on a kind of work which requires a new kind of interpretive strategy altogether. Stine unapologetically generates 'a calisthenics of perception' (Holquist 154) that produces, not intellectual muscles or psychological growth, but *goosebumps*.

Gary Crew, on the other hand, produces more complex literature for children and young adults that in some ways sublimates, in some ways fetishizes, the abject. Set in Australia, *Strange Objects* recounts the events that follow the finding of a 350-year-old iron pot containing a journal and a mummified hand. The abject is everywhere present in this story. Steven Messenger, the boy who finds the pot, immediately labels it 'the cannibal pot', suggesting his extreme suspicion of and distaste for aboriginal and non-white culture. Indeed, he says of the Asians, 'they all looked alike. I couldn't tell the difference and didn't have anything to do with them' (24), and of the 'Abo kids', '[t]hey needed a wash and looked as if they'd cut your throat. If one came near me I'd move' (24). His sense of disgust becomes more and more pronounced as the book proceeds. He takes a long shower after he has been touched by the elderly Aborigine Charlie Sunrise, and he even comes to resent being touched by his white friend Nigel Kratzman because Nigel works on cars and is always greasy. His dreams and his waking life are haunted by abject bodily fluids. He dreams of standing in pools of blood; while awake, he repeatedly coughs up phlegm and vomit.

His fear of contamination makes especially poignant his encounter with the first object he finds in the pot – a severed, mummified hand. It is the hand of a young white woman. This grisly discovery does the work that Kristeva says it will – it initiates a crisis in Messenger's sense of himself. The collision of worlds produces refracted images of himself in a dream double, and in the historical figure of mass murderer and rapist Jan Pelgrom. When Messenger discovers that he has inadvertently come into possession of a ring that was held to the hand with wax, he becomes more and more connected with other selves, and less connected with his body. The ring enables him to fly, it enables him to 'know' things that take him out of this world, with its contamination of bodies, into an other world that has a different relation to time, space, and morality. Crew employs the use of multiple perspectives to unfold the mystery of Messenger's find, but while others are relying on rational methods of inquiry, Messenger has dreams and visions, and is finally led to a sacred aboriginal site that contains a pictorial history of the former owner of the hand and the ring.

After this trip, during which he kills Charlie Sunrise, Messenger disappears. The ring has succeeded in wearing away time and space, blurring the boundaries of past and present, white and aboriginal. Thus the unfolding of the mystery only creates more mystery – we do not *know* what happens to Steven Messenger. We do not *know* what the connection is between him and Jan Pelgrom. Even Steven does not *know* what is happening to him – he ascribes knowingness to the ring, and he simply surrenders to it. He illustrates the way knowingness unravels as a defence in postmodernist culture. Knowingness inserts a haughty distance between the subject and the world. Steven collapses into the irrational world of the ring in order to avoid accepting the finitude of bodies in this one – in order to not know that his father is dead. In the end, he leaves a world that is too painful for him to live in.

But lest we feel too sorry for this abject hero, we must remember that he is a cruel, calculating, and strikingly amoral boy. Just as Pelgrom has no qualms about killing and eating a puppy that he had formerly frolicked with and apparently been fond of, Messenger kills seagulls and lizards just to try out his little inventions. In contrast, among the conventions at work in the creation of Nancy Drew, there was a strong commitment to an unfailingly competent, morally unambiguous heroine. In fact, knowledge is everywhere linked to morality; uncovering truth almost always means actively expelling evil from the society of the decent people whom Nancy counts among her friends. Strength of mind, strength of body, and strength of character form an indissoluble bond for our modernist heroes and heroines. But postmodern fiction is more likely to take up the position that Jacques Lacan attributes to Sade and the Romantics, that one can be well in evil. In traditional mysteries, evil is always bad, and the nefarious characters who practise evil almost always come to a bad end. But in Crew, as well as in Stine, being bad sometimes turns out okay, and certainly being scary is considered a good thing. Steven Messenger steals a ring, kills small animals and an old man, and escapes, just as his historical double Jan Pelgrom participated in over a hundred murders and rapes, and was set free. Justice is not served, and the fragility of the law is in fact exposed.

But the social is not the only site of evil in postmodernity. It is often the case that evil is located in an object, which indicates its ontological status in a postmodern context. If evil is located in a person, who has the opportunity to know and choose right from wrong, then it takes on the status of the epistemological; evil is a position one takes with regard to what one knows. But if evil resides in an object – say, monster blood or a haunted mask, a ventriloquist's dummy or a ring – then it is not something that can be altered or reformed, or even in some cases chosen. It exists. You run across it. It touches you. Maybe it changes you. But it itself does not change. It persists as the presence of a motivated irrationality. And you just have to live with its ongoing presence in your world. In her series *The Dark is Rising* (1965–76), Susan Cooper makes great use of 'things of power'. In a modernist, scientific, rational paradigm, power resides in the knowing subject's use of things, not the things themselves. In Stine's and Crew's postmodern vision, things have power, and in many cases knowledge as well. Messenger says of his ring that 'the best part was, when I wanted more, the ring seemed to know' (87). It is the ring that knows, the ring that has taken over Steven's identity, just as the mask takes over Carly Beth's identity in Stine's *The Haunted Mask* (1993). Objects are evil, and people are absolved of their responsibility.

Despite what we may think about the moral vision of these books, we have to acknowledge that they *are* read avidly. With the advent of cultural studies, critics who scorn them as unworthy of the kinds of attention one might give to a work of literary value have begun to consider them as, at least, conveyors of cultural assumptions and ideologies. We might also look at series mysteries as cultural and psychological symptoms which have an analogous, though not completely identical, relation to the more commonly understood bodily symptom in that their connection to the cause of the problem is not always readily apparent. For instance, a pain in one's side may be indicative of a bruise, a muscle strain, a neurological problem, or an advanced stage of cancer. The pain itself is not meaningful until it has been interpreted by a physician. However, often the symptom outlives its interpretation; that is, we may indeed have an explanation for it, but it persists nonetheless. Slavoj Žižek calls this particular virtue of the symptom its 'inherently ethical' character. Traumas should not be neutralized, but rather marked through repetition in order that they do not slip from cultural memory (272–3). Symptoms, then, are calls to pay attention to something we cannot see, or have forgotten or denied. The fact that much mystery fiction appears in series certainly supports the idea that it is of the order of the symptom; each book in a series exists as a repetitive gesture or phenomenon that cannot be stopped no matter how insistent we are in dismissing them as 'trash'. Moreover, the books are read and collected according to the logic of an obsessive symptom, no matter how much librarians, parents, and teachers might object.

So, if symptoms are those things that through repetitive action show us that there is something we cannot tell or even know about ourselves, then what need do these books address? What social, cultural, or psychological problem do they reveal, or perhaps even solve? At the personal level, the appeal of mysteries for the pre-adolescent and young adult reader stems from what Sigmund Freud and Melanie Klein call the *Wissentrieb*, or epistemophilic impulse – literally, the drive to know. Specifically, Freud relates this curiosity to Oedipal fantasies the preverbal child experiences regarding the sexual behaviour of his or her parents. The enigma of the primal scene, according to Geraldine Pederson-Krag, is precisely what keeps the allure of mystery active within us. Klein's emphasis, however, is on the child's desire to not only know but also control the contents of the mother's and his or her own body. She says that 'the epistemophilic instinct and the desire to take possession come quite early to be most intimately connected with one another' (204).

James Strachey finds this same dynamic at work in reading; reading involves the oral-sadistic gratification of 'devouring' a book. In the case of series mystery fiction, it is not unusual for a child's appetite to become voracious, not only for reading the books, but also for owning them. Klein hypothesizes that the preverbal child presumably has many questions regarding the way his or her world works, but they are questions that cannot be posed because the child has no language with which to ask them. These questions do not go away, but rather are repressed, and return in the form of a hatred and anxiety toward the position of both not knowing, and, inasmuch as he or she links knowledge with ownership, not having (Klein 204).

Nodelman emphasizes the importance of owning Goosebumps books as a kind of playground capital, but Klein also points out the connections between intellectual curiosity and sadism. If knowing is linked to owning and controlling, there is always the risk of damage to the thing I know. In order that the epistemophilic impulse not be inhibited, the child must believe that the body of the mother is safe from its intrusion – that I can know without necessarily affecting the thing known. In modernist mystery, knowing is an active position, yet the modernist stance of knowingness forecloses the possibility of inflicting harm in that it presents itself as 'already knowing'. It is interesting to note in this context that Nancy Drew's mother is dead. Either she is dead from Nancy's aggressive urge to know, or she is positioned so as to be invulnerable to it. For Klein, since the outside world is nothing other than an extension of the mother's body, we may read in the persistence of series mystery the manifestation of the desire to know and control a world that starts with the establishment of a certain attitude toward our indebtedness to that maternal body.

The hypothesis that I began with indicates that there has been a shift in the way mysteries work, that they have moved from epistemological concerns to ontological ones. The question that remains then is what exactly happens to the desire for knowledge when the status of knowledge itself changes? If it is true, as Jane Tompkins notes, that fiction provides 'solutions for the problems that shape a particular historical moment' (xi) then the mysteries of the Stratemeyer Syndicate in the 1930s understandably defined and solved different problems than those undertaken by contemporary writers like R. L. Stine and Gary Crew. Since mystery fiction is by definition concerned with questions of knowing, the challenge that postmodernism poses to the sufficiency of knowledge is certainly central to the work of contemporary writers. The modernist stance of knowingness can be read as an attempt to outrun the urge to know, to reach the conclusion quickly and cleanly, to deny any bodily residue that may threaten us with its irrationality. The postmodern response acknowledges the debt to the body, but as a fetishized commodity rather than an honoured or honourable site. The symptom of a disconnection between mind and body, mind and world, world and worlds, persists. Framed in terms ludic or deadly serious, Fear Street is a long way from River Heights.

Works cited

Benson, Mildred Wirt. 'The Nancy I Knew', in Carolyn Keene, *The Mystery at Lilac Inn* [1931], facsimile edn. Bedford: Applewood Books, 1994, n. p.

Crew, Gary. *Strange Objects*. New York: Simon & Schuster, 1991.

Grosz, E[lizabeth] A. 'Language and the Limits of the Body', in E. A. Grosz, Terry Threadgold, David Kelly, Alan Cholodenko and Edward Colless (eds), *Futur*Fall: Excursions into Post-Modernity*. Sydney: Power Institute of Fine Arts, 1986, pp. 106–17.

Holquist, Michael. 'Whodunit and Other Questions: Metaphysical Detective Stories in Post-War Fiction', *New Literary History*, 3 (1) (1971): 135–56.

Inness, Sherrie A. (ed.) *Nancy Drew and Company: Culture, Gender, and Girls' Series*. Bowling Green, OH: Bowling Green State University Popular Press, 1997.

Keene, Carolyn [Stratemeyer Syndicate]. *The Bungalow Mystery*. New York: Grosset, 1930.

Kelly, R. Gordon. *Mystery Fiction and Modern Life*. Jackson: University of Mississippi Press, 1998.

Klein, Melanie. *Contributions to Psychoanalysis 1921–1945*. London: Hogarth, 1948.

Kristeva, Julia. *Powers of Horror: An Essay on Abjection* [1980], trans. Leon S. Roudiez. New York: Columbia University Press, 1982.

Lacan, Jacques. 'Kant Avec Sade', *Critique: Revue Générale des Publications Françaises et Étrangères*, 191 (1963): 293–313.

Lear, Jonathan. *Open Minded: Working Out the Logic of the Soul*. Cambridge, MA: Harvard University Press, 1998.

McGillis, Roderick. 'R. L. Stine and the World of Child Gothic', *Bookbird* 33 (3–4) (1995–96): 15–21.

McHale, Brian. *Postmodernist Fiction*. New York: Methuen, 1987.

Milovanovic, Dragan. *Postmodern Criminology*. New York: Garland, 1997.

Moran, Barbara B. and Susan Steinfirst. 'Why Johnny (and Jane) Read Whodunits in Series', *School Library Journal*, 13 (7) (1985): 113–17.

Nodelman, Perry. 'Ordinary Monstrosity: The World of Goosebumps', *Children's Literature Association Quarterly*, 22 (3) (1997): 118–25.

Pederson-Krag, Geraldine. 'Detective Stories and the Primal Scene', in Glenn W. Most and William W. Stowe (eds), *The Poetics of Murder: Detective Fiction and Literary Theory*. New York: Harcourt Brace Jovanovich, 1983, pp. 13–20.

Siegel, Deborah L. 'Nancy Drew as New Girl Wonder: Solving it All for the 1930s', in Sherrie A. Inness (ed.), *Nancy Drew and Company: Culture, Gender, and Girls' Series*. Bowling Green, OH: Bowling Green State University Popular Press, 1997, pp. 159–82.

Stine, R. L. *The Haunted Mask*, Goosebumps 11. New York: Parachute Press, 1993.

——. *Night of the Living Dummy*, Goosebumps 7. New York: Parachute Press, 1993.

——. *Revenge of the Lawn Gnomes*, Goosebumps 34. New York: Parachute Press, 1995.

—— [Cathy Hapka]. *Attack of the Vampire Worms*, Ghosts of Fear Street 33. New York: Parachute Press 1998.

—— [Page McBrier]. *Escape of the He-Beast*, Ghosts of Fear Street 31. New York: Parachute Press, 1998.

Strachey, James. 'Some Unconscious Factors in Reading', *International Journal of Psychoanalysis*, 11 (1930): 322–31.

Tompkins, Jane. *Sensational Designs: The Cultural Work of American Literature, 1790–1860*. New York: Oxford University Press, 1985.

West, Diana. 'The Horror of R. L. Stine', *American Educator*, 19 (3) (1995): 39–41.

Žižek, Slavoj. *For They Know Not What They Do: Enjoyment as a Political Factor*. Phronesis. London: Verso, 1991.

13

Harry Potter and the Mystery of Ordinary Life

Christopher Routledge

'*Depend upon it there is nothing so unnatural as the commonplace'*
– Sherlock Holmes.

(Doyle 30)

The premise of J. K. Rowling's Harry Potter series is that there are two types of people, those who are magic like Harry, and those who are non-magic, known as 'Muggles'. Harry Potter, the series hero, is a young wizard who reaches the age of eleven before he realizes he has magic powers. Made an orphan in mysterious circumstances, he is brought up by his aunt and uncle, who mistreat him because they do not want him to grow up to be like his parents. But Harry Potter's development as a young wizard is presented as perhaps the least mysterious element of the series. It is shown to be a normal part of his growing up since he has been born with magical powers, and the natural course of things is mysterious only in the broadest sense. There is a hint here of Virginia Woolf's suggestion in 'Modern Fiction' that although it might seem dull and uninteresting, ordinary life is the 'proper stuff' of fiction (194–5). Extrapolating from Woolf's theory, it could be argued that Rowling's work implies that magic and mystery are the 'proper stuff' of real living, that everyday things are themselves magical and mysterious. I will argue here that while magic, witchcraft, and the supernatural are all central to the Harry Potter novels, it is the detective story elements that provide the main form of mystery in the series.

The first of the novels, *Harry Potter and the Philosopher's Stone* (1997) – published as *Harry Potter and the Sorcerer's Stone* in the US – opens mysteriously enough. The Dursleys, Harry's adopted family, are described as 'perfectly normal, thank you very much' (7). Much to his surprise

Mr Dursley wakes up one morning to find owls flying during the day, a cat reading a map on a street corner, and groups of people in strange clothes talking excitedly about 'Harry Potter'. These events, which herald the arrival of Harry in the Dursley household, are presented as unusual, but as we later learn, perfectly natural. They seem mysterious and strange to Mr Dursley only because he and his family, and the 'Muggle' community in general, refuse to acknowledge them as a part of life.

Perhaps by way of emphasizing this point, Rowling avoids depicting Hogwarts, the school for witchcraft and wizardry, with its trainee wizards as mysterious in any deeper way than that it is unknown to Harry. The endless corridors, wandering ghosts, and moving paintings, for example, are described in realistic terms; their oddity is not dramatized as such, but rather juxtaposed with the arrival of the pupils at the school:

> [Harry] was too sleepy even to be surprised that the people in the portraits along the corridors whispered and pointed as they passed ... Harry was just wondering how much further they had to go when they came to a sudden halt.
>
> A bundle of walking sticks was floating in mid-air ahead of them and as Percy took a step towards them they started throwing themselves at him.
>
> 'Peeves,' Percy whispered to the first-years. 'A poltergeist.' (*Philosopher's Stone*, 96)

However strange and unusual Hogwarts may seem, its peculiarities are accepted by the children, much as they might become used to any new situation. Harry and his friends have a full timetable of lessons, fixed mealtimes, and regulated bedtimes. The lessons are in such fascinating subjects as 'Muggle Studies', 'Defence Against the Dark Arts' and 'Divinations', and the building is patrolled by enchanted cats and 'nearly headless' ghosts, but above all, Hogwarts is a school. An extreme example of how normal all this seems to them is the children's opinion of History of Magic: '[e]asily the most boring lesson' and 'the only class taught by a ghost' (*Philospher's Stone*, 99). The novel goes to great lengths to show that the children find nothing particularly mysterious or even unusual in their lessons. Harry and his friends are like ordinary children; it is almost incidental that they have extraordinary powers.

Each of the books concludes with a return to normal school life, to exam results, and the train home: '[t]he rest of the summer term passed in a haze of brilliant sunshine. Hogwarts was back to normal, with only a few, small differences: Defence Against the Dark Arts classes were cancelled' (*Chamber of Secrets*, 250). Young witches and wizards have similar concerns to their Muggle counterparts; they discuss the relative merits of consumer items (in their case wands and broomsticks rather than games consoles and mountain bikes), worry about their exams, and avoid doing their homework. In the world occupied by Harry Potter, witchcraft and wizardry are as real as electricity and the telephone, and a good deal more useful. Bearing in mind the controversy the Harry Potter series has aroused in South Carolina and elsewhere over its apparent promotion of Satanism, it is worth pointing out that the stories have a strong, even rather conservative, moral structure. The distinction between evil Lord Voldemort and good Harry Potter could not be clearer, and while individual mysteries may be solved in each novel, the plots are open-ended enough to suggest a continuing struggle between good and evil which Harry must accommodate if he is to become a responsible adult.

Pico Iyer emphasizes the realism in Rowling's depiction of life at a British boarding school, confirming the lack of mystery in the series. Iyer argues that the Harry Potter series does for British boarding schools what magical realist writers such as Salman Rushdie and Gabriel Garcia Marquez have done for Bombay and Colombia respectively. While to outsiders Hogwarts seems a 'strange and wonderful' place, to initiates it is grounded in reality:

> For those who passed through these eccentric [English boarding school] playgrounds, though, much in the Harry Potter universe ... [is] familiar ... the cryptic list of instructions that would appear through the mail, describing what we must – and mustn't – bring to school ... the trip to dusty old shops with creaky family names – New & Lingwood or Alden & Blackwell – where aged men would fit us out with the approved uniform and equipment ... the special school train that would be waiting in a London station to transport us to our cells. (39)

There is much that is real then, in the Harry Potter novels, despite the veneer of wizardry and fantasy, and this combination of normality and adventure is perhaps what makes the novels so appealing.

Although magic and the supernatural are everywhere in the novels, they are presented as a normal part of life for the children at Hogwarts; they are not mysterious as such. Instead, the real source of mystery at the centre of each of the Harry Potter novels is a detective mystery. Harry and his friends, Ron and Hermione, solve mysteries of mistaken identity and uncover the perpetrators of evil deeds. A recurrent motif in the stories is wrongful accusation, and much of the detective work undertaken by the trio is to do with establishing the innocence of their friends. Although they do so with the aid of magic, their underlying method is one of gathering clues and forming theories about 'whodunit?'

The detective mystery in each of the books is connected in some way with the murder of Harry's parents at the beginning of the first book in the series, *Harry Potter and the Philosopher's Stone*. Harry Potter's struggle with Lord Voldemort and his supporters even has similarities with Sherlock Holmes's ongoing battle with the evil genius, Professor Moriarty. Each of the novels sees Harry and friends investigate a new attempt by supporters of the 'Dark Lord' to restore him to power. In the first novel, for example, they work out who has been trying to steal the Philosopher's Stone – the key to immortality – on Voldemort's behalf, while in the second, *Harry Potter and the Chamber of Secrets* (1998), Harry manages to thwart an attempt to take over Hogwarts. In the third, *Harry Potter and the Prisoner of Azkaban* (1999), he learns a little more about his parents and the betrayal that led to their murder.

It is finding justice for the wrongly accused, however, that is the main aim of detection in the novels. The stories depend at all levels on the tension deriving from false accusations. For example, Harry is treated unfairly by the Dursleys who think he is not to be trusted, while Dumbledore's suspension as headmaster in *Chamber of Secrets* rests on a false accusation of incompetence. Most of these injustices stem from the conflict between members of a conservative elite and others by whom they are threatened. This is perhaps most explicitly stated at the beginning of *Philosopher's Stone*, when the Dursleys express their distrust of Harry's parents by refusing to acknowledge their existence. While Mr Dursley represents conservative Muggle middle-class values to which Harry poses a challenge, in a more general sense the conflict between establishment figures and rebellious characters like Harry is built into the structure of the narratives.

The most obvious example of such conflict is the fact that the Wizard community keeps itself secret from the Muggles; whenever the two communities come into contact, a forgetfulness charm ensures the Muggles know nothing about it. Harry has a tendency to break the rules that keep magic secret; in *The Chamber of Secrets* he receives a warning from the Improper Use of Magic Office for having performed a hover charm at the Dursley's house. Within the school itself there are divisions between some children from long-established wizarding families, such as the Malfoys, and 'Muggle-born' children like Hermione, neither of whose parents are 'magic'. Like a child who is at a private school on a scholarship, rather than being paid for by her family, Hermione works extra hard because she feels she has something to prove. Despite being 'Muggle born', in *The Prisoner of Azkaban*, one of the courses the conscientious Hermione takes is Muggle Studies. By contrast, Draco Malfoy, through his powerful father, can influence what goes on at the school. When Malfoy is injured by Buckbeak, one of the magical creatures the children are studying, Hagrid the gamekeeper worries for his job:

> 'You haven't been sacked, Hagrid!' gasped Hermione.
> 'Not yet,' said Hagrid miserably, taking a huge gulp of whatever was in the tankard. 'But s'only a matter o' time I'n't it, after Malfoy ...' (*Prisoner*, 92)

It is within the Wizard community itself, rather then between Muggles and wizards, that the conflict between conservatives and modernizers is drawn in most detail, however. The books may be read as a critique of British society in the 1990s, during which an old aristocratic hierarchy gave way, theoretically at least, to a more meritocratic social structure. For example, in Britain a debate is currently raging over what proportion of the population should be allowed to have access to a university education, and over the quality of state-funded education in general. In the Harry Potter series, the 'dark forces' of conservatism hope to remove all Muggle influences from Hogwarts, thus reviving one of the aims of a founder of the school, Salazar Slytherin, described here in *Harry Potter and the Chamber of Secrets*:

> 'Slytherin wished to be more *selective* about the students admitted to Hogwarts. He believed that magical learning should be kept within all-magic families. He disliked taking students of Muggle parentage, believing them to be untrustworthy.' (114)

Harry's revulsion at Slytherin's elitist aims finds resonance in overdue reforms to the UK's governmental system, which are reducing the influence of the unelected House of Lords, many members of which have access to government by right of birth alone. Bearing this in mind, it is perhaps significant that the villain behind the mysteries investigated by Harry and friends is known as *Lord* Voldemort. An example of the diminishing influence of 'aristocratic' wizard families occurs at the end of *The Chamber of Secrets* when Lucius Malfoy realizes that his influence has been reduced by the growing power of bureaucratic and more accountable government. Having had the school's charismatic headmaster Albus Dumbledore temporarily suspended from his duties, Malfoy is threatened at the end by the reinstated head with being reported to Arthur Weasley of the Ministry of Magic.

If detective mystery is the principal form of mystery in the novels, the effect of that detection on the society in which it takes place differs significantly from more archetypal detective fiction. At least part of the appeal of detective heroes such as Sherlock Holmes lies in their ability to restore order where crime has brought chaos. The 'country house' type of detective fiction, in which the quiet life of a peaceful village is disrupted by a murder, is probably the most obvious example of this but, as John Carey points out in *The Intellectuals and the Masses*, Holmes's analytical skills can bring reassurance of a different kind. Confronting the demoralizing effects of large-scale urbanization that took place in the nineteenth century, Sherlock Holmes is able to reassure a mass audience of their value as individuals by examining an individual's clothing to ascertain her or his habits, occupation and tastes (Carey 8). In doing so, Carey suggests, Holmes shows that the person concerned is a unique individual. While Holmes's ability to reassure us that we are all unique individuals may be comforting, it also depends on a rigid social structure and a relatively stable system of signifying identity. Sherlock Holmes is able to see through disguises simply because they are just that; real identities cannot be concealed.

While many of the mysteries in the Harry Potter series depend on discovering the real identity of certain characters – Professor Lupin's identity as a werewolf, in *The Prisoner of Azkaban*, for example, or Tom Riddle's as Lord Voldemort in *The Chamber of Secrets* – Rowling's message is rather less comforting than Conan Doyle's. Harry Potter's role as a detective is not to restore order to a long-established and hierarchical social structure, but to make sure such a structure is prevented from reasserting itself. Indeed, the hierarchical structure represented by Lucius Malfoy and the other followers of Voldemort is presented as something evil and dangerous. In *The Chamber of Secrets*, for example, Harry discovers he is a 'parsel-mouth', able to talk to snakes. This explains how he was able to release the snake from the zoo in book one, and in this respect he is like the evil Salazar Slytherin:

'It matters,' said Hermione, speaking at last in a hushed voice, 'because being able to talk to snakes was what Salazar Slytherin was famous for. That's why the symbol of Slytherin house is a serpent.'
Harry's mouth fell open.
'Exactly,' said Ron. 'And now the whole school's going to think you're his great-great-great-great-grandson or something.' (147)

Even if Harry does turn out in later books to be related to Slytherin, the series as it exists so far emphasizes the extent to which identity is determined more by personal choices than by heredity. In Rowling's novels, individuals are responsible for their actions and their identities. For example, in *The Prisoner of Azkaban*, Lupin explains how Sirius Black, Peter Pettigrew, and Harry's father, James, chose to become Animagus (able to change into animals) so they could help their were-wolf friend. Similarly, even though he is a werewolf, predisposed to killing and violence, Lupin tries to avoid harming people. In *The Chamber of Secrets* Harry reflects on the possibility that he might be descended from Slytherin, and that he is destined to become associated with 'dark magic', but by the end of the novel he realizes that it is up to him to choose. This is an important lesson; Harry learns in *The Chamber of Secrets* to be proud of his parents, his family, and background, but not limited by them.

Most of the 'good' characters in the book tend not to do what is expected of them; characters such as Hagrid try to do what they think is right, rather than being bound to long-standing conventions. By righting injustices against 'ordinary' characters such as Hagrid, and by remaining loyal to the eccentric but brilliant headmaster Dumbledore in *The Chamber of Secrets*, Harry and his friends champion those whose idiosyncrasies make them appear dangerous to the conservative forces of evil. The search for solutions is not therefore a search for a stable truth, or a single answer, but a search for alternative, individual responses to the world.

The Harry Potter series describes a society in which witches and wizards, magical creatures and strange potions, are far from mysterious. Harry Potter is a normal boy who just happens to have magical powers, and the real mystery in the novels is a detective mystery. Where detective fiction as a literary form has tended to defend a conservative view of society as a hierarchical construct in which status is bestowed rather than necessarily earned, the Harry Potter novels describe a society with a long history which is nevertheless in a state of flux. Where classical detective fiction stories usually conclude with the restoration of order to social groups disrupted by crime, it is the 'evil' characters in the Harry Potter books who tend to be those whose social status has been undermined or diminished. Lord Voldemort himself is the principal example of this, the pure blood of his distant ancestor Salazar Slytherin diluted in his view by the Wizard–Muggle intermarrying of his parents.

The final mystery in Rowling's books, then, would seem to be the mystery of social class, in particular the mystery of what gives one group of people the right to dominate another. Harry's celebrity, based as it is on achievement rather than inherited social position, suggests for the moment that Rowling is making of him a liberal hero. His decision not to join the Slytherin house at school underlines an existential message that identity and social position can be a matter of choice. It remains to be seen whether the later novels in the series contradict this by making Harry's infant defeat of Voldemort a consequence of his being the 'rightful heir' to an ancient wizarding family.

Works cited

Carey, John. *The Intellectuals and the Masses: Pride and Prejudice Among the Literary Intelligentsia, 1880–1939*. London: Faber & Faber, 1992.

Doyle, Arthur Conan. 'A Case of Identity', in *The Adventures of Sherlock Holmes* [1892], ed. Richard Lancelyn Green, The World's Classics. Oxford: Oxford University Press, 1994, pp. 30–48.

Iyer, Pico. 'The Playing Fields of Hogwarts', *The New York Times Book Review*, 10 October 1999: 39.

Rowling, J. K. *Harry Potter and the Chamber of Secrets*. London: Bloomsbury, 1998.

——. *Harry Potter and the Philosopher's Stone*. London: Bloomsbury, 1997.

——. *Harry Potter and the Prisoner of Azkaban*. London: Bloomsbury, 1999.

Woolf, Virginia. 'Modern Fiction', in *The Common Reader*. London: Hogarth Press, 1925, pp. 184–95.

14
Enigma's Variation: the Puzzling Mysteries of Avi, Ellen Raskin, Diana Wynne Jones, and Chris Van Allsburg

Adrienne E. Gavin

Formulaic mysteries are appropriate for child readers, it is sometimes claimed, not because formula fiction has its place in anyone's reading fare, but on the grounds that, as they read, children are learning about the mode of mystery writing itself. The young, it is implied, do not require nuanced, complex, or allusive mysteries. Similarly, it is asserted:

> The researcher of children's literature cannot operate in the categories of 'originality, novelty, stylistic experiment' ... as are applied to modern (that is, 20th century) adult literature. Devices and patterns that may seem to betoken lack of originality, plagiarism, secondarity, in adult literature are a deliberate creative approach in children's books. (Nikolajeva, *Magic*, 118)

Comments like these, which are surprisingly common, have as their subtext a notion that in some way our expectations of children's literature can be 'lower' than our expectations of adult literature. While formulaic writing and derivativeness may be a 'deliberate creative approach' in some children's texts (as they are in some adult works), it is surely reductive to suggest that we should not expect stylistic experiment and originality in children's literature. This essay examines fiction by Avi, Ellen Raskin, Diana Wynne Jones, and Chris Van Allsburg in order to show the varieties of innovation and originality that are possible in children's mysteries.

Carol Billman describes three levels of sophistication in mystery writing for children. Child readers, she suggests, progress from the formula of fairy tales to formulaic mysteries like the Nancy Drew series which are 'conventional, rather than idiosyncratic or inventional' (32) and 'encourage what Tzvetan Todorov calls "metareading," a process by which "we note the methods of the ... narrative instead of falling under its spell"' (33). They then move onto more sophisticated mysteries which are 'rooted in the "real" world' and contain 'equivocal rather than completely stereotyped characters' (39). In a third stage, she argues, children read more complex, less codified mysteries which overlap with other genres such as time travel fantasies or historical fiction. Her suggestion that child readers progress consecutively through these levels of mystery is overly schematic. Her admission, however, that mystery's 'best offerings, for whatever age, urge upon their readers [a] constant balancing of the mysterious and the recognized, of the unsettling unknown and the reassuring known' (37) stresses the enigmatic and puzzling elements of the most innovative mysteries for children.

Every mystery, whether formulaic or innovative, requires a secret which lies at its heart and which, by text's end, is either explained or left mysterious. Every mystery also involves the provocation of puzzling in characters and/or readers who are compelled to ponder over possible solutions to the mysteries presented. What distinguishes creative, innovative, and original mystery writing from the more formulaic and derivative is the presence of enigma. Enigma is defined in *The Collins English Dictionary* as 'a person, thing, or situation that is mysterious, puzzling, or ambiguous'. As 'mysterious' and 'puzzling' are already inherent within mystery, it is 'ambiguous' that is the key word here. Innovative children's mysteries contain ambiguity; within them there is a slippery indeterminacy of meaning and solution; something enigmatic and shifting lies at their core, making it impossible to reach absolute conclusions. They encourage puzzling that extends beyond the bounds of the plot and which connects with deeper mysteries of life and art, involving issues of identity, reality, and fictionality. As Joan Aiken suggests, '[t]hings not understood have a radiance of their own. It is a challenge to go back to them, to puzzle and puzzle' (45). As this essay shows, Avi's *The Man Who Was Poe* (1989), Raskin's *The Westing Game* (1978), Jones's *Archer's Goon* (1984), and Van Allsburg's *The Mysteries of Harris Burdick* (1984), each in its own enigmatic variation, reveals the possibilities of innovation and originality in children's mystery fiction.

At first glance Avi's *The Man Who Was Poe* might appear to be a formulaic detective mystery. The mother, aunt, and sister of Edmund, the central child character, have all disappeared in separate and mysterious circumstances; there has been a robbery of California gold from the

Providence Bank; a dead woman's body is fished out of the water, and various characters are being trailed by other characters through the dark streets of Providence, Rhode Island in November 1848. A dark and mysterious stranger helps Edmund solve these mysteries, the criminals are revealed, the case seems closed. The case, however, is not closed and enigmatic questions remain to puzzle both the reader and Edmund.

Avi's innovation is to introduce into his historical detective novel that pre-eminent and originary detective created by Edgar Allan Poe, Auguste Dupin. In doing so he goes back to the origins of detective formula, but transforms that formula into something far less certain. Avi's Dupin is not a simple borrowing but a complex fictional construct who operates on occasion with the original Dupin's rational and clear-thinking powers of detection. At the same time, however, he is the alcoholic, death-obsessed Edgar Allan Poe himself. He tells Edmund that he is '"the man who *was* Poe. Now I am Dupin"' (143), but later says '"I'm no longer Auguste Dupin. I am the man who *is* Edgar – Allan – Poe"' (161). Avi's text uses intertextuality, metafictional elements, and circularity to create its enigma. It blurs distinctions between creator and created, fiction and reality, and 'Dupin-Poe' and Edmund.

The greater the knowledge a reader has of Poe's work and life the more intertextual significance that reader can see. By adding an appendix – 'Something about Edgar Allan Poe' – and by weaving among the more arcane links some specific and explanatory references to Poe's work, Avi ensures, however, that even child readers who know nothing of Poe see mysterious interlinkings between the novel they are reading, Poe's life, and Poe's fictional creations. It is the metafictional qualities of the novel, however, that create most enigma. The mysterious Dupin-Poe (as I call him here, although in the novel he goes by both names severally) agrees to help the desperate Edgar solve the mystery of his missing family, which he Dupinesquely does. He also, however, Poe-like, uses the situation as material for a story he sketches out soon after meeting Edmund: '*Edmund ... a boy ... Missing sister ... The sea – bringer of death ... abandonment. Release/death ... The ... necessity ... of death ... The certainty of death*' (30). Dupin-Poe's insistence on his story and the emphasis that story has on the inevitability of the death of Edmund's family members and especially his sister 'Sis' – whose name is the same as Dupin-Poe's late wife – deeply disturbs and horrifies Edmund who insists that his experience is real and that his sister is still alive and can be saved. The twisting together of 'real' and story puzzles both Dupin-Poe and Edmund. Dupin-Poe thinks to himself 'have I gone beyond the writing of words? Could I be writing this boy's *life*?' (56). Edmund is shocked when Poe refuses to help him find his mother and sister and instead writes his story: '"this *isn't* a story,"' he insists (161). Enraged at Dupin-Poe's saying Sis is dead, he tears up pages of the story and eventually has to battle physically free of Dupin-Poe to save his sister.

'Puzzling questions ... are not beyond *all* conjecture,' Dupin-Poe thinks to himself when considering whether his characters have come to life (173). Such questions are not beyond conjecture, but they are, the novel reveals, beyond answers. Dupin-Poe leaves Edmund with just such a puzzling question on the final page of the novel when he asks him: '"I ask you: in what fashion will your sister live longer. In her life? Or, in this, *my* story that would have been?"' (198). The novel ends in ambivalence. The undestroyed scrap of his story that Dupin-Poe tosses to Edmund is the first paragraph of Avi's novel, with the name Edgar crossed out and the name Edmund added. This drives the reader circularly back to the start of the novel and also confirms the enigmatic nature of the puzzling questions the novel has raised but not answered about the parallels between Dupin-Poe and Edmund. Dupin-Poe notes that for a mystery *'to be effective [there] must be a puzzle'* (80), and speaks of a '"puzzle which, if we could fully understand it would bring ... truth"' (118). Yet he also claims: '"[l]ies have their own truth"' (144). Avi's novel raises postmodernist questions about truth and lies, life and fiction, and creates a sense of enigmatic mysteries which must be puzzled over but which cannot be solved.

Ellen Raskin's novel *The Westing Game* innovates mystery in different ways. It is overtly a puzzle mystery, designed as a game not just for readers but for the characters themselves who are desperately seeking the solutions to the clues they hold. The 16 heirs of the mysterious Sam Westing, directed by his will, motivated by thoughts of inheriting his two hundred million dollars, and working in teams of two, are trying to figure out who among them has murdered Westing. Each team has different clues and must come to solutions in its own way. Mystery piles upon mystery: Is any one a twin? Who plays chess? Who is exploding bombs? Was Westing murdered? Is he actually dead?

Raskin, as Peter Hunt states, is 'consistently experimental' in her work (150), and a Raskin mystery, as Constance B. Hieatt points out, 'is not of the common or garden variety. All of them offer more than the simple appeal of what Graham Greene calls "an entertainment"' (128). Her works are 'playful and fundamentally mysterious' in postmodern ways (McGillis 154). Billman classes *The Westing Game* as 'a mystery novel of the second degree of difficulty' (35). She demonstrates that the novel moves beyond formula in its use of an 'omniscient narrator [who] flits quickly from one character's mind to that of another' and in its lack of a central detective character (36). She does not, however, see enigma within the novel:

> Raskin presents what readers know to be the familiar ingredients of mystery fiction – wills, detectives, clues, red herrings, even a potential corpse – and serves them up in a new and truly adventurous guessing game. Her variation is not, however, ultimately so lacking in clues for its unraveling as to stymie readers. (Billman 37)

Billman claims that Raskin 'gives the necessary information to solve the ever shape-shifting crime' (38). This is partially true in that it does become clear to readers that Sam Westing, still alive, must be operating this extraordinary puzzle, but it is not true to say that readers can solve the mystery. The enigma at the heart of this novel is that its puzzle is so confusingly difficult that none of the players except Turtle Wexler ever completely solve it and most readers are unlikely to either without the novel's explanation. Mystery remains as to how all the intricate clues fit together. In a different way than Avi's, Raskin's novel also drives readers back to the beginning to re-look at clues. It also leaves open the question why Turtle does not ever tell anyone else that she has discovered Westing.

Raskin's mystery is innovative, too, in its acute and witty observation of characters' public facades and the private truths that lie beneath. She enters into the puzzling nature of human relationships. As the shin-kicking of Turtle, the highly decorated but unneeded crutches of Sydelle Pulaski, and the social-climbing and bigoted remarks of Grace Windsor Wexler reveal, the characters seek individual attention. Through their involvement in the Westing Game each finds a new and confident sense of themselves and they all go on to live out successfully the American dream that 'Uncle Sam' Westing has urged upon them.

Like Raskin's novel, Diana Wynne Jones's *Archer's Goon* makes use of humour which underneath contains darker puzzles. Like Avi's novel it makes use of metafictional techniques and of characters who have mysteriously mixed identities. As Maria Nikolajeva claims:

> Diana Wynne Jones is an indisputable innovator, and in her books the hesitation principle is most tangible ... The play with alternative

worlds in [her] books becomes a discussion of existential questions: what is reality? Is there more than one definite truth? (*Children's*, 74)

Archer's Goon is a complex fantasy whose mystery begins with puzzling questions about who is intimidating Howard's father, the famous writer Quentin Sykes, and then moves on to more perplexing mysteries connected with identity, time, and the self.

The enigma at the heart of the novel is 13-year-old Howard himself. He begins with a stable self-identity and then is encompassed by a mysterious and threatening situation which destroys his sense of himself. His family live in a town which is secretly run by seven supernaturally powerful and giant siblings who have, gangster-like, divided up the town and corruptly 'farm' their patches. When Howard's father refuses to write his regular payment of two thousand new words for an unknown member of the giant family, Howard's own family are beset. A goon arrives and takes up residence in their house, music blares constantly, their road is dug up, their gas, electricity and banking are cut off, they are driven to borrow food, and a gang is ready to attack Howard and his sister, Awful, at any opportunity.

Howard tries to solve the mystery of which of the seven beings – Archer, Dillian, Shine, Torquil, Erskine, Hathaway, and Venturus – is causing these terrible problems for his family. In what Nikolajeva describes as a 'paradigm shift' in fantasy structures (*Magic*, 117) and 'an identity variable which seems almost unique' (*Magic*, 117), Howard discovers that he himself is the 'criminal'. Tracking down Venturus, the last and youngest giant sibling, who lives in the future, Howard discovers that *he* is Venturus. He discovers, too, that his giant siblings have been trapped in the town and prevented from moving beyond it to 'farm' the rest of the world, not by Quentin Sykes's words as they had believed, but by Venturus himself who has muddled with time in order to perfect his spaceship. He learns that, because of this, everyone has lived through two repeated sets of 13 years and might be entering into a third identical loop if he does not act to stop his Venturus self.

In her analysis of some other Jones novels, Margaret Rumbold points to the shifting selves in Jones's work and to her use of 'multiple signifiers to reflect the heterogeneous nature of the subject' (22). She suggests that within Jones's *Hexwood* (1993) 'selfhood remains essentially enigmatic (at times arbitrary) and cannot be nailed down' (25). This is also true of *Archer's Goon* in which Howard-Venturus's self is the central enigma which is never fully solved. Learning that he is Venturus both horrifies and embarrasses Howard. He feels his magical powers coming upon him, but knows, too, that this third time through life: 'he [will] have to bring himself up not to be Venturus' (241).

Howard acts to rid the world of the three older giant siblings and in a wonderfully metafictional scene in which observing characters run from window to typewriter to see the same scene unfold, his father finally writes the requested words which, as they are typed onto the page, force the greedy older siblings into Venturus's spaceship, to be shot far into the universe. In Jones's novel 'good and evil are no longer absolute categories' (Nikolajeva, *Children's*, 74). The Goon, for example, changes from being a knife-throwing threat, to being virtually a part of the Sykes family, to revealing himself as Erskine and imprisoning the family, to emerge at the end a loved family friend. Jones's novel innovates through the extremely complex position in which it places its protagonist as both solver of and source of mystery, and ends with an indeterminate future ahead for Howard-Venturus.

Most puzzling and mysterious of all the texts discussed here is Chris Van Allsburg's postmodernist picture book *The Mysteries of Harris Burdick*. At the time it was published it was, as John Rowe Townsend notes, 'the enigmatic Van Allsburg's most enigmatic book so far' (329). The book contains 14 discrete and apparently unconnected black and white illustrations, each accompanied by a title and a caption. Van Allsburg claims in his introduction (interestingly written from the Providence, Rhode Island setting of Avi's novel) that these drawings had been handed to him by a retired children's publisher, one Peter Wenders. Wenders told him, he recounts, that they had been drawn thirty years earlier by a man named Harris Burdick who had brought them in to Wenders as samples to gauge his publishing interest in 14 different stories. Having left the drawings with Wenders, 'Harris Burdick was never heard from again ... To this day Harris Burdick remains a complete mystery' ('Introduction', n.p.). Burdick's disappearance, Roderick McGillis suggests, 'serves to remind us of the supposed "death of the author" in postmodern art' (154). It also suggests the missing person or body that supplies the impetus to much detective mystery or the fleeting appearance of a ghostly being in supernatural mystery.

Apart from the claims about their mysterious origins, which raises postmodernist questions about truth and fiction, the drawings are in themselves mysterious. Their blackness and whiteness is shaded and slightly indistinct; edges are blurred, creating images of dreamscape. They hint at magic and are uncanny, strange, and eerie in effect. They depict puzzling or impossible things such as a chair with a nun in it flying through a cathedral, or a bird flying off bird-patterned wallpaper. As McGillis puts it, 'they "unclose" [rather than disclose] their meaning, keeping it always mysterious and relative' (154). They disrupt 'expectations based on [the mystery story] genre' by not providing solutions (McGillis 154).

The book encourages readings of different types of mystery: the magical, the frightening, the natural, and the fantastic, and the captions heighten mystery further. Providing clues to the stories behind the drawings, they serve to mystify through their provocative nature. The title 'Archie Smith, Boy Wonder', for example, is captioned '*A tiny voice asked, "Is he the one?"*' while 'Another Place, Another Time' is captioned '*If there was an answer, he'd find it there.*' Each title and caption raises more questions than it answers.

David Lewis, discussing indeterminacy within postmodernist picture books, suggests that

when we have too *little* information, we often find that issues within a story which we would normally expect to have resolved are in fact undecidable ... outcomes are left unresolved or relationships remain permanently unclear. (261)

Van Allsburg's book is a perfect example of such indeterminacy. Each illustration is in itself an enigma, its mystery unsolvable and its readers left puzzling. As the back cover of the book states 'the puzzles, the mysteries, presented by these drawings, are not what we are used to. They are not solved for us ... The solutions to these mysteries lie ... in our imagination.'

McGillis suggests that the '"perfect lift-off" in the final illustration ... suggests a departure from the known to the unknown' (68–9). In its plotlessness and indeterminacy Van Allsburg's book clearly moves into 'the unknown', as far from the 'rational', solved world of early detective mysteries as it is perhaps possible to go. He is not alone in this move towards inexplicable mystery. Meena G. Khorana notes that within the work of the nominees for the 1998 Hans Christian Andersen Illustrator Award a common motif is 'the evocation of a mysterious, haunting atmosphere by combining magical and realistic elements' (3).

Collocates of the word mystery such as 'wrapped', 'shrouded', or 'cloaked' suggest something covered-up and secret. In formulaic mysteries the cloak, shroud, or wrapper is removed, exposing what lies beneath. In innovative mysteries such as those by Avi, Raskin, Jones, and Van Allsburg the wrapper or cloak remains in place. It perhaps lifts slightly on rare glimpsing occasions or is seen through dimly when the light is at strange angles, but what is beneath is never clearly revealed. Each of the texts discussed here creates an enigma that cannot be solved and that stimulates readers' puzzlement beyond the bounds of any outline plot. In creating that enigma, these authors use postmodernist techniques such as intertextuality, indeterminacy, and incomplete solutions and introduce metafictional elements. In this way their variations on mysteries sustain puzzles, insist that some mysteries are inexplicable, and reveal the innovative and non-formulaic possibilities of mystery literature for children.

Works cited

Aiken, Joan. 'A Thread of Mystery', *Children's Literature in Education*, 2 (1970): 30–47.
Avi. *The Man Who was Poe* [1989]. New York: Avon Books, 1997.
Billman, Carol. 'The Child Reader as Sleuth', *Children's Literature in Education*, 15 (1) [52] (1984): 30–41.
Hieatt, Constance B. 'The Mystery of *Figgs & phantoms*', *Children's Literature*, 13 (1985): 128–38.
Hunt, Peter. *An Introduction to Children's Literature*. Oxford: Oxford University Press, 1994.
Jones, Diana Wynne. *Archer's Goon*. London: Methuen, 1984.
Khorana, Meena G. 'To the Reader', *Bookbird*, 36 (3) (1998): 2–4.
Lewis, David. 'The Constructedness of Texts: Picture Books and the Metafictive', in Sheila Egoff, Gordon Stubbs, Ralph Ashley, and Wendy Sutton (eds), *Only Connect: Readings on Children's Literature*, 3rd edn. Toronto: Oxford University Press, 1996, pp. 259–75.
McGillis, Roderick. *The Nimble Reader: Literary Theory and Children's Literature*. New York: Twayne, 1996.
Nikolajeva, Maria. *Children's Literature Comes of Age: Towards a New Aesthetic*. New York and London: Garland, 1996.
——. *The Magic Code: The Use of Magical Patterns in Fantasy for Children*. Stockholm: Almqvist & Wiskell International, 1988.
Raskin, Ellen. *The Westing Game* [1978]. New York: Puffin, 1997.
Rumbold, Margaret. 'Taking the Subject Further', *Papers*, 7 (2) (1997): 16–28.
Townsend, John Rowe. *Written for Children: An Outline of English-language Children's Literature*, 6th edn. London: Bodley Head, 1995.
Van Allsburg, Chris. *The Mysteries of Harris Burdick*. London: Andersen Press, 1984.

Index